Russian Minimalism

Russian Minimalism

FROM THE PROSE POEM TO THE ANTI-STORY

Adrian Wanner

NORTHWESTERN UNIVERSITY PRESS / EVANSTON, ILLINOIS

Northwestern University Press
Evanston, Illinois 60208-4210

Copyright © 2003 by Northwestern University Press.
Published 2003. All rights reserved.

Printed in the United States of America

10   9   8   7   6   5   4   3   2   1

ISBN 0-8101-1955-2

Library of Congress Cataloging-in-Publication Data

Wanner, Adrian, 1960–
  Russian minimalism : from the prose poem to the anti-story / Adrian Wanner.
     p. cm. — (Studies in Russian literature and theory)
  Includes bibliographical references and index.
  ISBN 0-8101-1955-2 (cloth : alk. paper)
  1. Russian poetry—19th century—History and criticism. 2. Prose poems,
Russian—History and criticism. 3. Russian prose literature—20th century—
History and criticism. 4. Minimalism (Literature)—Russia. I. Title. II. Series.
PG3064.P74W36 2003
891.709′11—dc21

                                                                    2003002704

The paper used in this publication meets the minimum requirements of the American National Standard for Information Sciences—Permanence of Paper for Printed Library Materials, ANSI Z39.48-1992.

For Cathy

Contents

Preface

The oxymoronic genre of the prose poem, a marginal form of literature by definition and par excellence, has begun to galvanize the interest of critics and theoreticians in recent years. The past decade has witnessed a flurry of articles, monographs, anthologies, and special journal issues devoted to this genre in French, German, English, and American literature.[1] This book is the first study of the Russian prose poem. It addresses the extent to which the genre of the *stikhotvorenie v proze* in Russia is rooted in the French tradition of the *poème en prose,* and traces the trajectory leading from Ivan Turgenev's "Poems in Prose" (1882) to Daniil Kharms' minimalist anti-stories of the 1930s. Turgenev and Kharms form the opposite poles in a wide chronological and typological spectrum of Russian prose miniatures, encompassing realist, symbolist, and futurist texts. In this sense, the book could be called a study of Turgenev's prose poems and their descendants, or, conversely, of Kharms' mini-stories and their antecedents. The implied link is less of a directly genealogical than of a typological nature. As I will show, the various prose miniatures discussed in this book raise related theoretical issues that concern the nature of literary minimalism.

At first sight, Turgenev and Kharms may seem an unlikely couple. The development of their careers and reputations make them almost antipodes. Turgenev (1818–83), the first Russian writer to win international fame in his lifetime, has lost some of his former exalted status. His prose poems in particular, perhaps because of the fact that some of them were imposed on generations of Soviet schoolchildren as mandatory reading, have a reputation for being rather dated and dull. By contrast, Daniil Kharms (1905–42), a virtual unknown in his time except for his children's stories, has emerged half a century after his death in a Stalinist prison as "a true giant of the new Russian literature"[2] with a growing popular and academic cult following.

Reading Turgenev after Kharms can be an illuminating experience, if only to open our eyes to some features in Turgenev's work of which in all likelihood the author himself was unaware. It also becomes obvious that Kharms' minimalist absurdism did not emerge ex nihilo. Some features of the Kharmsian anti-story can be detected in earlier miniature works of Russian literature that have only received scant critical attention, such as Fedor Sologub's "Little Fairy Tales," Aleksei Remizov's dreams, or Vasilii Kandinskii's prose poems. As for Turgenev, it would no doubt be problematic to call him a "minimalist" or adherent of an avant-garde aesthetic. As we will see, he was in fact more conservative than Charles Baudelaire, his French predecessor in the genre of the prose poem. Nevertheless, a closer look reveals that Turgenev's prose poems contain elements that will come to full fruition in twentieth-century modernism.

The more immediate history of the Russian prose poem in the wake of Turgenev can hardly be called a success story. Unlike the French *poème en prose*, which became a mainstay of modernist poetry, the Russian *stikhotvorenie v proze* looks at first like an anemic plant struggling to survive in an inhospitable environment. In consequence, the recent enthusiasm for the prose poem among literary critics has not yet spilled over into the Slavicist community.[3] If we limit our inquiry to texts with the explicit label *stikhotvorenie v proze*, we might indeed gain the impression that the oblivion into which many Russian prose poems have fallen is well deserved. However, if we approach the problem in a wider sense and look at texts that embody the "minimalist" principle of the prose poem without being necessarily labeled as such by their authors, we will discover that this type of writing forms an important, if understudied, subcurrent of twentieth-century Russian literature.

The chronological framework of this book coincides more or less with the rise and fall of modernism in Russian culture. The oeuvre of Daniil Kharms constitutes in many respects a culmination and at the same time a turning away from the legacy of the modernist avant-garde. As has been noted more than once, Kharms' prose work seems to anticipate the transition from modernism to postmodernism.[4] Some critics have even attempted to proclaim minimalism as the postmodern form par excellence. Vladislav Kulakov asserts that "the transition from modernist maximalism to postmodernist minimalism is the most essential fact (*sushchestvenneishaia iz realii*) of the postmodern situation."[5] If we subscribe to this belief, the writers and artists of the early twentieth century discussed in this study would have to be classified as "protominimalists."[6] Kulakov also draws a sharp distinction between minimalism and miniaturism. The former does not necessarily entail smallness, but can consist of unwieldy, large-scale structures, whereas the latter, with its aestheticization of the miniature form, follows different, and nowadays rather outdated, artistic principles.[7] One might conclude then that this book is really misnamed and that its real title should be something like "Russian Protominimalist Miniaturism." However, as

Iurii Orlitskii has noted in his afterword to the recent collection of essays on minimalism in the journal *Novoe literaturnoe obozrenie,* the neat dichotomies of "unconscious protominimalism vs. conscious minimalism," or "modernist maximalism vs. postmodernist minimalism," suffer from the fact that "in such oppositions, regardless of their external effectiveness, the number of exceptions is usually higher than the number of 'exact hits.'"[8]

If not every prose poem presents an example of minimalist literature, one could argue that the miniature form typical for the prose poem entails at least a potential minimalism. This development from miniaturism to minimalism constitutes, as it were, the master plot of this book. It can be observed in the creative development of various authors discussed in this study, including Ivan Bunin, Aleksei Remizov, Velimir Khlebnikov, or Elena Guro. In this sense, the writer's individual career parallels the evolution of the genre as a whole. The "poetic," impressionist or ornamental prose of earlier miniatures gives way to an extremely condensed and sparse diction. Much of the stylistic bombast in the prose miniatures of the fin de siècle looks like a desperate rearguard action to salvage the "poeticity" of the prose poem from the negativity inherent in the genre's very principle. Once the form is allowed to follow its own internal logic, the prose poem realizes what we could call its Aristotelian entelechy. Poetic prose lyricism is replaced by an ascetic starkness, as the prose poem mutates into the minimalist anti-story.

With this somewhat teleological scheme I do not mean to imply that the historical development of the prose poem in Russia followed a strictly predetermined course. The hybrid nature of Turgenev's prototype allowed in fact for various directions and sub-branches, including a "decadent" variant (which became more or less extinct with the end of symbolism) and a didactic type, which has remained alive to this day in the prose poems of Aleksandr Solzhenitsyn. From an artistic and aesthetic point of view, however, it seems to me that the "minimalist" branch of the prose poem is the one most deserving of critical attention.

It is not my goal to give an exhaustive account of the history of the Russian prose poem in this book. Rather, I will note the various trends of writing prose poems by highlighting some of the most salient examples. If exhaustiveness is impossible, I will strive nevertheless for a certain comprehensiveness, given the uncharted territory in which I travel. The opening chapter provides a theoretical introduction, discussing the notion of minimalism, which is borrowed from the realm of American visual arts, and its implication for the theory of the prose poem. Chapter 2 is devoted to the prototype of the Russian prose poem, Ivan Turgenev's *Stikhotvoreniia v proze,* and its relation to Charles Baudelaire's *Petits poèmes en prose.* The following chapters discuss the prose miniatures of various literary schools, with the proviso that such classificatory attempts are always arbitrary to some degree and that significant overlap may exist between these trends.

Chapter 3 explores what is perhaps the most uniquely Russian contribution to the genre, the "realist" prose poem, focusing mainly on the work of Ivan Bunin. Chapter 4 provides an overview of the symbolist prose miniature, including such authors as Dmitrii Merezhkovskii, Konstantin Bal'mont, Valerii Briusov, Innokentii Annenskii, Andrei Belyi, Aleksandr Blok, and others. Although Fedor Sologub and Aleksei Remizov are also usually classified as symbolists, their miniature fairy tales and dreams are sufficiently independent and significant to warrant chapters of their own (chapters 5 and 6, respectively). A survey of futurist prose miniatures, in conjunction with avant-garde painting, is offered in chapter 7, and addresses such authors as Velimir Khlebnikov, Benedikt Livshits, Vasilii Kandinskii, and Elena Guro. Chapter 8, finally, is devoted to Daniil Kharms' minimalist prose. At the same time, it summarizes the discussion by highlighting the various correspondences between Kharms' oeuvre and previous Russian prose miniatures. The epilogue brings the discussion into the present time by contrasting Lev Rubinshtein's postmodern card catalogues with Aleksandr Solzhenitsyn's conservative prose miniatures.

Earlier versions of parts of this book have appeared in *Comparative Literature Studies, Slavic Review, Russian Review, and Slavic and East European Journal.*[9] I wish to thank the publishers for granting permission to incorporate the materials here. Research on this project has been supported by the Institute for the Arts and Humanistic Studies at Pennsylvania State University and by the Research and Graduate Studies Office in the College of the Liberal Arts. An IREX short-term travel grant enabled me to consult libraries and archives in Moscow in the summer of 1997. I am indebted to Pennsylvania State University for granting me a teaching release in the spring semester of 2000, which allowed me to work full-time on this project. Most of all, I am grateful to the numerous colleagues who have read and commented on earlier drafts of parts of this book, including my colleagues Michael Naydan and Linda Ivanits of Penn State and the two anonymous referees of Northwestern University Press. I thank Saul Morson for his early encouragement of the project and Caryl Emerson for agreeing to include the book in the "Studies in Russian Literature and Theory" series. My biggest gratitude is owed to my wife, Cathy Wanner, who has read every single draft of this book and has always been generous with her advice and judicious criticism. My work, and life, would be unthinkable without her. It is to her that I dedicate this book.

Russian Minimalism

Chapter One

Russian Minimalism and
the Theory of the Prose Poem

RUSSIAN LITERATURE has a reputation for giganto-mania. Ever since Henry James coined the phrase of the "loose baggy monster," the typical Russian novel has been seen in popular lore as an unwieldy behemoth with a bewildering array of characters and subplots. This verbosity is sometimes ascribed to the alleged maximalist mentality of the Russian people. Logorrhea and graphomania seem somehow the natural cultural consequences of living in the world's largest country. Like most stereotypes, of course, this perception does not hold up under closer scrutiny. The elegant conciseness of Pushkin's prose fiction, or the laconic "slice of life" realism of Chekhov's stories, which exerted such a seminal influence on much Western twentieth-century writing, are obvious counterexamples.

However, this is not a book about short stories. It deals with an even shorter genre, which I will tentatively call minimalist prose. This label requires some explanation. The term "minimalism" first gained prominence in the plastic arts as a designation for a group of New York artists who came to the fore in the 1960s, including Carl Andre, Dan Flavin, Donald Judd, Sol LeWitt, Robert Morris, and others. Although these artists never formed a coherent school (some of them in fact rejected the minimalist label), they shared a common concern with arranging industrial materials, such as steel, copper, brick, plywood, mirrored glass, or fluorescent light into regular, symmetrical, or gridded structures. Starkly presented, these works disposed of any pretense of craft or ornamental composition and were resistant to symbolic or metaphorical interpretation. Analogous to this development in the plastic arts, the minimalist label was also used by musicologists to characterize the reductionist and repetitious compositions of a Philip Glass or Steve Reich. In the realm of literature, the use of the term "minimalism" is somewhat less established. In the United States, it has become the designation for a type of short fiction popular during the 1980s, most prominently the stories of Raymond Carver. Sometimes dubbed "K-Mart realism," "hick chic," or "Diet Pepsi minimalism," the salient features of this style have been described as formal sparseness, a detached, deadpan tone, a relative lack of plot and depth, and a concern with surface detail and brandnames rather than with personal, social, political, or cultural history. The prevalent mode of this type of writing is realist or hyperrealist, and the subject matter is domestic, regional, quotidian, and banal.[1]

Of course, literary minimalism is not limited to American fiction of the 1980s. Nothing prevents us from applying the minimalist label in a wider sense and to claim it as a tendency of reductionist or sparse writing that can become productive in any literature at any time. From such a perspective, Heraclitus or Aesop might qualify as proto-minimalists. As Warren Motte has pointed out in his recent monograph on minimalism in contemporary French literature, France has a particularly rich tradition of prose miniatures, stretching from Pascal, La Rochefoucauld, La Fontaine, and La Bruyère all the way up to a host of contemporary writers. Another author who is sometimes referred to as a founding father of modern literary minimalism is Samuel Beckett. Beckett's thirty-five-second play *Breath,* according to Motte, qualifies as "the most radical example of minimalism . . . in English literature."[2] Motte never mentions Russian literature, yet Russia too produced a tradition of minimalist writing which deserves to be analyzed as such. It is interesting to note that the term *minimalism* itself is of Russian origin. The two individuals credited with coining the expression are the Russian-born artist John Graham (né Ivan Dombrovskii, 1886–1961) and the former cubo-futurist David Burliuk (1882–1967).[3] In addition, the Russian avant-garde in general, and Kazimir Malevich in particular, have been identified as precursors of New York minimalism of the 1960s.[4]

The tradition of Russian minimalism is little explored. So far, the term has mostly been applied to contemporary "postmodern" Russian poetry.[5] Yet one could argue that the effect of minimalism is more striking in prose than in verse. In poetry, miniature forms are not an uncommon phenomenon, given the natural tendency of poetic discourse toward condensation and heightened attention to the material side of language. The brevity of a quatrain, a tercet, or even a distich is unlikely to raise eyebrows. The critical limit is reached only with the monostich, which hovers uneasily between verse and prose, since in order to recognize the principle of lineation as such, we need more than one line.[6] A minimalist effect can also be achieved by repeating the same word or phrase a multitude of times. Theoretically, this repetition can go on ad infinitum. As an example, one could mention German Lukomnikov's poem "100 tysiach pochemu," which repeats the word "Pochemu?" ("Why?") a hundred thousand times.[7] In a prose text, the minimalist "threshold" is reached sooner than in verse. A text of only a few lines, while quite ordinary in lyric poetry, seems unusually short in the context of narrative prose. The device of repetition, which is to some extent

4

natural to poetry, will be perceived immediately as a kind of "fault" in the linear texture of prosaic discourse.

There is no universal agreement on the meaning of narrative minimalism. Motte defines "smallness" and "simplicity," converging into the notion of "lessening," as minimalist key terms. It is important to realize, however, that not everything small or simple qualifies ipso facto as minimalist. Minimalism entails a polemic thrust. It is characterized as much by what it negates as by what it affirms. The starkness and sparseness of minimalist sculpture has to be seen as a reaction against the exuberance and mystic pretentiousness of abstract expressionism, its precursor movement in the visual arts. "Lessening" entails not only a reduction in scope and complexity, but also a rupture of the beholder's horizon of expectation. The public is likely to perceive the minimalist object not just as small and simple, but rather as "too small" and "too simple" when measured against the prevalent standard of aesthetic norms. An unprepared viewer is likely to be baffled or disturbed by minimalist sculpture, which defies most parameters in which art has been traditionally defined. Its production does not seem to require any particular artistic talent or even simple craftsmanship. *Anybody*, after all, could assemble a pile of bricks or a stack of wood and declare it to be a work of art. Its anonymous, industrial outlook disposes with the notion of the artistic genius conveying a unique, individual vision—to borrow Walter Benjamin's terms, the aura of the work of art is shattered in the process of mechanical reproduction.[8] Perhaps even more disturbing is the apparent lack of referential or allegorical meaning. The minimalist object has no mimetic function; it does not symbolize anything. It simply exists.

To be sure, not every pile of bricks or stack of wood is a work of art. But there is no inherent, ontological difference between a "mere" pile of bricks and a minimalist sculpture consisting of a pile of bricks. The only difference between the two lies in the approach of the viewer, which in its turn is conditioned by the object's presentation: we look differently at a pile of bricks exhibited in an art gallery or museum than we do at the same object encountered on a construction site. In other words, matters of framing and labeling are central to the notion of minimal art. The minimalist object becomes art not by its essence, but by fiat: the fact that it is presented and labeled as a work of art is sufficient to constitute it as art (in some instances, the hefty price tag of the object may provide additional validation in terms of capitalist market value—a pile of bricks worth $100,000 obviously cannot be a "mere" pile of bricks). What is at stake here is a radical redefinition of art from an essentialist to a purely relational category. Marcel Duchamp's ready-mades, which have been named among the avatars of minimal art, present a well-known example of this trend. As far as literary minimalism is concerned, the same observations can be applied. Minimalist texts defy traditional generic expectations, constituting themselves as literature by fiat rather than by adhering to any received literary conventions. By doing so, they force the reader to revisit personal assumptions of generic classification.

John Perreault has described the generic shifts produced by minimal art forms thus:

> Paradoxically, the closer an artist gets to the mythological "essence" of his particular medium the faster his medium becomes something else. Frank Stella's shaped-canvases become a kind of flat sculpture for the wall. Cage's "music" becomes theatre. Concretist poems become graphic art. Prose becomes poetry or music. Film becomes a kind of projected painting. Architecture as it tries more and more to be simply architecture becomes sculpture. And sculpture as it strives for "sculptureness" becomes architecture or merely interior design. This paradoxical "media transportation" indicates perhaps that just as there is no ideal gameness that relates all games, there is no ideal art or essence of painting or sculpture, no "nature."[9]

Under conditions of extreme brevity, prose can become "poetry." This has little to do with a changed essence of the text. Rather, what is at stake is the perception of the text by the reader. "Poetry" implies a slowed-down process of reading which pays minute attention to details of form, style, prosody, and phonetics. In the same manner the viewer of a minimalist "white on white" painting will give special importance to shades and minute irregularities on the pictorial surface, the pigmentation of the paint on the canvas, and the physical "factuality" of the picture in its spatial surrounding.

The transformation of prose into poetry is intimately linked with the genre of the prose poem. Popularized in France by Charles Baudelaire and in Russia by Ivan Turgenev, the prose poem occupies a privileged position in the birth of literary minimalism. This is not to say that every prose poem follows a minimalist aesthetic. Rather than the actual practice, it is the *theory* of the prose poem that makes it fruitful for a discussion of minimalism. As Michael Riffaterre said, the prose poem "has the distinction of being the literary genre with an oxymoron for a name."[10] Located in the no-man's-land between poetry and prose, it raises a host of theoretical questions about the nature of poetry and prose as well as general problems of generic classification and labeling.

The oxymoronic nature of the prose poem is particularly evident in the Russian term *stikhotvorenie v proze,* since the word *stikhotvorenie* (literally "verse-making") implies versification. If we define poetry as versified literary discourse, the notion of poetry in prose seems nonsensical, a contradiction in terms. On the other hand, it is of course a long-acknowledged critical stance that the "poeticity" of a text may rely on factors other than versification. The conceptual split between versification and poetry can be traced as far back as Aristotle, who in his *Poetics* refused to acknowledge versified scientific and historic texts as poetry. The discovery of the "emotive function" of lyric poetry in Sentimentalism and Romanticism gave a further boost to the notion of a free-flowing, verseless, and rhymeless form of poetic expression. If we understand poetry as an outburst of lyrical energy, regular metric patterns would seem at best irrelevant and at worst a hindrance to what Wordsworth has dubbed the "spontaneous overflow of powerful feelings." From this perspective, the prose poem appears to be a lyric text that compensates for the lack of regular prosodic features by other means.

Until the 1960s, most critics considered the prose poem to be a form of "poeticized prose." How exactly the text established its poeticity remained a matter of contention, however; criteria ranged from formal features (rhythm, euphony, and textual patterning) and semantic tropes (symbolism, metaphors) to style (sublime vocabulary, ornamental syntax) and content (emotions, lyric expression). In an attempt to overcome the dated notions of the lyric on which some of those criteria relied, some scholars defined the poeticity of the prose poem as a structural *Gestaltqualität* (Ulrich Fülleborn) or "intertextual semiosis" (Michael Riffaterre).[11] What all these approaches have in common is the assumption of a necessary and demonstrable difference between the language of a prose poem and "ordinary" language. By virtue of its poetic status, the prose poem belongs to a higher aesthetic or semiotic level than simple narrative, descriptive, or expository prose. In his massive, but theoretically underdeveloped study of the prose poem in France, Germany, and England, John Simon states that "[u]ltimately, a *prose* poem is a prose *poem* because it is more beautiful than prose."[12] For Ulrich Fülleborn, the historian of the German *Prosagedicht,* the question becomes a matter of quality: an aesthetically polished essay, sketch, or anecdote is *eo ipso* a prose poem, whereas a bad prose poem is no prose poem at all.[13] Such an approach raises certain problems: after all, nobody would claim that a bad novel or a bad sonnet is no longer a novel or a sonnet. Does a prose poem have to be good in order to exist? And what does "good" mean, anyway?

A closer look at the textual evidence reveals that none of the criteria mentioned above really proves satisfactory in catching the elusive phenomenon of poeticity in the prose poem. While it is indeed possible to find individual prose poems by Baudelaire or Turgenev that feature a distinct rhythmic structure, an abundance of metaphors, or an emotional lyric content, it is also possible to find other prose poems by the same authors that lack all of those features. Some texts, far from shining examples of "poetic prose," seem to be written in a deliberately plain, "prosaic" fashion. This fact has proved unsettling to critics with a "poetic" concept of the prose poem and has led them to blame the author for not adhering to the rules established by the critic. Suzanne Bernard, the author of a monumental history of the French *poème en prose,* found many of Baudelaire's prose poems "too prosaic."[14] John Simon also bemoaned the fact that Baudelaire's prose poems "[do] not always escape prosaism, and often become merely anecdotal."[15]

Turgenev's prose poems have provoked similar evaluations. The East German scholar F.-J. Schaarschuh, for example, claimed that "by far not all of Turgenev's *Stikhotvoreniia v proze* are prose poems," since some of them fail to conform to Schaarschuh's definition of the prose poem as a lyric prose text "woven through" (*durchwebt*) with verse elements.[16] Schaarschuh is not the only critic who was lured by the semantic implications of the term "*stikhotvorenie v proze*" to search for metric elements in Turgenev's prose poems. Leonid Grossman believed that he had detected a whole row of various meters supposedly underlying Turgenev's texts.[17] However, besides the fact that random metric elements can be found in any prose text if one looks for them hard enough, Viktor Zhirmunskii has shown that Turgenev's *Stikhotvoreniia v proze* are in fact less rhythmical than some of the lyrical digressions in Turgenev's prose narratives.[18] In other words, if Turgenev's prose poems are defined as something "more than prose," it is hard to determine what exactly causes their alleged surplus value.

In light of the problematic and ultimately unsatisfactory attempt to grasp the phenomenon of the prose poem as poetic prose, an opposite approach began to emerge in Western criticism in the 1960s. In a seminal study on Bertrand and Baudelaire, Fritz Nies approached the genre in terms of *Entwirklichung* (de-realization) and *Verfremdung* (estrangement).[19] According to Nies, the prose poem reflects the crisis of lyric poetry in a prosaic age, where traditional notions of the lyric have become increasingly problematic. Bertrand and Baudelaire, as pioneers of the French *poème en prose*, tried to cope with this situation by creating a new, dynamic aesthetic of surprise, turning the unaesthetic and "prosaic" into the object of poetic discourse, and replacing the traditional emotive voice of the lyric with that of an ironically detached *flâneur*. In other words, rather than an upgraded form of prose, the prose poem becomes an intentionally degraded form of poetry. With this "destructive" potential, it undermines and explodes traditional generic boundaries and conventional lyrical and narrative forms. As the subsequent development in France and elsewhere has shown, the prose poem evolved from an "anti-poem" to a sort of avant-garde "anti-prose," whose most important pioneer was Arthur Rimbaud. Such texts radically depart from traditional models of plot construction, logical cohesiveness, and even conformity to syntactic and grammatical rules. As we will see, Russian literature of the twentieth century offers multiple examples of "disruptive" prose miniatures, including Fedor Sologub's "Little Fairy Tales," Aleksei Remizov's dreams, and the experimental prose of the futurist avant-garde, culminating in Daniil Kharms' absurdist mini-stories.

In the age of deconstruction and gender criticism, the "subversive" potential of the prose poem has been put to full use by a number of critics.

The authors of three American books on the prose poem published in the 1980s and 1990s all agree in their view of the genre as a form of "counter-discourse" (Richard Terdiman), the "place within literature where social antagonisms of gender and class achieve *generic* expression" (Jonathan Monroe), and a "genre-breaking genre" establishing a "tradition of subversion" (Margueritte Murphy).[20] Both Monroe and Murphy make ample use of Bakhtinian terminology, defining the prose poem as a locus of heteroglossia, a "dialogical genre" which, like Bakhtin's novel, constantly tests the limits of genre. While there is certainly some truth to these observations, especially as far as the French tradition of the *poème en prose* is concerned, they still fail to establish a definition that accounts for all existing examples of the *stikhotvorenie v proze.* Do we have to exclude, for example, "monological," or otherwise nonsubversive texts from the canon of prose poems? As an empirical observation shows, not every text labeled *stikhotvorenie v proze* lives up to the ideal of subversive agitation (some of them actually seem rather bland and conventional). One could also argue that the modern verse lyric is not always and not necessarily as single-voiced and hostile to experimentation as theoreticians of the prose poem have claimed. Steven Monte points out that "there is nothing preventing verse poems from including all but maybe one feature of the prose poem, the absence of line breaks."[21] In consequence, Monte denounces the assumption that prose poems have to be subversive as an "essentialist" stand.[22] If subversiveness, just like "poeticity," fails to provide a common denominator for all prose poems, it seems hard not to agree with Michel Beaujour, who has noted that "one can of course describe discrete texts, but the genre, type, sort of 'speech act,' kind of discourse, what have you, is so elusive that the theoretician may well wish to decide that there is after all no such thing as a prose poem, since this notion cannot be construed as the object of a poetic enquiry."[23]

For a theorist who nevertheless wishes to study the phenomenon of the *stikhotvorenie v proze,* a possible solution to this problem might be to adopt a "nominalist" rather than a "realist" stand. In other words, the prose poem may not exist as a *Ding an Sich* or Platonic form, but it still exists as a label that certain authors or interpretive communities choose to apply to certain texts. The choice of this label reveals certain ideas with which a given author (or a whole society or period) associates the nature of "poeticity." Furthermore, by choosing the label "prose poem," an author also enters into an implicit dialogue with other authors who have used the same label before. For the readers of such texts, the label functions as a signal exhorting them to approach the text in a certain manner defined by their own notion of poeticity. Again, this notion will vary from reader to reader and from period to period: it might be a quest for aesthetic pleasure, or, quite to the contrary, for the provocation of the unaesthetic shock experience. Of course, it is also possible to *mislabel* a text and frustrate the reader's expectations.

9

Given the anarchic nature of the prose poem, any attempt at formal characterization is fraught with problems. The following three features have been seen by many critics as pertinent to a definition of the genre:

1. *Prosaic form.* In order to qualify as a prose poem, a text obviously should be written in prose. This implies that it has to be printed as a continuous text without line breaks (otherwise it would be free verse). It is important to note that this is a purely typographical criterion and does not say anything further about the prosodic nature of the text. In most cases, a prose poem features no regular meter, but there are some borderline cases such as Maksim Gor'kii's "Burevestnik" ("The Stormy Petrel"), which is written in trochaic tetrameters, but printed with sentence rather than line breaks, or some of Konstantin Bal'mont's symbolist miniatures.[24] An interesting case of mislabeling is Turgenev's "Ia shel sredi vysokikh gor" ("I walked among high mountains"), which is clearly a verse poem (it features line breaks, regular iambic tetrameters, and rhymes), but was published as a *stikhotvorenie v proze*.

2. *Brevity.* Most critics agree that a prose poem has to be short.[25] The theoretical justification for this requirement may be based on a historically dated and debatable equation of poetry with organicist and expressionist lyricism, as Michel Beaujour has noted.[26] Still, it is an empirical fact that texts labeled as *stikhotvorenie v proze* do not usually exceed a length of one or two pages. Many of them are even shorter, congealing into micro-texts that offer, to quote David Young's whimsical characterization of the prose poem, "life histories reduced to paragraphs, essays the size of postcards, novels in nutshells, maps on postage stamps, mind-bending laundry lists, theologies scribbled on napkins."[27] Baudelaire took care to state brevity as a constitutive feature of the genre by labeling his texts "*Petits* poèmes en prose" (my italics). The situation seems even clearer in Russia, where the term *stikhotvorenie* (as opposed to *poema*) implies in itself a short text.[28] Perhaps it is this built-in notion of brevity in the semantics of the generic label that explains why Turgenev's *Stikhotvoreniia v proze* are on average shorter than Baudelaire's.

3. *Autonomy.* The prose poem is not part of a larger narrative framework. For this reason, "lyric digressions" in narrative prose do not in themselves constitute prose poems, although critics have sometimes described them as such.[29] On the other hand, prose poems usually appear as part of a series or cycle.[30] However, this series does not constitute a sequential narrative. Both Baudelaire and Turgenev described the order of their collection of prose poems as random and invited the reader to "browse" through it without following the typographical arrangement of the book.[31]

Prosaic form, brevity, and autonomy may be necessary features of the prose poem, but one could object that the same criteria also apply to other short prose genres such as aphorism, anecdote, or parable. In fact, many prose poems are *also* aphorisms, anecdotes, or parables in that they exist in an overlapping system of genres. Because of the fluidity of its contours, the prose poem is able to accommodate a variety of preexisting forms. In the case of Baudelaire's *Petits poèmes en prose,* Marie Maclean mentions the "*Märchen* or wonder-tale, the *Sage* or anecdote, the fable, the allegory, the cautionary tale, the tale-telling contest, the short story, the dialogue, the novella, the narrated dream."[32] Michel Delville, in his investigation of the contemporary American prose poem, lists "the fable, the parable, the dream narrative, the aphorism, the journal entry, the *pensée,* the dictionary definition, or even the stand-up comedy joke."[33] These lists seem rather similar to the inventory of sub-genres that Neil Cornwell has drawn up for Daniil Kharms' mini-stories, which includes "the fable, the parable, the folk-tale, the children's story, the philosophical or dramatical dialogue, the comic monologue, pantomime (or *commedia dell'arte*), carnival and the silent movie."[34]

The distinction between a "regular" fable and a fable-like prose poem has less to do with any intrinsic "poetic" textual qualities of the latter than with the manner of its presentation. A prose text becomes a prose *poem* in the same manner as a pile of bricks becomes a minimalist sculpture—by being labeled as such. What distinguishes a "parabolic prose poem" from a "mere" parable is the fact that the former is presented in a frame that invites the reader to regard the text as a poem. The notions of labeling and framing point to the crucial role of what Gérard Genette calls the *paratexte* in establishing a definition of the prose poem.[35] As Margueritte Murphy rightfully notes, "such features as title and subtitle, preface and preamble, help us recognize a text as a prose poem, as well as the typographical presentation of the text on the page, and the fact of its inclusion in a volume marked as 'poetry' or 'poems.'"[36]

To be sure, this definition of the prose poem still begs the question as to why anyone would want to label a prose text "poetry." The shock value of a seemingly incongruous designation, denoting an impossible *coincidentia oppositorum,* lies at the core of the prose poem. Thomas Beebee has described the genre as "a dehiscence between two opposing use-values of language."[37] To borrow a term from Gary Saul Morson, we could call the prose poem a "boundary genre," a form of literature governed by "two mutually exclusive sets of conventions." Morson explains that "a boundary genre may be compared to disputed territory over which neither side has clear sovereignty at a given moment or to a person with dual citizenship in time of war."[38] In problematizing the traditional dichotomy between poetry and prose, the prose poem belongs really to neither category. As Barbara John-

11

son puts it in her groundbreaking study of Baudelaire's *poèmes en prose:* "Neither antithesis nor synthesis, the prose poem is the place from where the polarity—and therefore the symmetry—between presence and absence, between prose and poetry, *disfunctions.*"[39]

Ultimately, the prose poem questions not only the status of poetry, but of any kind of generic classification as well. The boundaries rendered problematic include not only the dichotomy between poetry and prose, but also the distinction between literature and nonliterature. As Stamos Metzidakis notes, "[i]n the final analysis, the prose poem's greatest value [. . .] lies in its intrinsic capacity to proclaim more boldly perhaps than any other type of literary text does the following: If you want 'literature,' here it is! Unfortunately though, after reading prose poems closely, we still do not really know what it is we have."[40] Russell Edson, one of the foremost writers of prose poems in contemporary American literature, states it more colloquially and bluntly: "Heck, one can call most anything a prose poem. That's what's great about them, anything that's not something else is probably a prose poem; that's why they offer unique ways of making things."[41]

If any prose text can function as poetry, then any text, of whatever provenance or whatever aesthetic quality, can qualify as a work of literature. The notion of "literariness" shifts from a textual quality to a relational category involving the rapport between reader and text. In this sense, the prose poem partakes in a major trend in twentieth-century art: in its deconstruction of poeticity, and ultimately, literariness, it illustrates, perhaps more than any other literary genre, the principle of minimalism. The notion of "lessening," which we have introduced as a key term of minimalist aesthetics, is crucial for the definition of the prose poem. In the generic context of prose literature, it is "less than a story," given its brevity; as a work of poetry, given its lack of meter, rhyme, and lineation, it is "less than a poem." Essentially, the nature of the genre consists in a cluster of minus-functions, defining itself primarily by what it *is not* rather than by what it is. In addition, the generic indeterminacy of the prose poem is also a defining feature of minimalist art. The postmodern interest in the subversion of boundaries may be one reason for the current fashionable status that this genre enjoys in American literature and criticism.[42]

To be sure, this does not mean that every *stikhotvorenie v proze* necessarily follows a minimalist aesthetic. As we will see, Ivan Turgenev, the founder of the genre in Russia, was driven simultaneously by "subversive" and conservative impulses. Nevertheless, it was Turgenev who laid the groundwork for the more radical prose experiments of his twentieth-century modernist successors. In this sense, a discussion of Russian minimalist prose has to begin with Turgenev's "Poems in Prose," to which we now turn.

Chapter Two

Ivan Turgenev's Rewriting of Baudelaire

NOT EVERY LITERARY GENRE has a clearly discernible origin. Yet the birth of the Russian prose poem, or *stikhotvorenie v proze,* can be dated rather precisely. On August 12, 1882, M. M. Stasiulevich, the editor of the St. Petersburg journal *Vestnik Evropy* (*The Herald of Europe*), paid a visit to Ivan Turgenev in his Bougival residence near Paris. In conversation with the aging and ailing novelist, Stasiulevich mentioned that English newspapers had been reporting a piece of "pleasant news"—allegedly, the eminent writer was about to complete a new novel. Turgenev vehemently denied such rumors. Not only was he not writing a novel, he declared, but he would never write one again, and he had proof. With these words, Turgenev pulled from his desk drawer a folder containing a jumble of loose manuscript sheets of various sizes and colors. He told the astonished Stasiulevich that this folder contained something like a collection of sketches that an artist would draw before completing a large painting. "These are my materials," Turgenev explained. "They would serve a useful purpose if I were to undertake a big project; but, in order to prove to you that I am not writing anything now or in the future, I will seal all this and give it to you for safekeeping until my death."[1] Stasiulevich confessed to be confused about what such "materials" could possibly amount to and asked his host to read him some excerpts. Turgenev obliged this request, and Stasiulevich was highly impressed by what he heard. He begged Turgenev to reconsider his decision to keep these manuscripts under lock and key. Turgenev finally gave his consent to the publication of fifty pieces, which appeared in the December issue of *Vestnik Evropy.*[2]

The title under which these texts were to be published elicited some debate. In his first drafts, Turgenev had used the designation "Posthuma," suggesting a publication only after his death. This label seemed now no longer appropriate. Stasiulevich rejected Turgenev's subsequent title, "Senilia," probably because he feared the potentially unflattering associations that such a designation might provoke.[3] Instead, Stasiulevich proposed "Zigzagi" ("Zigzags"). He justified this choice in a letter to A. N. Pypin with the observation that Turgenev's prose miniatures are "short like lightnings, and

like a lightning they suddenly illuminate before you enormous perspec-
tives."[4] In the same letter, however, Stasiulevich admitted that Turgenev
himself preferred a different title: the generic designation "Poems in Prose"
(*Stikhotvoreniia v proze*). It is under this label that the pieces finally appeared in *Vestnik Evropy*. A new genre was thus born to Russian literature.

How is this new genre defined? Setting aside for the moment the
crucial question of Turgenev's indebtedness to Charles Baudelaire's *Petits
poèmes en prose,* a few preliminary observations are in order. We note that
Turgenev defines his new genre *negatively*. Not only is the prose poem not
a novel, but the author uses it as justification for his refusal to write any
more novels. We could almost call it an anti-novel. In fact, the new genre
suggests not only the breakdown of the novelistic form, but—if we are to
take literally Turgenev's assertion that he "is not writing anything"—the end
of literature *tout court*. The original title, "Posthuma," could be read as a
reference to the death of the author, but also to the death of the novel, or
perhaps the death of literature. In this sense, the prose poem looms as a
spectral presence, part of the debris from the shipwreck of the novelistic
form. Turgenev's last novel, *Nov'* (*Virgin Soil,* 1877), had in fact been a critical fiasco.

It is interesting to note that the theme of posthumous life surfaces in
one of Turgenev's earliest prose poems, "Sopernik" ("The Rival," February
1878, PSS 10:130). The first-person narrator, an agnostic, scoffs at the notion
of life after death. His "rival," who is a religious believer, announces that, if
he dies earlier than the narrator, he will pay him a visit from the other world.
The rival dies and one night he appears before the narrator. He does not
utter a single word, however. To all questions, he merely nods his head
"silently and sadly." When the narrator breaks into laughter, the ghost disappears. Given Turgenev's original intention to call his prose miniatures
"Posthuma," it is tempting to read this text as a meta-generic allegory of the
prose poem as a "posthumous text." As the disembodied ghost of the deceased novelistic form, the new genre stubbornly refuses to answer our
inquiries about immortality, the meaning of life, and other "ultimate questions," the topics on which other Russian novelists such as Dostoevskii and
Tolstoi had expatiated so freely. Ultimately, the prose poem, like the ghost
in Turgenev's story, appears not to be saying much at all. Similar to a flash
of lightning "zigzagging" through the sky, it is visible only for an ephemeral
moment before everything reverts to darkness. The epistemological gain offered by this brief illumination seems dubious at best.

The publication of Turgenev's prose poems in *Vestnik Evropy* caused
some consternation among literary critics. The most negative assessment
came from the leading radical, Nikolai Chernyshevskii, the author of the influential novel *Chto delat'?* (*What Is to be Done?*). In a letter to his son in
Paris, who had sent him a few of his own prose poems inspired by Turgenev,

Chernyshevskii condemned the new genre in unequivocal terms. He alleged that such texts cannot claim a literary status at all. At best they are "themes" or "rough drafts" (*chernovye nabroski*), which require an act of painstaking labor to be transformed into a work of art. As Chernyshevskii put it: "Peasant huts are built with rough-hewn logs. But giving the public a wood chip (*shchepku*) betrays a lack of respect for one's gift. The chip has to be transformed through thoughtful carving into a very beautiful little thing of regular outlines; only then will it be a suitable gift."[5] Chernyshevskii argues that while unadorned, "plain" language is fine for a longer narrative, the miniature form requires a heightened concentration of artistic means. In another letter to his son, Chernyshevskii drew a connection with the visual arts to illustrate his point (as Turgenev had done himself when he presented his prose poem to Stasiulevich as artist's sketches). Suspecting the authors of prose poems to be lacking in poetic talent and schooling, Chernyshevskii argued that someone who does not have the proper technique should not engage in painting at all.[6]

With his example of the wood chip as a work of art, Chernyshevskii provided an unwitting anticipation of the twentieth-century concept of the "ready-made." Thirty years before Marcel Duchamp scandalized the New York art world with his urinal, Chernyshevskii had already furnished the standard arguments that would later be raised against minimal or conceptual forms of art: How can something be called art if it displays no evidence of craft and technique? After all, the word "art" (Latin *ars*) implies technical mastery, or, as the Germans like to put it, *Kunst* comes from *können* ("to be able"). If *anybody* can do it, how can it be special? Interestingly enough, Chernyshevskii's assessment of Turgenev's prose poems as "materials," "themes," or "rough drafts" in need of further elaboration corresponds exactly to the way Turgenev had first presented his texts to Stasiulevich. As we remember, he introduced his pieces as "materials" for a never-to-be-written novel and agreed only with some reluctance to make of them a "gift" to the public.

How then does a rough draft become a prose poem? Chernyshevskii's Parnassian notion of an elaborately chiseled "thing of beauty" is not absent from Turgenev's creative concept. This can be illustrated with another metafictional text. The prose poem "Kubok" ("The Goblet," January 1878, PSS 10:178) has been read as a metapoetic comment on its own generic raison d'être. According to Peter Brang, "Kubok" could even serve as the motto for all of Turgenev's prose poems:[7]

Кубок

Мне смешно . . . и я дивлюсь на самого себя.

Непритворна моя грусть, мне действительно тяжело жить, горестны и безотрадны мои чувства. И между тем я стараюсь придать им блеск и красивость, я ищу образов и сравнений; я округляю мою речь, тешусь звоном и созвучием слов.

Я, как ваятель, как золотых дел мастер, старательно леплю и вырезываю и всячески украшаю тот кубок, в котором я сам же подношу себе отраву.

The Goblet

It amuses me . . . and I am astonished about myself.

My sadness is not faked, life is indeed hard for me, bitter and joyless are my feelings. And at the same time I am striving to give them polish and beauty, I search for images and comparisons; I am rounding off my speech, taking pleasure in the sound and harmony of words.

Like a sculptor, like a master goldsmith, I painstakingly mould and carve and decorate in various manners the goblet in which I give myself poison.

Rather than as a piece of untreated "raw material," the prose poem appears here as a carefully crafted work of art. We notice the self-reflective character of this text: its content consists entirely of the description of its own writing. The image and comparison that the poet claims to be looking for is the one already presented to the reader in the title. The process of stylistic elaboration described in the text—"the sound and harmony of words"—is illustrated by Turgenev's carefully crafted sonorous cadences. In chiseling and polishing his object to perfection, Turgenev's poetic persona seems to closely follow Chernyshevskii's advice. However, the text as a whole hardly supports the notion of an unproblematic celebration of impassive beauty, presumably as an aesthetic sublimation of life's pains and sufferings. It turns out that the beautifully decorated goblet serves as a vessel of death. Filled with poison, it becomes an instrument of suicide. The poetic *homo faber*, while patiently sculpting and crafting his text, engages in a form of self-destructive behavior that elicits both wonder and derision.

In trying to define the essence of Turgenev's prose poems, we are left with a confusing conglomerate of contradictory questions. Is the prose poem a piece of untreated raw material? A specter arising from the dead body of the novel? A beautifully crafted vial of poison? The mutual incompatibility of these concepts points to a general aporia that arises each time we try to grasp the nature of this problematic genre. In another piece that can be read as a metageneric allegory, Turgenev suggests that the poeticity of the prose poem is a phenomenon of reader response rather than of any inherent formal or linguistic quality. The prose poem "Dva chetverostishiia" ("Two Quatrains," April 1878, PSS 10:139–42) tells the story of two poets, Iunii and Iulii, who live in a country where everyone craves poetry so much that the absence of new poems is considered a national calamity. Iunii and Iulii compete for the favor of the public with two quatrains that are virtually identical (in fact, Iulii seems to have plagiarized his text from Iunii). But while Iunii is driven from the podium with enraged boos and hisses—

the irate crowd even threatens to lynch him—Iulii is hailed as a new poetic genius. A wise old man explains to the flabbergasted Iunii that his problem was simply bad timing: "You said your own—but not at the right time; and he said not his own—but at the right time." Turgenev's jab at the fickleness and stupidity of the reading public may be related to the disappointing reception of his own works—attacks against journalists and critics are indeed standard fare in many of his prose poems. Yet the story also raises an interesting theoretical issue. As it turns out, the same text, depending on shifting parameters of presentation, can be received as either worthless trash or splendid poetry. In other words, poeticity is entirely in the eye of the beholder.

It becomes clear that Turgenev's prose poems acquire their poetic status as a result of a particular framing and labeling. Rather than by a shared essence, the various texts labeled as prose poems are connected by a "family resemblance." Wittgenstein's observation that the various phenomena we call "games" do not have one thing in common, but are related to each other in many different ways, provides a compelling model both for genre theory in general and for the prose poem in particular.[8] This is true even for the limited corpus of Turgenev's *Stikhotvoreniia v proze*, which, besides brevity, seem to have little else in common. Lyric and prosaic, dramatic and idyllic, narrative and descriptive, and sentimental and aphoristic pieces mingle on a random basis. As we know from Stasiulevich's memoir, even the paper on which they were written came in various sizes and colors. And yet, the mere fact that all these pieces were gathered together in a folder marked "Posthuma," then "Senilia," and finally "Poems in Prose," forces us to consider them as a unified corpus in need of a definition. At the same time, in their stubborn resistance to this classificatory attempt, the *Stikhotvoreniia v proze* make Turgenev look like an unwitting ancestor of the modernist, or even postmodernist, avant-garde.

Of course, all of this does not tell us much about Turgenev's originality. Should we see him as the originator of a new literary form, or was he simply following in the footsteps of Charles Baudelaire, who is usually credited with the invention of the modern prose poem? As the most recent monograph on this topic asserts, "it is generally agreed that Baudelaire's prose poems constitute the model, which was to determine the parameters of the genre and validate all such literary enterprises in the future, establishing expectations and conditioning the reader's response to such texts."[9] Having spent the first years of his creative career as a verse poet, Baudelaire began to experiment with prose poetry in 1855. A complete edition of his fifty prose poems appeared posthumously in 1869. Later editions were published either under the title *Petits poèmes en prose* or *Le Spleen de Paris*. After a long hiatus of critical neglect, during which Baudelaire's prose poems were overshadowed by the verse poetry of *Les Fleurs du Mal*, the prose poems have emerged in recent years as a major focus of critical interest.[10] The innovative genre of the *poème en prose* has been increasingly recognized as Baudelaire's breakthrough to poetic modernity, or, to borrow the subtitle of Barbara Johnson's influential 1979 deconstructionist monograph, as "Baudelaire's second revolution."[11] For most contemporary critics, the "subversive" character of Baudelaire's oxymoronic genre has by now become a commonplace.

In his famous dedication to the editor Arsène Houssaye for the twenty prose poems published in *La Presse* in 1862, Baudelaire provided a genealogy and a poetics for his new genre. He pointed to Aloysius Bertrand's little-known *Gaspard de la nuit*, published in 1842, as the source of his inspiration, and evoked his dream of "le miracle d'une prose poétique musicale sans rhythme et sans rime, assez souple et assez heurtée pour s'adapter aux mouvements lyriques de l'âme, aux ondulations de la rêverie, aux soubresauts de la conscience" ("the miracle of a musical poetic prose without rhythm and without rhyme, flexible and rugged enough to adapt itself to the lyrical movements of the soul, to the undulations of reverie, the spasms of conscience").[12] This formula, as suggestive as it sounds, has not proven very helpful for a definition of the genre. A closer inspection casts doubt upon both the genealogical and the poetic claim in Baudelaire's preface. Critics have not failed to note that Baudelaire's prose poems have little in common with Bertrand's (Baudelaire himself states as much in his preface, acknowledging that he wrote "quelque chose . . . de singulièrement différent"). Furthermore, as noted earlier, Baudelaire's allegedly "poetic" prose seems in part rather antipoetic and antimusical. Fraught with ironies, Baudelaire's preface is therefore best understood as a sort of prose poem in itself. To complicate things even more, Rosemary Lloyd has noted the "slippage between meaning and statement" in Baudelaire's description of poetic prose, since "no language, however prosaic, can be without rhythm."[13]

In a further attempt to explain his project, Baudelaire located his new genre specifically in the modern metropolis. In his words, "c'est surtout de la fréquentation des villes énormes, c'est du croisement de leur innombrable rapports que naît cet idéal obsédant" ("it is mostly from exposure to enormous cities, from the intersection of their innumerable connections, that this obsessive ideal is born"). Besides providing a thematic and stylistic characterization, this statement can also be understood as a meta-generic allegory: the prose poem itself is located at a crossroads, in constant dialogue with other genres, a dynamic rather than a static entity. Since Baudelaire began his career as a verse poet, the relation between his verse and prose poems is of special interest. In an 1866 letter, Baudelaire claimed that his prose poems were "encore *Les Fleurs du mal,* mais avec beaucoup plus de liberté, et de détail, et de raillerie" ("another *Fleurs du mal,* but with much more liberty, detail, and mockery").[14] The notion of "raillerie" points to the importance of irony in Baudelaire's project. Evidently, the prose poem can be used to undermine not only traditional notions of poetry, but also of narrative prose. It particularly renders questionable any straightforward moralizing claims of literature. This point becomes evident in another letter of the same year, in which Baudelaire describes his project as that of a *flâneur* who extracts "de chaque objet une morale désagréable."[15]

Since the modern prose poem originated in France, any consideration of the Russian *stikhotvorenie v proze* has to address the question of its indebtedness to the Baudelairean model. Turgenev's residence in Paris and his intimate knowledge of the French literary world make it extremely likely that he was familiar with Baudelaire's prose poems. Although Turgenev never mentions Baudelaire in any of his critical essays or letters, there is some circumstantial evidence pointing to a link between Turgenev's and Baudelaire's texts.[16] The generic title *Stikhotvoreniia v proze* seems to be inspired by Baudelaire. This parallel becomes even more obvious if we look at the French translation of Turgenev's prose poems, which was done partially by the author himself, and appears under the exact Baudelairean title, *Petits poèmes en prose.* In the margins of his rough drafts, Turgenev characterized his pieces as "poems without rhyme and meter" (PSS 10:445), a designation that closely resembles Baudelaire's "prose poétique . . . sans rhythme et sans rime" (although we note that Turgenev replaced Baudelaire's problematic absence of rhythm with a more commonsense absence of meter).

In the original publication, both Baudelaire's and Turgenev's collections contained fifty pieces, and both authors ultimately intended to augment this number to one hundred. Like Baudelaire's, Turgenev's prose poems are heterogeneous in nature and defy easy generalizations. Rhetorically highly elaborate, lyrical pieces mingle with rather "prosaic," narrative, anecdotal, or aphoristic texts. In his drafts, Turgenev divided his already completed and yet-to-be-written pieces into three subcategories, entitled "Themes" (*siuzhety*), "Dreams" (*sny*), and "Landscapes" (*peizazhi*).[17] Baudelaire's draft project of prose poems included similar categories ("Choses parisiennes," "Onéirocritie," and "Symboles et Moralités").[18] It is noteworthy that the dream appears as a subgenre of the prose poem with both authors. As noted before, similarities also exist on the level of the suggested reception that both authors propose for their texts. In his preface to the *Vestnik Evropy* publication, Turgenev recommends a random, nonsequential mode of reading for his prose poems. As he puts it: "My dear reader, do not run through these poems one after the other: you will probably get bored—and the book will fall from your hands. Read them separately: today one, tomorrow another—and one of them, perhaps, will arouse something in your soul" ("K chitateliu," PSS 10:125). This aleatory approach echoes the advice Baudelaire gives in the preface to his prose poems, encouraging his readers to interrupt the reading wherever they want to, without paying attention to a "superfluous plot."[19]

Even though the idea and framework of Turgenev's prose poems seem inspired by Baudelaire, more concrete parallels are harder to detect. This is hardly surprising, of course, if we remember the vast difference between the two writers in personality, social status, and literary practice. The Russian realist, political moderate, and solid establishment figure had little in common with the French bohemian enfant terrible and revolutionary founder of poetic modernity. The few critics who looked at both Baudelaire's *Petits poèmes en prose* and Turgenev's *Stikhotvoreniia v proze* have not failed to stress the differences between the two authors' personalities, worldviews, and literary practices.[20] The links that critics have unearthed between the prose poems of Baudelaire and Turgenev are for the most part quite vague. Allen mentions a common preoccupation with "death, evil, nature, beauty, dreams, and time."[21] Other critics point to a common "tragic worldview,"[22] the tendency toward allegory,[23] or the "interpretation of human existence through contrasting philosophical generalizations."[24] Many of those parallels are part of the larger postromantic European heritage and do not in themselves indicate a concrete linkage between Baudelaire and Turgenev. The Soviet editors of Turgenev's complete works deemed it necessary to include a word of warning to those bent on hunting for concrete parallels between the prose poems of Baudelaire and Turgenev. They dismissed such an endeavor as a fruitless enterprise that could yield only "unconvincing" results.[25] Yet a closer look reveals that there are indeed some specific thematic links between Baudelaire's and Turgenev's prose poems. These parallels are interesting not so much for what they show about Turgenev's indebtedness to Baudelaire, but for what they reveal about the *differences* between the two authors. While borrowing certain elements from Baudelaire, Turgenev fundamentally transformed them in order to make them palatable to his own poetic system.

Turgenev's rewriting of Baudelaire can be illustrated with his treatment of "La Corde" ("The Rope"), which served as a source not just for one, but for two of his own prose poems. First published in *Le Figaro* in 1864, Baudelaire's "La Corde" is based on a true story about the painter Edouard Manet (to whom the prose poem is dedicated). The narrator, a painter, begins by declaring that his tale will demonstrate the illusionary nature of something that is taken by most people as an "evident, trivial phenomenon": maternal love. The story relates how the painter takes in a poor boy whose appearance he finds striking. He uses him as a model, dressing him up in various poses such as a gypsy with a violin, the crucified Christ, and Eros with a torch. Finally, he is so enraptured by his model that he asks the child's parents for permission to have the boy live with him to do various odd jobs in the workshop. The boy moves in with the painter and soon develops an immoderate taste for sugar and liquor. One day, the exasperated painter threatens to return him to his parents. When he comes back to the workshop, the boy has hanged himself. The painter is horrified, but when he informs the boy's parents, they seem strangely unmoved. No tears appear in the mother's eyes, a fact that the narrator first interprets as a result of excessive grief. Later, the mother comes to see him in his workshop and asks for the nail and rope with which her child hanged himself. The painter first assumes that she sees these things as a sort of "horrible and dear relic." The next day, he receives numerous letters from people begging him for a piece of the rope. Now the mother's true intention dawns on him: she wants to make money by selling the rope in pieces as a good-luck charm to superstitious people.

The startling behavior of this "bad mother," which provides the moral of the painter's story and serves to justify his dim view of motherly love, is really rooted in a popular saying. The semantic kernel of Baudelaire's prose poem is a French idiomatic expression: "avoir de la corde de pendu" (having a piece of a hanged person's rope) means "to have good luck."[26] This does not mean that people were actually peddling ropes of suicide victims in nineteenth-century France. Baudelaire, as he does in some other prose poems, takes a figure of speech literally.[27] No such saying, let alone such a tradition, exists in Russia. If the same motif appears in Turgenev's prose poems, this can only be explained as a borrowing from Baudelaire.

However, Turgenev uses the figure of the "lucky" noose in a radically different context. The prose poem "Chernorabochii i beloruchka" ("The Worker and the Man with White Hands," or literally, "Black-worker and White-hand," PSS 10:143–44), written in 1878, relates the dialogue between a worker and a member of the radical intelligentsia. The intellectual tries to convince the worker that they are "brothers," despite his white hands. He explains that his hands smell of iron because he spent six years in a forced labor camp. He was sent there because he wanted to free the working people and rebelled against their oppressors. The worker is unimpressed. "They locked you up?" he asks. "It serves you right: what did you have to rebel for?" The second half of the prose poem relates the dialogue between the worker and a co-worker two years later. The intellectual has now been sentenced to death and is going to be executed. The two workers are unmoved by his fate. They are only interested in the event because they hope to obtain the rope with which "white-hand" will be hanged. As they explain, it brings "good luck to the home."

The differences between Baudelaire's and Turgenev's treatment of the motif are obvious. Turgenev situates his story in the political context of the failed populist "going-to-the-people" movement of the 1870s (which was also the subject of his novel *Virgin Soil*). The suicide is replaced by the genuine—if useless—martyrdom of the Russian revolutionary. In Baudelaire's text, the theme of martyrdom is present on a subliminal level: one of the poses in which the painter depicts the child is that of the crucified Christ, bearing "the Crown of Thorns and the Nails of the Passion." As Marie Maclean has noted, the boy is "finally granted a sort of blasphemous *pietà* as his mother clasps to her bosom, not the body, but the rope whose fragments have acquired a miraculous value almost like those of the Cross."[28] Turgenev's hero is comparable to Jesus inasmuch as his martyrdom also becomes a source of commercially exploitable relics. Their commercial value has no relation to his personality or deeds, and those engaged in the relic trade obviously have no appreciation for the sacrifice made on their behalf. Turgenev's satire targets both the obtuse ignorance of the Russian laborers and the quixotic idealism of the radical intelligentsia.[29]

Baudelaire's narrator, as we remember, declares his disillusionment with the notion of motherly love to be the point of his story. If "La Corde" is a parody of the Passion of Christ, the boy's mother certainly does not act like the Virgin Mary; instead of grieving the death of her son as one would expect, she immediately engages in the profitable trade of relics associated with his suicide. Turgenev developed this theme of Baudelaire's prose poem in a separate text, "Shchi" ("Cabbage Soup," PSS 10:151–52), which he wrote one month after "The Worker and the Man with White Hands." Ironically, by cutting and recycling "La Corde" in this way, Turgenev treated his Baudelairean subtext in a fashion similar to the manner in which the mother in Baudelaire's story treats the fatal noose: he, too, cuts the "Rope" into smaller pieces to use them for separate purposes.[30] Baudelaire's rope thus becomes the virtual intertextual string that ties together some seemingly disparate and unrelated elements in Turgenev's prose poems.

"Shchi," the second of Turgenev's texts related to "La Corde," is the story of a peasant widow who has lost her only son, twenty-year-old Vasya, "the best worker in the village." The landowner's wife pays her a visit to express her condolences. To her surprise, she finds the peasant woman sitting at the table eating cabbage soup. The noble lady is shocked by this behavior: "My God! She can eat in such a moment. . . . What vulgar feelings all these people have!" The landlady remembers how, when she lost her nine-month-old daughter a few years back, she was so grief-stricken that she refused to rent a charming *dacha* in the countryside and stayed the entire summer in St. Petersburg. She asks the peasant woman for an explanation:

> "My Vasya is dead," muttered the woman quietly, and tears of pain run again over her hollow cheeks. "That means that my end is near too: I have lost all [literally: my head has been chopped off (*s zhivoi s menia sniali golovu*)]. But the cabbage soup must not go to waste: it has been salted, you know."
>
> The lady only shrugged her shoulders and walked away. Salt did not cost *her* much.

In both Baudelaire's and Turgenev's prose poems, a mother's grief over her dead son seems compromised by a concern with money. However, Turgenev clearly exculpates the mother's behavior. The upper-class lady who is shocked by the peasant woman's seeming lack of grief is presented as a figure of satirical scorn; it is she who lacks real feelings, not the peasant woman, who appears instead as a monument of quiet moral dignity. Unlike the mother figure in Baudelaire's text, she does have tears on her face. Her economic motivation is thrift, given that salt was heavily taxed in Russia and therefore a luxury item for the poor. The mother in "La Corde," however, seems driven only by a desire for profit.[31]

It appears that Turgenev's design was to correct "La Corde" by rehabilitating Baudelaire's "bad mother." In the context of Turgenev's prose poems, the virtues of motherhood are celebrated rather than questioned. In the prose poem "Vorobei" ("The Sparrow," PSS 10:142), which was written in the same month as "Chernorabochii i beloruchka," Turgenev portrays a heroic sparrow mother who defends in kamikaze-fashion her fledgling from the potential attacks of the narrator's dog. Turgenev explains her self-sacrificing behavior with the concluding comment that "love is stronger than death and the fear of death. Only through it, only through love is life maintained and sustained" (tol'ko liubov'iu derzhitsia i dvizhetsia zhizn'). In its sententious ponderousness, this comment echoes the initial statement of Baudelaire's narrator in "La Corde": "If there exists an evident, trivial phenomenon, always alike, and of a nature of which it is impossible to be deceived, it is maternal love."[32] Of course, the narrator then proceeds to question the truth of this statement, whereas Turgenev's intention, quite to the contrary, is to reaffirm and reinforce the ideal of motherly love.

The theme appears once again in one of the last of Turgenev's prose poems, "U-a . . . U-a . . ." (PSS 10:188–89), written in November 1882. The narrator relates how he was about to commit suicide by throwing himself from a precipice in the Swiss Alps when he suddenly heard the voice of a baby crying. He rushed toward the origin of this sound and discovered, in a simple peasant hut, a young woman who was nursing her child, with a shepherd, "probably her husband," sitting next to her. This sight relieved him instantly from his "Byronic" and suicidal moods: "O ardent cry of a newborn human life, you saved me, you cured me!" One suspects that it was exactly this kind of rhetoric that Baudelaire set out to undermine in his *Petits poèmes en prose.* Turgenev's strategy, on the other hand, consists of defending the truth in the commonplace from Baudelaire's subversive attacks: for *him,* motherly love is indeed "an evident phenomenon."[33]

Turgenev's texts operate in a straightforward, nonironic mode. The reader is invited to identify with the narrator and his conclusions. This is doubtless how Turgenev himself read "La Corde": he took the narrator's comment on motherly love at face value and found it necessary to rebut it. Turgenev was not alone in taking Baudelaire's attack against the mother seriously. According to Robert Kopp, the editor of a critical edition of *Petits poèmes en prose*, Baudelaire's "precise and cold" narrative illustrates indeed "the deep perversity—natural, according to Baudelaire—of which a woman is capable."[34] René Galand concluded that the central figure of "La Corde" is the "Terrible Mother," a theme connected with Baudelaire's hatred of women in general and mothers in particular.[35] In his monograph on Baudelaire's prose poems, Edward K. Kaplan characterized "La Corde" as "Baudelaire's most brutally skeptical fable of modern life, suspending the certainty at the foundation of all ethics: maternal love."[36]

More recent critics, however, have shed some doubt on this view. J. A. Hiddleston was the first to point out that the narrator of "La Corde" is himself a deeply suspicious character, employing self-complacent, empty rhetoric that hides his fundamental insensitivity toward human suffering.[37] In his very thorough reading of "La Corde," Steve Murphy has analyzed how the narrator tries to shift the blame for the boy's death by changing the focus of the narration and turning the mother into an object of horror.[38] Both Hiddleston and Murphy agree that the real target of Baudelaire's text is not the boy's mother, but the narrator of the story. Although seemingly identical with Manet, this narrator also shares certain features with Baudelaire himself. His paintings serve as a *mise en abyme* for the art of the poet and the suspicious attempt to turn human suffering into a work of aesthetic enjoyment. To quote Murphy once again: "Baudelaire speaks not only for Manet, but for himself. As the painter has turned his model into art, into a corpse and into a witty and picturesque narrative, Baudelaire has turned the resulting narrative into poetry."[39]

Since Baudelaire undermines his own narrative by discrediting the narrator, it becomes extremely difficult to distill any kind of unequivocal moral message from his prose poem. The real message, according to Hiddleston, "would appear to be that art, whether the painter's or the poet's, is unable to come to grips with reality, which it avoids or fails to recognize."[40] His rhetorical modus operandi is the paradox and the strategy of Menippean satire: it turns out that the painter's rejection of the commonplace is yet another commonplace, his belief to be without illusions is yet another illusion. Consequently, the reader is left questioning the validity of any moral judgment. This does not mean that Baudelaire's text precludes a moralized reading, but the interpretation will shift according to the context in which we approach it. "La Corde," depending on our perspective and the other prose poems with which it is juxtaposed, can be seen as either an attack on the bad mother, with its concomitant undermining of bourgeois stereotypes of motherhood, or as an illustration of the dehumanizing effects of poverty. This moral indeterminacy allows for a multiplicity of readings and explains the wide diversity in Baudelaire's critical reception. In Russia, Baudelaire became a champion of both the radical and the decadent camp and was seen in turn as a social critic, symbolist, revolutionary, reactionary, nihilist, and religious prophet.[41]

Turgenev must have been disturbed by Baudelaire's refusal to take a clear-cut position and by his open-ended approach to what is usually a closed genre, the moral tale. Perhaps this attitude explains Turgenev's strange silence with regard to his French predecessor in the genre of the prose poem. Obviously, the *Petits poèmes en prose* were not a model to be imitated, but rather an irritant to be overcome and replaced by "improved" prose poems of his own making. This can be observed in another example of a direct intertextual borrowing, the prose poem "Nishchii" ("The Beggar," February 1878, PSS 10:132). The motif of the narrator's encounter with a beggar is related to Baudelaire's penultimate prose poem, "Assomons les pauvres!" ("Let's beat up the poor!"). This rather unsettling piece, which a contemporary critic has called "as cruel and zany as a Monty Python sketch,"[42] displeased Baudelaire's editor so much that he refused to publish it (it appeared only in the 1869 posthumous edition). The story relates in brutal and grotesque detail how the narrator, who had studied books about the "art of making people happy, wise and rich in twenty-four hours," beats up an old beggar who accosts him in the street. This action is triggered by a sort of Socratic demon who whispers in his ear that "only he is equal of another who can prove it, and only he is worthy of freedom who can conquer it." After being thoroughly drubbed by the narrator, the old beggar suddenly recovers his strength and leaves his attacker with a black eye and several knocked-out teeth. At the end of the struggle, the narrator tells the beggar, "Monsieur, *vous êtes mon égal!*" and offers to share his purse with him. The beggar in turn declares to have learned his lesson.

Turgenev's "Nishchii" opens with a similar situation: the narrator encounters a miserable old beggar who stretches his hand out for help. To his dismay, he discovers that he has no money in his pockets. In a sudden flash of inspiration he seizes the beggar's outstretched hand and gives him a firm handshake. A smile lightens up the ravaged features of the beggar as he mutters, "I thank you all the same. That too is alms, brother." The narrator concludes with the observation, "I understood that I also had received alms from my brother." In a narrative shortcut of the Baudelairean subtext, Turgenev procedes immediately from the initial encounter to the final proclamation of equality. Baudelaire's exchange of black eyes, knocked-out teeth, and money becomes in Turgenev's rewriting an exchange of uplifting words— the brutal physicality of the beating metamorphoses into the reassuring handshake.

The gesture of the unexpected handshake, which gives "Nishchii" both its narrative punchline and moralizing emblem, reoccurs in various permutations throughout Turgenev's prose poems. In "Morskoe plavanie" ("A Trip on the Sea," November 1879, PSS 10:169–70), the narrator is greeted by a monkey, the only other passenger on his trip from Hamburg to London. As with the beggar, the gesture establishes a sentiment of intimate fellowship and shared "humanity," an effect created by the anthropomorphic description of the animal, which looks at the narrator with "sad, almost human little eyes." In "Poslednee svidanie" ("The Last Encounter," April 1878, PSS 10:146–47), a prose poem inspired by Turgenev's visit to the dying poet Nekrasov, the narrator seizes the outstretched hand of his former enemy as a gesture of reconciliation in the face of death. In "Kogda menia ne budet . . ." ("When I won't be here anymore . . . ," December 1878, PSS 10:182), the addressee of the text, presumably Pauline Viardot, becomes the recipient of a posthumous handshake. Turgenev advises his beloved against visiting his grave after his death. Instead, he recommends that in hours of sadness she should take one of their mutually beloved books, find a passage that had moved them both to tears, close her eyes, and stretch her hand out toward him. Of course, at this time his hand will "lie immobile under the earth," but he imagines that she will perhaps feel nevertheless on her hand a "light touch" (*legkoe prikosnovenie*). The emotionally charged gesture of the handshake came to symbolize for Turgenev the ultimate expression of shared love.[43] Evidently, the handshake of "Nishchii" locates this text at the polar opposite of Baudelaire's "Assomons les pauvres!"

Baudelaire's prose poem has provoked a flurry of contradictory interpretations—is it a statement of pure cynicism, social Darwinism, revolutionary agitation, or is it perhaps an allegory of reading, with Baudelaire inviting his reader to "fight back?"[44] In comparison with the complexities of Baudelaire's text, Turgenev's "Nishchii" delivers a straightforward and somewhat facile message of brotherhood. While the ending of "Assomons les pauvres!" can be read as a "grotesque satire of social harmony,"[45] Turgenev takes the egalitarian rhetoric of Baudelaire's narrator at face value, shifting, as it were, from *égalité* to *fraternité*. Baudelaire ridicules this type of philanthropic banality when his narrator exclaims, "Monsieur, vous êtes mon égal!" As J. A Hiddleston has noted, exposing this kind of commonplace and *idée reçue* was one of Baudelaire's major preoccupations in his prose poems.[46] Baudelaire's unsettling play with ironic double entendres and his modernist provocation appear "sanitized" in Turgenev's somewhat simplistic and rather humorless appropriation.[47]

The generic model for both Baudelaire's and Turgenev's text is the moral tale. However, Baudelaire's version radically subverts the reader's expectation of an uplifting, unequivocal moral message. Turgenev, by contrast, reinstates the moral sense by making his story an allegory of spiritual richness hidden beneath material poverty. To be sure, this is a concept deeply rooted in the Russian cultural tradition. Turgenev's prose poem constitutes a secularized version of an age-old model of religious parables and *exempla*.[48] Rather than exposing social antagonisms and class struggle, Turgenev's "Nishchii" works toward a harmonized image of universal brotherhood. In this sense, Turgenev appears once again as Baudelaire's foil. Whereas the French poet introduces in his prose poems the social theme of urban poverty as a deliberate break with the traditional subjective emotionalism of the lyric genre, the Russian novelist *begins* with what looks like socially engaged "critical realism," only to transform it into a spiritual allegory.

As if to leave no doubt about his didactic intentions, three months after writing "Nishchii," Turgenev once more explored the theme of begging and charity in the prose poem "Milostynia" ("Alms," PSS 10:149–50). This is the story of a once-rich man who lost his fortune by giving it away to needy people. He is reduced to a state of penury, his friends have abandoned him, and he fears the ultimate humiliation of having to beg for money from strangers. At this moment, the man is approached by a mysterious person who bears a certain resemblance to Turgenev's secularized image of Christ.[49] The stranger explains that the existence of beggars is a necessary condition for the exercise of charity. He urges the man to forget his pride and to give "other good people the opportunity to demonstrate by deeds that they are good." The man follows the stranger's advice. The piece of bread that he buys with the first small sum received fills his heart with a feeling of "quiet joy." Rather than deploring social inequality, "Milostynia" thus justifies the dichotomy between rich and poor as the necessary framework for the give-and-take of charitable brotherly love.[50]

It is interesting to note that Baudelaire, too, doubled up his beggar story with a companion piece, entitled "La fausse monnaie" ("The Counterfeit Coin").[51] The contrast with Turgenev's "Milostynia" could not be more dramatic. The story relates how the narrator's companion deliberately hands a counterfeit coin to a beggar. The narrator condemns this behavior, but not for the reasons one would expect. He is even excited about this "experiment" at first, but when he realizes that his companion is only trying to "carry off paradise economically" by doing a good deed on the cheap, he concludes: "I might have found it curious, unique, that he would enjoy compromising poor people; but I will never forgive him for the incompetence of his calculation." Baudelaire's sententious conclusion espouses a rather more complex morality than Turgenev's injunction to philanthropy: "It is never excusable to be mean, but there is some merit in knowing that you are; and the most irreparable of vices is to do evil through stupidity."[52]

Turgenev's texts operate in a radically different rhetorical mode from Baudelaire's. His didactic message is easily decipherable, whereas Baudelaire presents the startled reader with a conundrum of conflicting interpretive strategies. "Assomons les pauvres!" seems to lampoon the discourse of both socialist egalitarianism and capitalist "survival of the fittest." The *poème en prose,* with its subversion of the traditional prose–verse dichotomy, appears as the appropriate genre for a text that places itself at a crucial ideological divide without embracing either position. Turgenev's prose poem of the beggar, by contrast, looks like a conscious attempt to correct its Baudelairean subtext. Turgenev's design is to create not a paradoxical multiplicity of meanings, but a unifying text that mediates between opposites in order to unite them in a harmonious whole.

Still, the theme of struggle, which permeates many of Baudelaire's prose poems, is not absent from Turgenev's work either, but it takes on a different role. The story "Bliznetsy" ("Twins," February 1878, PSS 10:175) allows for a comparison. Turgenev's very compact prose poem describes a fight between hostile identical twins. The word "identical" (*odinakovo*) serves as the structural backbone of the text. Everything is the same: the enraged facial expression of the twins, their irately glistening eyes, their curses, their voices, their distorted lips. The narrator, who witnesses this scene, finally takes one of the twins by the hand and leads him to a mirror, telling him: "You better fight here, before this mirror. . . . For you, it will make no difference, but for me it will be less terrifying." We might see in this story another echo of the struggle between "equals" alluded to in "Assomons les pauvres!" An even more pertinent connection can be drawn with another of Baudelaire's prose poems, "Le Gâteau." The narrator of this story witnesses a fierce, drawn-out struggle between two poor boys over a piece of bread that he had given to one of them. The two look so much alike that they seem to be twins. At the end of their fight, which is described in brutally graphic detail, the piece of bread has crumbled into pieces.

Turgenev's prose poem reduces the Baudelairean intertext to a single key scene—the struggle between twins—without providing any explanatory context. We do not know what the twins are fighting about. His minimalist, bare-bones narrative contrasts with Baudelaire's more elaborate story, which is embedded in an absurdly overdone romantic travelogue. The contemplation of an idyllic mountain landscape prompts the narrator to indulge in Rousseauian dreams about the natural goodness of man, which are then thoroughly shattered by the bellicose behavior of the two "savages." Unlike Turgenev's narrator, Baudelaire's does not intervene in the struggle, although he is responsible for having started it by providing the contested piece of bread. He merely notes that his previous elated mood has been thoroughly spoiled. As he states rather sadly: "So there exists a magnificent land where bread is called cake, a delicacy so rare that it suffices to beget a perfectly fratricidal war!"[53]

As in "La Corde," Baudelaire's story features a smugly comfortable narrator who seems insensitive to true suffering. The title, "Le Gâteau," echoes Marie Antoinette's famous "Let-them-eat-cake" quip. The expression refers to a semantic confusion in the text: one of the boys refers to the narrator's bread as "cake." This allusion raises the implicit question of whether the boys, instead of fighting each other, would not be better advised to turn their joint aggressive energy against the narrator, who still holds a large chunk of bread. The situation is quite different in Turgenev's text, where the twins struggle without any external motivation. Rather than as displaced, but potentially justified behavior, their struggle is presented as senseless. As identical twin brothers, they literally embody the notions of *fraternité* and *égalité* while violating at the same time the standard of moral behavior that one would expect to ensue from these principles. Turgenev's narrator, unlike Baudelaire's, acts with unquestioned authority as a voice of reason and common sense. The solution he proposes seems borrowed from another Baudelairean prose poem, "Le Miroir."

Le Miroir

Un homme épouvantable entre et se regarde dans la glace.

"—Pourquoi vous regardez-vous au miroir, puisque vous ne pouvez vous y voir qu'avec déplaisir?"

L'homme épouvantable me répond: "—Monsieur, d'après les immortels principes de 89, tous les hommes sont égaux en droits; donc je possède le droit de me mirer; avec plaisir ou déplaisir, cela ne regarde que ma conscience."

Au nom du bon sens, j'avais sans doute raison; mais, au point de vue de la loi, il n'avait pas tort.[54]

The Mirror

A frightful man enters and looks at himself in the mirror.

"Why do you look at yourself in the mirror, since you must see yourself there only with displeasure?"

The frightful man replies, "Sir, according to the immortal principles of '89, all men are by right equal. Thus I possess the right to see my reflection; with pleasure or displeasure, that only concerns my conscience."

According to common sense, I was probably right; but, from the legal viewpoint, he was not wrong.[55]

The quest for self-knowledge, implied by the presence of the mirror, has been interpreted in different ways. According to Hiddleston, the "frightful man" represents the untroubled self-acceptance of the democrat who is unmindful of original sin. His self-examination in the mirror is pointless, since it does not lead to a true "examen de conscience"—he accepts his (moral) ugliness as an example of natural man.[56] Rosemary Lloyd, on the other hand, has cast doubt on the first-person narrator and his "good sense." In her view, the hideous man represents Baudelaire's poetic persona who fearlessly confronts his own ugliness in the poems of *Les Fleurs du Mal*, while "the exponent of good sense is the credulous and unimaginative public."[57] According to Kaplan, "Le Miroir" simply presents a "legal conundrum," demonstrating that certain theories can be right and wrong at the same time.[58]

In comparison, Turgenev's use of the mirror-image is far less ambivalent. The narrator uses it to demonstrate the absurdity of fraternal struggle by turning it into a confrontation against the self. Fighting one's mirror-image because one mistakes it for another person precludes by definition any form of self-knowledge. The spectacle of the fighter before the mirror is less terrifying than the struggle of twins only because it is a form of self-destruction, and in this sense causes less collateral damage.

Turgenev's use of language differs considerably from Baudelaire's. Although irony and sarcasm occur in both Baudelaire's and Turgenev's prose poems, Turgenev's irony is generally decipherable. In "Shchi," for example, the reader knows not to identify with the landlady, but with the peasant woman. The situation is somewhat more complex in "Chernorabochii i beloruchka," where both the worker and the intellectual seem problematic characters. However, the reader can find firm ground by adopting Turgenev's own liberal, reformist, middle-of-the-road position, which is equally critical of autocratic repression, lower-class ignorance, and radical extremism (while this position is not stated in the text, it is silently implied). In Baudelaire's prose poems, as we have seen, there is no such firm ground; the reader is thrown into a vortex of conflicting meanings. Of course, this is less of a surprise if we remember the genre in which the text is written: the oxymoronic and paradoxical nature of the *poème en prose* is Baudelaire's contribution to the poetics of modernity.

Turgenev, with his conservative attitude, needed to "stabilize" the unsettling implications of the modernist genre that he appropriated from Baudelaire. This explains why he countered Baudelaire's unsettling beggar story with his own moralistic tale of brotherhood, why he transferred the motif of the "good-luck noose" from the frivolous world of the painter's studio to the arena of Russian societal struggle, and why he replied to Baudelaire's attack against the "bad mother" with his own praise of motherhood. Baudelaire's rejection of the cliché crystallized into reaffirmation in Turgenev's prose poems.

We might observe that craving for affirmation is not necessarily part of a secure worldview. On the contrary, it could be interpreted as a symptom of profound malaise. Indeed, a deep pessimism permeates many of Turgenev's prose poems. "Vanitas vanitatum vanitas" could serve as a motto for most of them. Society, especially as far as the writing profession is concerned, is not treated kindly—most of it seems to consist of mean-spirited, presumptuous careerists of limited intellectual capabilities. Human existence in general is presented as an inconsequential trifle in the face of the indifferent immensity of nature.[59] Old age, with its ailments, destroys what is left of life's zest. Death in various allegorical guises—as an old woman, a young woman, a veiled woman, a stinging insect—is a constant theme. The prose poem "Nessun maggior dolore" (June 1882, PSS 10:187) demon-

strates programmatically how a rather parodistically overdone world of "poetry" is undermined by the intrusion of the "prosaic":

Nessun Maggior Dolore

Голубое небо, как пух легкие облака, запах цветов, сладкие звуки молодого
голоса, лучезарная красота великих творений искусства, улыбка счастья
на прелестном женском лице и эти волшебные глаза . . . к чему, к чему все
это?

Ложка скверного, бесполезного лекарства через каждые два часа—вот,
вот что нужно.

Nessun Maggior Dolore

Blue sky, clouds light like fluff, the fragrance of flowers, the sweet sounds of
a young voice, the radiant beauty of great works of art, the smile of happiness
on a charming female face and these enchanting eyes . . . what, what is all this
for?

A spoonful of foul, useless medicine every two hours—this, this is what is
needed.

However, Turgenev's pessimism does not reach the level of artistic self-
doubt. If many of Baudelaire's prose poems can be read as a self-reflective
and self-critical comment of the poet about his own art, Turgenev's metapoetic stance in his prose poems veers toward the self-celebratory. This becomes evident in "Russkii iazyk" ("The Russian Language," PSS 10:172),
the closing piece in the *Vestnik Evropy* publication of 1882, and perhaps
Turgenev's best-known prose poem. His praise of the "great, powerful,
righteous and free" Russian language implies also a celebration of the writers and poets who make use of this superior idiom (including, of course,
Turgenev himself). The task of the Russian writer is a sacred mission—to
preserve and perpetuate the great Russian language and literary tradition.
Elizabeth Allen has speculated that Turgenev "saw his own explorations of
the prose poem as his final contribution to that mission, hence as his ultimate moral responsibility." Such a lofty aim entails a different generic concept of the prose poem. According to Allen, Turgenev's objective, unlike
Baudelaire's, consisted not in breaking boundaries, but in affirming them:
"Turgenev endeavored to demonstrate that the discrete boundaries of prose
poems, joined together, could trace the shape and disclose the strength of
the entire Russian literary tradition in all its poetic and prose fullness as no
other, traditional genre could do."[60]

While such a grandiose task seems somewhat at odds with Turgenev's
own self-deprecatory characterization of his *Stikhotvoreniia v proze* when
he first introduced them to Stasiulevich, it is undoubtedly true that his concept of the prose poem differs significantly from Baudelaire's. An important
difference between Baudelaire and Turgenev concerns the context in which
the genre of the prose poem emerges in their oeuvre. Both writers explored

the prose poem late in their lives, after they had made their mark in other genres. For both of them the prose poem constitutes, so to speak, their final poetic word. *Posthuma,* one of the titles envisioned by Turgenev for his collection of prose poems, literally applies to Baudelaire's *Petits poèmes en prose,* which appeared in book form two years after the poet's death.

It is important to stress, however, that Baudelaire and Turgenev approached prose poetry from opposite directions. For Baudelaire the prose poem came after the verse poem. In fact, some of his *poèmes en prose* are prose reworkings of texts that had been originally written in verse. By comparing these "doublets," critics have gained valid insights about the generic specificity of the *poème en prose.* Barbara Johnson in particular has shown how Baudelaire "disfigured" his verse poetry in the process of rewriting it in prose.[61] Turgenev's prose poems, by contrast, are more organically linked with his earlier work. "Lyric prose" had been a hallmark of his narrative style from the beginning. Some of his *Zapiski okhotnika* (*Sketches of a Hunter*), as Allen observes, almost qualify as prose poems. One could also argue that Turgenev, with his turn to prose poetry at the end of his career, completed a circle that began with the lyric verse poetry of his youth.[62] An interesting case of a Turgenevan "doublet" is presented by "Vstrecha" ("An encounter"), which exists both as an independent prose poem narrated in the first person, and in reworked form as a dream of the protagonist Aratov in the novella "Klara Milich." In a detailed comparison of the two versions, the Hungarian scholar Zsuzsa Zöldhelyi has shown how the text becomes "prosaified" through its integration into the narrative genre, whereas the prose poem features a comparative abundance of rhetorical flourish and lyric expansion.[63] As we can see, Baudelaire and Turgenev had opposing concepts of prose poetry: while Baudelaire was rewriting his earlier verse poetry in prose and thereby problematizing the very notion of lyric poetry, Turgenev was poetically "upgrading" his earlier narrative prose.[64] As Christa Gasde has noted, Turgenev's seemingly nonsensical inclusion of a rhymed verse poem into the corpus of his prose poems could be explained by this movement from prose to poetry. Turgenev simply went "a step too far," committing a "little exaggeration." In the case of Baudelaire the inclusion of a verse poem in his collection of prose poems would have been contrary to the author's artistic design.[65]

Whether Turgenev was successful in his transformation of the Baudelairean prose poem remains a controversial question. Critics have disagreed considerably on the literary merit of Turgenev's *Stikhotvoreniia v proze,* as early enthusiasm gave way to a more skeptical or even negative attitude by the middle decades of the twentieth century.[66] Koschmal and Allen, the most recent critics of Turgenev's prose poems, deemed it necessary to preface their discussion with a caveat about the relative artistic inferiority of

Turgenev's *Stikhotvoreniia v proze* compared to Western European examples of the genre.

In spite of their relative marginality, Turgenev's prose poems nevertheless exerted a certain influence on Russian literature. Since personalities do matter in literary history, it is tempting to ascribe the strikingly different development and status of the prose poem in France and Russia to the differences between the founders of the genre, Baudelaire and Turgenev. With his *Petits poèmes en prose,* Baudelaire provided both a convenient label and a practical example of a prosaic anti-poetry that could be further developed and radicalized by his successors Rimbaud, Mallarmé, and the twentieth-century avant-garde. In comparison, Turgenev appears as a figure solidly ensconced in the style and value system of the nineteenth century. His more traditional notion of prose poetry as lyrically condensed prose, while to some extent inspirational to the aesthetics of the fin de siècle, proved to be of little consequence for the further development of modern poetry in Russia. The fact that some of Turgenev's prose poems, such as "Russkii iazyk" or "Kak khoroshi, kak svezhi byli rozy . . ." ("How beautiful, how fresh were the roses . . ."), were singled out by generations of Russian schoolteachers for compulsory admiration did not do much to endear the genre to writers of a more innovative bent.

Nevertheless, we are left with the fact that, with all his conservative recuperation of Baudelaire's subversive model, Turgenev still introduced a form into Russian literature that by its name alone could only subvert any sort of standard notion of genre. In their hybrid mixture of realism and decadence, conservatism and innovation, Turgenev's prose poems lead to a two-pronged juncture in the history of the Russian prose miniature. On the one hand, as will be seen in the following chapter, they inspired a tradition of realist prose poems. Unlike the French *poème en prose,* which was practiced mainly by poets, the Russian *stikhotvorenie v proze* remained a genre practiced by prose writers—notwithstanding a few exceptions, such as Iakov Polonskii.[67] Moreover, what had been a harbinger of modernism in France became in Russia a genre rooted in the realist tradition of the nineteenth century. However, as the later chapters will demonstrate, the innovative features implied in the notion of the prose poem also foreshadowed a tradition of modernist formal experimentation, which resulted in the breakdown of generic boundaries and the creation of subversive anti-poetic and anti-narrative texts just as radical as anything written in France.

Chapter Three

The Russian Prose Poem as a Realist Genre

THE REALIST PROSE POEMS written in the wake of Turgenev seem at first sight quite different from the French model that prevailed elsewhere in Europe. As noted before, the Russian *stikhotvorenie v proze* appealed rather to writers of prose fiction than to poets. Stylistically it had little in common with modernist experimental writing. Thoroughly traditional in its realism, it shared the general realist commitment to socially "progressive" causes. Nevertheless, the distinction between realism and modernism is not as watertight as one might think. A premonition of modernist developments already began in the later works of the Russian nineteenth-century realist novelists. In his study of Tolstoi's *Anna Karenina,* Boris Eikhenbaum points to elements of "impressionism" and "philosophical lyricism" in this novel. He adds: "It is interesting, that at the same time Turgenev writes his 'Senilia.' This influence of poetry on prose prepares the coming development from realism to symbolism."[1] Among the Russian prose writers who gained prominence in the last two decades of the nineteenth century, lyric styles became a common practice. Anton Chekhov in particular is known for his impressionistic focus on atmospheric details and attention to minute mood swings reflected through the subjective lens of an individual consciousness.

As we have seen, Turgenev's prose poems already contain a "decadent" streak, and many of their morbid and pessimistic features became a hallmark of the prose miniatures that followed in their wake. With their eclecticism and melancholic mood, they exemplify the spirit of the 1880s, a period characterized by a sense of malaise after the death or silence of virtually all the great Russian novelists around 1880 and the dashing of liberal hopes after the murder of Tsar Alexander II in 1881.

The spiritual depression of the period becomes visible in the three prose poems left behind by the short-story writer Vsevolod Garshin (1855–88).[2] Originally written as entries into various albums, Garshin's untitled miniatures were published posthumously (thereby fulfilling Turgenev's original project of the prose poem as a posthumous text). Their generic designation as prose poems was not Garshin's own decision, but arose through the classification attempts of his Soviet editors.[3] In fact, the earliest of Garshin's prose poems, written in 1875, antedates Turgenev's generic model by a few years. In this sense, Garshin's miniatures present an example of how a text can acquire the status of a prose poem through an ulterior process of framing. Quite independently of the author's original generic intention, his pieces became de facto *stikhotvoreniia v proze* simply by dint of being anthologized as such. Nevertheless, the prose poem label is not without foundation, given Garshin's personal acquaintance with Turgenev and certain stylistic and thematic parallels. The dominant mood, as in Turgenev's "Senilia," is morbid and melancholic. The earliest text was inspired by the suicide of Garshin's brother in 1873. Another prose poem renders Garshin's thoughts during a concert given in honor of his close friend, the poet Semen Nadson, who was dying of consumption at the age of twenty-four. The most laconic text recalls certain of Turgenev's prose poems in its sententiousness and oriental packaging.[4] Most of all, it resembles Turgenev's "Nessun maggior dolore," with its sharp contrast between the aesthetic splendor of nature and the misery of human existence marked by sickness and death. One wonders whether the youth of the story is not an allegorical disguise for Garshin himself, who seeks advice from the elder Turgenev:

> Юноша спросил у святого мудреца Джиафара:—Учитель, что такое жизнь?
>
> Хаджи молча отвернул грязный рукав своего рубища и показал ему отвратительную язву, разъедавшую его руку.
>
> А в это время гремели соловьи и вся Севилья была наполнена благоуханием роз.

> A youth asked the holy wise man Djafar: "Teacher, what is life?"
>
> The hajji silently rolled back the dirty sleeve of his rags and showed him a repulsive ulcer eating away his hand.
>
> Meanwhile the nightingales were ringing out, and all of Sevilla was filled with the fragrance of roses.

The ending of Garshin's piece recalls the beginning of Turgenev's "Nessun maggior dolore," with its accumulation of romantic clichés steeped in the Mediterranean picturesque. The Italianate nature of Turgenev's text (which uses as its title a quote from Dante's *Inferno*) corresponds to Garshin's evocation of crepuscular Sevilla reminiscent of Dostoevskii's "Legend of the Grand Inquisitor" or Pushkin's "Don Juan." In both Turgenev's and Garshin's texts, the intrusion of illness—with its repulsive realism—clashes with the world of romantic escapism and renders any form of naive lyric expression highly problematic. Like the hand of the hajji, the poetic experience is eaten away by the ulcer of the "reality principle," leaving in its wake a stunted minimalist text.

Garshin's laconicity was not to provide the predominant model for the coming generation of Russian prose poems. At the turn of the century, the genre became popular with various writers of the socially committed camp (who, in all likelihood, were unaware of Chernyshevskii's earlier hostility to the very idea of a poem in prose). Left-wing Russian "thick journals" of the 1890s and 1900s regularly featured *stikhotvoreniia v proze,* some of them translations and some original Russian works.[5] Several writers of Maksim Gor'kii's neo-realist *Znanie*-entourage, such as Skitalets and A. Kornev, published prose poems in the Marxist journals *Zhizn'* (*Life*) and *Sovremennyi mir* (*Modern World*).[6] Most of these texts are not particularly exciting reading. Strangely enough, with their fin de siècle mood of elegiac preciosity, they resemble the contemporaneous Western European models of the genre that became popular in the wake of French *décadence.* Considerable overlap also exists with the decadent Russian prose miniatures of the time, which will be discussed in the next chapter. Although inspired in part by Turgenev, these prose poems lack his sense of formal restraint, instead indulging in a free-flowing stream of lyrical effusion.

A. Kornev's prose poem "Gasnet zaria" ("Dusk is waning") provides a good example.[7] The title represents the author's allegiance to two conflicting poetic systems. The optimistic implications of "zaria" (which usually means "dawn" rather than "dusk," with concomitant metaphorical connotations of revolutionary upheaval) are canceled out by the word "gasnet," conjuring up the image of a dying flame. The text begins with the topos of a nature scene rendered with the full palette of impressionistic coloration:

> The sun has set, the dusk is waning. . . . Rhythmically and silently breathes the majestic breast of the river. In the distance, it has colored its waters all over in purple and golden hues, and here—at the landing—golden ribbons run over it, they bend, wind themselves into rings, draw together into a narrow circle and again run into various directions—and it seems that thousands of unknown beings romp and play in the blue expanse of the river.

Kornev's social commitment surfaces in the second paragraph, which describes the peasants and workers waiting at the landing. Here, Kornev supplements his purple prose with the critical realism of a populist ethnographic sketch:

> The faces of most of them are covered with premature wrinkles; the flush of their cheeks has faded from the misfortunes of life; many of their faces and hands are withered; all of their faces are marked by a concentrated seriousness; the eyes of most of them look bleak, severe, and mournful.

The narrator laments his own loneliness in the third paragraph and follows with another impressionistic symphony of colors in paragraph four. The dusk now turns from pink to crimson and the river from gold to smoke-colored purple and lilac. In paragraph five, the narrator expresses his desire to meet a young woman, but nothing comes of that. The prose poem ends with another poetic evocation of the river at night and a statement of the poet's loneliness. Perhaps the most remarkable feature of this otherwise not very remarkable text is the way in which it combines purple fin de siècle prose lyrics with social realism. Aubrey Beardsley, as it were, meets Ilya Repin.[8]

Kornev's text poses a challenge to those theorists who define the prose poem as a necessarily "revolutionary" genre symbolizing "the very locus of class struggle within literature."[9] Although the author had no doubt a negative attitude toward the political status quo and meant to highlight some unappealing features of Russian reality, his prose poem hardly presents an example of a subversive counterdiscourse. His social engagement does not propel him to write a disruptive text. Rather, he engages in a purely monological form of writing. The "men of the people" are not given a voice of their own, but are smoothly integrated into a discourse laced with neoromantic and decadent clichés.

Perhaps the only example of politically *and* aesthetically revolutionary Russian prose poetry can be found in the oeuvre of the proletarian bard Aleksei Gastev (1882–1941). However, his concept of the prose poem, although it departs from customary standards of realism, is essentially affirmative rather than subversive. Gastev's collection of hymns to factory work, *Poeziia rabochego udara* (*Poetry of the Worker's Blow,* published in 1918), mixes revolutionary agitation with cosmic symbolism and a futurist cult of the machine age. His best-known work, the prose poem "My rastem iz zheleza" ("We grow out of iron," 1914), evokes a sort of transsubstantiation from flesh into steel, as the narrator merges with the metal girders of a blast furnace to become a gigantic human machine. As Rolf Hellebust has observed, "Gastev's strategy puts the vocabulary and style (inventories, terse physical descriptions, simple commands) of a technical manual at the service of unbridled Promethean lyricism."[10] Gastev's genre had few followers, however, and in the 1920s he gave up literature altogether to devote his energy to the education of Soviet workers in the Taylorist method of industrial labor.

The term *stikhotvorenie v proze* fell into almost complete disuse after the first decade of the twentieth century.[11] Nevertheless, at least one major Russian writer of the twentieth century, Ivan Bunin (1870–1953), continued in his own way the realist strand of Turgenev's prose poetry. The rest of this chapter will be devoted to a reading of Bunin's prose poems. Although Bunin himself never used the generic label, literary critics have repeatedly applied it to his work. Usually, such a qualification has been explained by references to the "poetic," "lyric," or "rhythmic" quality of Bunin's prose. However, this generic attribution rests on the dubious equation of the prose poem with "lyric prose." Such a paradigm really fits only

Bunin's early prose miniatures written at the turn of the century. As almost plotless, emotional mood-pieces, they have much in common with the decadent prose of some of Bunin's contemporaries and friends of that time. In the late 1890s, Bunin was in close contact with the two leading decadent poets, Konstantin Bal'mont and Valerii Briusov. He published their works in the Odessa newspaper *Iuzhnoe obozrenie* (*Southern Review*), where he worked as an editor, while his own prose miniatures were included in the first symbolist almanacs.[12] As V. N. Afanas'ev has shown, Bunin's miniature "Pozdnei noch'iu" ("Late at night"), which appeared in the symbolist almanac *Severnye tsvety* (*Northern Flowers*) in 1901, bears a close resemblance to Bal'mont's prose poem "Zimnye sumerki" ("Winter Dusk"), published in 1898 in *Iuzhnoe obozrenie*. After the turn of the century, Bunin's relation to Briusov and Bal'mont cooled, while he grew closer to Gor'kii and his entourage. However, this change of allegiance did not immediately affect the style of his prose miniatures. As we have seen before, the neo-realists of the time practiced a manner of writing that was influenced by decadence. One of Bunin's impressionist sketches of that time, "Tuman" ("Fog," 1901), appeared in the same journal, *Zhizn'*, that had featured Kornev's prose poem "Gasnet zaria" the year before.

It was only later in his career that Bunin adopted a much more restrained, "objective" approach, documenting, in James B. Woodward's words, "the fiction writer's gradual liberation from the power of the lyricist."[13] After his emigration to France, Bunin wrote a series of laconic prose miniatures that were published in 1930 in the Parisian newspaper *Poslednie novosti* under the title *Kratkie rasskazy* ("Shortest Stories") and *Dalekoe* ("The Far Away"). Some of these texts are so brief that they hardly qualify as short stories in any conventional sense of the term. Galina Kuznetsova describes a conversation with Bunin in 1930 in which he expressed his preference for "extremely small, compact stories of a few lines." As a justification for this minimalism, Bunin mentioned that "even with the greatest writers, there are only isolated good passages, and between them—water."[14] Bunin's pursuit of brevity was conditioned, as he explained in a different context, by his experience of writing verse poetry.[15] The very compactness of Bunin's miniatures invites a mode of reading attuned to minor details. In her text-linguistic analysis of three kratkie rasskazy, Maria Langleben asserts that "each of the stories is a laconic over-condensed text drained of all redundancies. Rather than being expressed in words, most of the author's intentions are left hidden in the formal minutiae—in the syntactic structures, in the design of paragraphs, in the morphology, and even in the phonetics."[16]

In this sense, Bunin's minimalist prose conforms to the generic paradigm of the prose poem as it has been outlined earlier. It actualizes a confrontation of two opposed modes of reading. On the one hand, the reader's expectation of a "story," triggered by the generic heading *rasskazy*, is frustrated by the extreme brevity of the text that precludes any kind of elaborate plot. On the other hand, the hallmarks of lyricism suggested by the frame (shortness and the serial arrangement of the pieces in a cycle) clash with the prosaic form and the lack of an emotional, subjective content usually associated with the lyric genre. The difference between Turgenev's and Bunin's approach to the prose poem lies in the latter's increased "prosaism." As Vladislav Khodasevich put it in his review of Bunin's miniatures collected in the book *Bozh'e drevo* (*God's Tree*): "Bunin is infinitely drier and sharper (*terche*), because he wrung out and poured away all the water of Turgenevan profundity, and removed without a trace all the sugar of Turgenevan lyricism."[17]

It is curious to note that both Bunin himself and his critic Khodasevich resort to metaphors of drainage in their attempt to define a "shortest story." A conventional narrative, so it appears, contains too much "water" that must be eliminated in order to arrive at the real literary substance. This concept of the minimalist story as the concentrated essence of a long narrative is reminiscent of Joris-Karl Huysman's famous panegyric to the prose poem in the novel *A Rebours* (*Against the Grain,* 1884), which later gained the status of a decadent cult book. Huysman's hero, Des Esseintes, conceives of the prose poem as an entire "novel condensed in one or two pages." As he explains:

> Handled by an alchemist of genius, [the prose poem] should store up in its small compass, like an extract of meat, so to say, the essence of the novel, while suppressing its long, tedious analytical passages and superfluous descriptions. Again and again Des Esseintes had pondered the distracting problem, how to write a novel concentrated in a few sentences, but which should yet contain the cohobated juice of the hundreds of pages always taken up in describing the setting, sketching the characters, gathering together the necessary incidental observations and minor details. In that case, so inevitable and unalterable would be the words selected that they must take the place of all others; in so ingenious and masterly a fashion would each adjective be chosen that it could not with any justice be robbed of its right to be there, and would open up such wide perspectives as would set the reader dreaming for weeks together of its meaning, at once precise and manifold, and enable him to know the present, reconstruct the past, divine the future of the spiritual history of the characters, all revealed by the flash-light of this single epithet. [. . .]
>
> In a word, the prose poem represented in Des Esseintes' eyes the concrete juice, the ozmazone of literature, the essential oil of art.[18]

Incidentally, the same metaphor of a liquefied narrative concentrate, only minus Huysman's decadent exuberance, also underlies the concept of the miniature "story in drops" developed by Bunin's fellow Parisian émigré Aleksandr Kuprin. In the preface to his *Rasskazy v kapeliakh,* written in

1929, Kuprin claims that his stories are "full of such a dense essence that there would be enough for an entire novel. After all, a drop of pure aniline colors an entire grown-up's bathtub in green and purple."[19]

Like Kuprin's "stories in drops," Bunin's prose miniatures are marked by the émigré experience. Although written in postrevolutionary Paris, they are overwhelmingly located in prerevolutionary Russia. What they present is far from an idyllic picture, however. One gets the impression that the author depicts a world on the brink of doom. The predominant theme of Bunin's *kratkie rasskazy* is death. Both the opening and the closing piece of the cycle ("Lando" and "Pis'mo") explicitly evoke images of death. At the same time, Bunin's approach differs considerably from Turgenev's allegorically constructed memento mori. This becomes evident in the opening text, "Lando":

Ландо

У смерти все свое, особое.

Возле ворот дачи стоит огромное старое ландо, пара черных больших лошадей: приехал из города хозяин дачи. Что-то необычное, чрезмерное в этом ландо и в этих лошадях. Почему? Оказывается, что лошадей и ландо дал хозяину дачи его приятель, содержатель бюро похоронных процессий. Кучер, сидевший на козлах, сказал:—Это ландо из *погребательной* конторы.

И, в довершение всего, черная борода кучера имеет цвет сухой ваксы: крашеная.[20]

The Landau

With death everything is special, particular.

At the gate of the dacha stands a huge, old landau, a pair of big black horses: the owner of the dacha has arrived from the city. There is something unusual, excessive in this landau and in these horses. Why? It turns out that the horses and the landau were given to the owner of the dacha by his friend, the owner of a funeral home. The coachman, sitting on the box, said: "This landau is from the *funererial* office."

And, to crown all, the black beard of the coachman has the color of dry wax: dyed.

Bunin's deadpan narrative approaches the death theme metonymically rather than in Turgenev's favorite allegorical mode: instead of a female character shrouded in white veils, we encounter the ordinary accoutrements of the burial industry. This enforced prosaism extends to the stylistic level with its plain, laconic sentence structure, and the substandard vocabulary of the coachman, who says "pogrebatel'noi," instead of the correct "pogrebal'noi." This process deflates the solemnity usually associated with death, creating a sense of irony (Shakespeare's gravediggers come to mind). Is the text supposed to be funny? The words of the coachman seem to offer a punchline, which falls flat, however. Read as an anecdote, the story does not work particularly well. One senses something incongruous, something "not quite right." The uncanny nature of this seemingly innocuous snapshot of ordinary life stems from the concealed presence of death. Although nobody dies in the story, an air of "deadness" permeates everything. The funeral vehicle intrudes into an environment where it does not belong: a dacha, a locus of rural enjoyment. The incongruous presence creates a sense of displacement and acts as a powerful reminder of life's precariousness. The story crystallizes in the final image of the coachman, who has taken on the waxen outlook of a dead man.[21]

In a more open and violent form, death permeates many of Bunin's prose miniatures. Some of them are murder stories, such as the text immediately following "Lando" ("Ubiitsa" ["The Murderer"]), where an excited crowd watches the arrest of a young woman who has stabbed her lover to death.[22] "Teliach'ia golovka" ("The Calf's Head") contains the graphic description of a butcher's shop, ending with the image of a calf's head being split in two. The last piece of the cycle *Kratkie rasskazy*, "Pis'mo" ("A Letter"), renders the letter of a soldier describing the pitiless slaughter of World War I. Beginning rather innocuously with the information that the railway cars carrying the troops to the front were well-heated, and some observations about the weather, the tone becomes suddenly pathetic when the soldier sends a last farewell to his loved ones in the face of his certain death. The letter ends as a fragment: "Two next to me were digging a trench, and a shell came flying and killed both of them, one a newlywed, not one of ours, and the other our Vanya, he fell to the glory of Russian arms . . ." (*on pogib vo slavu russkogo oruzhiia*).

In his minimalist style of narration, Bunin eliminates any trace of a morally evaluative or emotionally resonant narrative voice. At best, the narrator provides dry comments, such as the gnomic opening statement of "Lando." Spatial settings are evoked in the laconic shorthand of a film scenario. Mostly, the described objects "speak for themselves." The effect of "Teliach'ia golovka" relies on the minute, blood-curdling description of a severed calf's head. The heart-wrenching words in "Pis'mo" appear as a sort of *objet trouvé*, a fragment of a document presented without any further comment. The style of the letter betrays a character with little education. The only incongruous expression is the "glory of Russian arms," which the writer appropriates from the vocabulary of war propaganda. The text undermines the jingoistic solemnity of such rhetoric by exposing it as a cover-up for senseless slaughter.

To what extent Bunin wrote his minimalist prose in a conscious awareness of the Turgenevan generic model of the *stikhotvorenie v proze* remains difficult to determine. Most of the *kratkie rasskazy* were composed shortly after André Mazon published the complete text of Turgenev's prose poems in 1930, which may have provided a source of inspiration. Bunin himself, however, categorically rejected the comparison of his *kratkie rasskazy* to Turgenev's prose poems.[23] But one wonders whether the vehemence with which Bunin reacted against any suggestion of possible similarities between his work and Turgenev's may not be evidence of an "anxiety of influence." There are certainly thematic parallels between Turgenev's and Bunin's writing, with both authors emphasizing the *vanitas* of human existence and the inevitability of death. Iurii Mal'tsev has pointed to a series of common elements between Turgenev's and Bunin's late works, including a "tragic consciousness of being doomed (*obrechennosti zhizni*), a keen feeling for life's sadness and beauty, the rejection of any comforting illusions, a lyrical emotionalism and musical prose."[24]

At least one of Bunin's miniatures seems to establish a specific intertextual link with a prose poem that has been mentioned earlier, Turgenev's "Nishchii." The story "Slepoi" ("The Blind Man"), written in 1924, relates the narrator's encounter with a blind beggar on the French Riviera.[25] Unlike Baudelaire's "Assomons les pauvres!" and Turgenev's "Nishchii," which frustrate the beggar's (and the reader's) expectation of a monetary gift, Bunin's narrator behaves in a most conventional manner: he drops "a few centimes" into the beggar's outstretched cap. The blind man reacts by saying: "Merci, merci, mon bon frère!" This exchange is followed by the narrator's musings about what he just heard. It is also tempting to read these remarks as Bunin's comment on Turgenev's celebration of brotherhood in "Nishchii." "'Mon bon frère . . .'. Yes, yes, we are all brothers," he begins. However, he maintains that only "death, great sorrow, or great misfortune" remind us of this truth, because they "remove us from the realm of everyday life." The blind man, who has been "touched by the hand of God," lives without a name, outside of time and space. "He is now simply a human being, to whom all are brothers." In addition to this shared human nature, a broader sense of cosmic belonging unites the two with the surrounding universe: ". . . my flesh, as the flesh of the entire world, is one with yours, because your sensation of life is a sensation of love, because every suffering is our common suffering, disturbing our common joy of life, that is, a sensation of each other and of all that exists!" This lyric evocation of cosmic unity is interrupted by the reality expressed in the two closing sentences, each separately set off as a paragraph: "Don't think about equality in ordinary life, with its hatred, envy, and fierce competition. There can be no equality there, there never was and never will be."

Bunin's treatment of the beggar story mediates, as it were, between Turgenev and Baudelaire. Although committed in principle to the ethics of compassion and brotherhood advocated in Turgenev's moral tale, Bunin also questions the relevance of those notions in the world of everyday "Darwinian" existence. Bunin's hostility to the Soviet experiment of enforced social equality provides an additional political context. Bunin's approach to "brotherhood" thus appears much more circumspect and tempered than Turgenev's; it is reduced to an abstract awareness of a common human essence. The relationship with the beggar remains more formal and distant. No embrace or handshake takes place—the encounter remains the traditional monetary transaction between almsgiver and recipient. The narrator has neither been morally regenerated or transformed through his encounter with the beggar, nor has he received "a gift from his brother." He merely uses this experience to engage in some philosophical musings of his own.

While Turgenev's beggar is an image of human misery, dressed in dirty rags and suffering from festering wounds, Bunin's blind man is presented as aesthetically appealing. With his head of grey hair, he has "an old man's good looks" (on . . . starcheski blagoobrazen). His erect, immobile pose reminds the narrator of an Egyptian statue. He appears as an organic part of the beautiful nature setting with which the text begins: the snow-covered peaks of the Alps in the background, the embankment lined with palm trees, the "dense blueness" of the sea, and the "white statue of an English King in a navy uniform, standing in the emptiness of the bright sky." The common sculptural element linking the blind man with the royal monument suggests that the beggar is also a "king." While bridging the polarized social spectrum with such a conflation of identities, the blind man's status as both beggar and king also sets him apart from the narrator and thus challenges any easy notion of "brotherhood" between the two.

A tempting approach to Baudelaire's, Turgenev's, and Bunin's beggar stories would be to read them as meta-narratives about the genre in which they are written. The encounter between the rich man and the beggar mirrors the dichotomy between poetry and prose, the "aristocratic" versus the "plebeian" genre. The three authors' solutions elucidate their different understanding of how the two contrapuntal discourses interact in the prose poem. Baudelaire's paradoxical confrontation and Turgenev's harmonious fusion assume an uneasy coexistence in Bunin's texts.

Several of Bunin's *Kratkie rasskazy,* just like Baudelaire's *Petits poèmes en prose,* feature encounters between rich and poor. "Pervyi Klass" ("First Class"), for example, relates the mutual feelings of unease between the well-to-do passengers of a suburban train and a dirty railway worker who is taking a brief ride in the first-class compartment.[26] "Kanun" ("Eve") juxtaposes the rugged peasants, whom the narrator observes from his cab on the way to the railway station, with a smug, well-dressed gentleman in gold-rimmed spectacles sitting opposite him in the train. Stylistically, the text shifts from a vernacular register in the first half to a more elevated vocabulary at the end. The story concludes with the laconic statement, "But it was already the fall of 1916."[27] This historical reference, placing the event on the eve of the catastrophe of 1917, retroactively endows the description with dramatic irony. Bunin's choice of genre enhances the intended effect. The single, seemingly insignificant moment captured by his minimalist narrative crystallizes into something larger through the frame in which it is presented. The unresolved tension is reflected in a text that, although labeled "*rasskaz*," refuses to tell a "story," while at the same time reverberating with potential narratives.

On the surface, of course, Bunin has more in common with Turgenev than with Baudelaire. This is not surprising if we remember both Bunin's self-chosen role as the heir to the great tradition of nineteenth-century Russian realism and his hostility toward modernist experimentation. If anything, Bunin appears even more conservative—or more "realistic"—than Turgenev. The prose miniatures of his mature years are devoid of the allegoric, fantastic, and dream-like features that endeared Turgenev's late work to the symbolists and decadents. If Turgenev's intention was to illustrate the richness of Russian literature, as Elizabeth Allen has claimed, the impetus for Bunin's writing was to preserve a cultural tradition that he believed had been lost in his homeland. At the same time, however, Bunin's minimalism, which in a way both represents and embodies the "death of literature," appears as an eminently modern feature. Some of his prose miniatures resemble those of the avant-garde writer Daniil Kharms, as we will see in a later chapter.

In summary, we have to note that the Russian realist prose poem hardly qualifies as a particularly productive genre. With a few exceptions, it remained a form of literature that was practiced mainly by second- and third-rate writers. One reason for this relative lack of success is certainly the contradiction between a style that requires a "life-like" descriptive and narrative evocation of reality and a genre that by its very "subversiveness" can only undercut any mimetic illusion and *effet de réel*. One possible consequence of this conflict is the dissolution of narrative content in a flow of impressionist lyric expansion, as happened in the prose poems written at the turn of the century and in Bunin's early writings. Bunin's turning away from this kind of prose lyricism to a form of laconic sparseness marks the successful transition from fin de siècle exuberance toward modernist simplicity. At the same time, it realizes the minimalist potential inherent in the very form of the prose poem. Rather than a hindrance, the tension between realist expectation and minimalist form becomes in Bunin's miniatures a calculated technique and source of artistic appeal.

Chapter Four

Symbolist Prose Miniatures

WHILE THE *POÈME EN PROSE* established itself as a major symbolist genre in France, the same cannot be said about its Russian cousin. If the Russian symbolists experimented with the genre of the prose poem at all, it was usually at the beginning of their career, only to abandon it in favor of more traditional forms. Juvenilia rather than "senilia," many of these texts were later disavowed by their own authors. Some of them remained unpublished drafts. This marginal status may seem surprising at first sight. As evidenced by their choice of the symbolist label, the first practitioners of symbolism in Russia were declared francophiles. In addition, the emergence of decadence and symbolism, first in France and then in many other European literatures of the fin de siècle, provided a fertile ground for the flourishing of prose poems. With its blurring of established boundaries, the new genre corresponded to the reigning *Zeitgeist* characterized by the crisis of traditional realist prose and the new valorization of lyric modes of writing.

Nevertheless, the Russian symbolist prose poem remained on the whole a rather marginal phenomenon. A possible reason might be the fact that the *stikhotvorenie v proze* had become a genre practiced by realist writers whom the symbolists did not find much to their taste. Unlike the realist authors of prose poems, the symbolists shunned the generic label *"stikhotvorenie v proze."*[1] They either resorted to alternative terms, such as "lyric fragment in prose" (Andrei Belyi) or, in most cases, provided no generic classification at all. This does not mean that the symbolist prose miniatures cannot be considered within the generic paradigm of the prose poem. As we will see, many of them relate either directly or indirectly to the example set by Turgenev. This chapter will survey the various manifestations of the Russian symbolist prose poem, beginning with the poets usually classified under the "decadent" rubric (Konstantin Bal'mont, Valerii Briusov, Innokentii Annenskii, Ivan Konevskoi, and Aleksandr Dobroliubov), followed by the "younger" mystic generation (Andrei Belyi and Aleksandr Blok). Some attention will also be paid to the prose miniatures published in the various symbolist almanacs in the first decade of the twentieth century, most of them written by nowadays more or less forgotten authors.

One of the earliest promoters of symbolism in Russia was Dmitrii Merezhkovskii (1865–1941), whose public lectures "On the Causes of the Decline and on the New Trends of Contemporary Russian Literature" (1892, published 1893) provided a sort of manifesto for the new aestheticist and spiritualist movements in Russia. Merezhkovskii acted as a champion for the prose poem, both in its Baudelairean and Turgenevan hypostasis. In 1884, two years after the appearance of Turgenev's *Stikhotvoreniia v proze,* Merezhkovskii published his translation of twelve prose poems by Baudelaire in the journal *Iziashchnaia literatura* (*Belles-Lettres*). In an introductory note, the then nineteen-year-old translator reminded his Russian readers of the fact that Baudelaire, rather than Turgenev, had to be credited as the originator of the prose poem. At the same time, given that two so different authors made use of the same genre, Merezhkovskii predicted a great future for this new literary form.[2] Eight years later, in his lecture about the new trends in Russian literature, Merezhkovskii singled out Turgenev's late work, his semi-fantastic tales and prose poems, for special praise. Unlike the author's realist novels, which Merezhkovskii dismissed as an outdated literary form overly concerned with "questions of the day," the prose poems, according to Merezhkovskii, provided a model for the new literature of the future. Merezhkovskii's dithyrambic praise for Turgenev's prose poems turns into a programmatic endorsement of literary aestheticism and idealism:

> In twenty lines of his "Poems in Prose," [Turgenev] makes entire poetic discoveries. [. . .] He continued Pushkin's deed, he expanded the boundaries of our Russian understanding of beauty, conquered whole new territories of a yet unknown sensitivity, discovered new sounds, new sides of the Russian language. [. . .] Turgenev is a great Russian impressionistic artist. And on the strength of this most important and unconscious feature of his work, which went almost unnoticed by our critics, he is the true herald of the new ideal art, which is coming to replace utilitarian vulgar realism in Russia.[3]

Merezhkovskii's assessment of Turgenev as a proto-symbolist was echoed by other poets of the emerging modernist movement. The poet Konstantin Bal'mont (1867–1942), one of the earliest and more prolific practitioners of the Russian symbolist prose poem, celebrated Turgenev on the tenth anniversary of his death in 1893 with an enthusiastic hymn, "Pamiati I. S. Turgeneva" ("To the Memory of I. S. Turgenev").[4] Several of the compliments that Bal'mont pays to Turgenev sound rather similar to his equally enthusiastic poetic praise of Baudelaire. For example, he commends Turgenev for descending into the "dark abyss of popular life," captivated by its "sad beauty," and finding "flowers in the dirty mud." A year later, these expressions reoccur in Bal'mont's introductory poem to P. F Iakubovich's translation of Baudelaire's *Les Fleurs du Mal,* where the French poet reaps praise for finding "the shining of beauty in the dirty mud of crime."[5]

In the 1890s Bal'mont composed a series of lyrical prose miniatures, some of which were included in his volumes of poetry *Pod severnym nebom* (*Under Northern Skies,* 1894) and *V bezbrezhnosti* (*In Boundlessness,* 1895). "Proshchal'nyi vzgliad" ("A Farewell Glance"), originally part of a triptych of three prose poems with the title "Teni" ("Shadows"), presents a good example of Bal'mont's approach to prose poetry.[6] The text consists of an extended elegiac reverie over the inexorable passing away of youth. The narrator, having returned to the village of his childhood, is strolling through a deserted park on a September evening, where "everywhere there is a premonition of death, both in the shining crimson of the sunset and in the sickly crimson of the last nasturtia." He remembers a recent trip to the "far north" in a style that sounds as if it were quoted from the promotional brochure of a travel agency, featuring "the blue lakes of dreamy Sweden, the green pastures of Denmark, the fjords and gray cliffs of stern Norway." Out of this cluster of images emerges the poem "Chaika" ("The Seagull"), evoking a seagull floating sadly over the "cold maritime abyss" into the "boundless distance."[7] This excursion into verse poetry is followed by two more pages of melancholic prose effusions. At the end, the allegoric personification of youth walks away, "humiliated and miserable."[8]

The second prose poem of the triptych, "Razluka" ("Separation"), also evokes the image of a seagull before the backdrop of a Scandinavian landscape, but this time the mood is confident and exuberant rather than melancholic. The narrator expresses his longing for a distant woman, the addressee of the text, while sailing on "blue-green waves in sight of the shores of Scandinavia." The idea of inseparable togetherness generates a series of images, linking the evening hour with the Evening Star, and the wave of the sea with a lonely, white-winged seagull, to which it is "singing lullabies." The flight of the bird over the sea is followed by an emotional homecoming:

> The seagull flies up to the heavy clouds, the seagull whirls away to distant countries—where and why, it barely knows itself—but again, like a wanderer who got tired from roaming in inhospitable lands, it will fly back to the blue familiar wave, it will cling to it with its snow-white breast,—and the sun laughs, shining on them, and sends them radiant caresses.[9]

It becomes evident that Bal'mont understands the prose poem as a form of poetry rather than as a prosaic genre. In his books of poetry, the prose miniatures mingle with verse poems without any clear demarcation. In an effort to poeticize his language, Bal'mont uses a rhythmic prose, which at times approaches regular metric patterns. Longer paragraphs alternate with very short units of two or three lines resembling stanzas of free verse. Two of his prose poems, "Razluka" and "El'zi," are even written in regular ternary meters, which means that they differ from a verse poem only typographically. In the later editions of his poetry, Bal'mont reprinted them as conventional poems with line breaks. In this sense, the insertion of the seagull poem into the prose of "Proshchal'nyi vzgliad" appears like a natural step. By breaking into metric and rhymed verse, Bal'mont simply takes his poetization of prosaic discourse a step further. Fulfilling its desire to become a poem, his prose reverts to the status of "pure" poetry, thereby abolishing the genre of the prose poem altogether.

Bal'mont's effort to create a "poetic" prose generates a style saturated with lyrical effusions and an impressionistic dwelling on half-tones and nuances. The description of the deserted park in "Proshchal'nyi vzgliad" mobilizes all the resources of fin de siècle coloration:

> On the evening sky the September dusk was burning out. Bright-red stripes were growing pale, rising above the lines of the horizon; they imperceptibly changed first into pink, then into pale yellow, then they drowned without a trace in the faded azure. There was something mysterious in the change of halftones, the eye tried in vain to capture the borderline between the separate stripes, tried in vain to understand how bright crimson can end up as pale azure. Barely audible a quiet wind was rustling in the thinned out foliage of the poplars, maples and lime-trees. The old park was as though quietly dying, and it was sweet and sad to listen to its premortal whisper. At times from one twig or another a lonely golden leaf would break off and, falling, spin around like a butterfly weary from its flight. All paths were strewn with dead leaves, and every step was accompanied by a rustling, every step reminded of the death of what had once lived.

Thematically, Bal'mont's prose poems offer a panoply of neo-romantic and decadent clichés: "exotic" northern landscapes, dreams and fairy tales, fatal love, morbid evocations of the beauty of dying. Manic-depressive mood-swings alternate between abject melancholy and an intoxicated fusion with the power of the elements and declarations of passionate love. The similarities with Turgenev's prose poems are undeniable, but so are the differences. Bal'mont's poetic effusions look like a parody of Turgenev's more sober and restrained approach. The theme of old age, for example, which seems a natural topic for the sexagenarian author of "Senilia," turns into somewhat of a pose when the twenty-seven-year-old Bal'mont laments that the youth who "not long ago used to laugh so light-heartedly" now sports a silvery-gray head.[10] Bal'mont appropriated certain motives from Turgenev's prose poems only to make them conform to his own poetics.

A case in point is the image of Alpine scenery clad in eternal ice, which appears in the prose poems of both authors. In "Razgovor" ("A Conversation," PSS 10:127–28), Turgenev evokes the dialogue between two peaks in the Swiss Alps, the Jungfrau and Finsteraarhorn. The conversation only takes a few minutes, but in fact, thousands of years have elapsed in human time, during which human civilization emerged and disappeared from the face of the earth. At the end, eternal silence reigns again in a world covered with snow and ice. This image of an eternally frozen landscape, both in its polar and Alpine manifestation, exerted a particular fascination on Bal'mont. A whole cycle of his poetry is located in the "Kingdom of ice."[11] The image also occurs in the prose poem "Skazka nochi" ("A Fairytale of the Night"),[12] where the narrator asserts that "in the silence of the mountains, covered with snowflakes, there are more words than in the empty talk of people, more sounds than in the singing of birds." After wandering through the world of humans, which is described as a nightmarish realm of the "living dead," the narrator returns to the mountains, seeing "how much beauty there is in their cold silence." He concludes that "in death there is more Life than in life."[13]

Turgenev's forbidding image of a depopulated desert of snow and ice becomes for Bal'mont a source of aesthetic frisson. The traditional romantic elation over the Alpine sublime takes on additional decadent connotations when the author celebrates the mountains as a realm of death. Bal'mont is not ready to admit one major consequence of Turgenev's tale, however. In the conversation between Jungfrau and Finsteraarhorn, human beings are referred to as utterly insignificant "small insects." By contrast, Bal'mont assumes not a diminished, but an aggrandized vision of his own persona. In the prose poem "Na vysote" ("On the Peak"),[14] the narrator evokes his ascent on a mountain peak so high "that even the clouds of the sky were below me." We learn that, like a prophet or law-giver, he will later descend to impart his new-found wisdom to his fellow humans.

If Turgenev constitutes one source for Bal'mont's prose poems, additional connections exist with the larger literary environment of the European fin de siècle and its preferred decor of dusk, autumnal parks, and languorous reverie. Although Bal'mont's poetry, criticism, and translations demonstrate a high opinion of Baudelaire,[15] the parallels between Bal'mont's prose poems and Baudelaire's *Petits poèmes en prose* remain rather superficial. An untitled miniature in V *bezbrezhnosti* was perhaps inspired by Baudelaire's "Un hémisphère dans une chevelure." Like Baudelaire, Bal'mont compares the beloved woman's body to a vast geographic expanse. The opening line reads: "In your eyes, there are the two spheres of the earthly world, and on top of that, the heavenly world."[16] Baudelaire's and Bal'mont's approaches differ in important respects, however. Baudelaire's text parodies "La Chevelure," the verse poem that he had devoted to the same topic, by disfiguring the love hymn with grating prosaisms. The narrator ends up chewing the woman's hair as if it were a dish of spaghetti. By contrast, Bal'mont's text follows the traditional symbolist path of access to an "other world" via the transfiguration of visible reality. While Baudelaire begins his text with the strange comparison of the woman's hair to a hand-kerchief, Bal'mont's opening points immediately to a transcendental "heavenly world." Bal'mont's text resembles less Baudelaire's prose poem than the verse poem it parodies, which establishes a correspondence between the woman's hair and the sky.[17] Unlike Baudelaire's prose poems, Bal'mont's texts completely lack a sense of irony. In this sense, Bal'mont is closer to Turgenev's "Senilia" than to Baudelaire's *Petits poèmes en prose*—rather than subverting clichés, his project seems to consist in affirming them.

In fairness to Bal'mont, it has to be pointed out that he himself remained unsatisfied with his prose poetry. With the exception of the metric pieces "Razluka" and "El'zi," which he republished as traditional lineated verse poems, he discarded all his prose poems from the later editions of his works.[18] It appears that in retrospect, the more mature Bal'mont viewed his youthful excursions into the realm of prose poetry as a failed experiment. Not only did he repudiate his earlier attempts, he also ceased working in this genre altogether.[19]

A similar turning-away from the prose poem can be observed with Valerii Briusov (1873–1924), the other leading decadent poet of the 1890s. The later *chef d'école* of the Russian symbolists did not share Merezhkovskii's and Bal'mont's enthusiasm for Turgenev as a harbinger of symbolism. As we know from the correspondence with his sister, he preferred Turgenev's realist novels to his mystery tales and prose poems.[20] Briusov's attitude toward the prose poem was much less exuberant than Merezhkovskii's. In a critical fragment that was first published in 1918, he gave the following assessment of this genre:

> I do not remember who compared the "poems in prose" to a hermaphrodite. In any event, this is one of the most insupportable forms of literature. For the most part, it is prose to which a certain rhythmicality has been added, i.e., which is smoothed over by a purely external method. In saying this, I have in mind not the principle, but the existing models. Genuine "poems in prose" (such as they ought to be) were written by Baudelaire, Edgar Poe, Mallarmé. The "poems in prose" of Turgenev are undoubtedly prose, but artistic and beautiful (*khudozhestvennaia i prekrasnaia*).[21]

The characterization of the prose poem as an androgynous genre can be traced back to Baudelaire. In "Le Thyrse," a text that must have been known to Briusov, Baudelaire evokes the image of the thyrsus as an emblem for the genius of Franz Liszt, equating the staff with his masculine will and the surrounding flowers with feminine fantasy. The thyrsus has also been interpreted as an allegory of the prose poem itself, with the masculine "straight line" of prose adorned by feminine poetic curlicues. The etymology of "prose" (*oratio prorsa*=discourse going in a straight line) and "verse" (from *vertere*=to turn) seems to support such an approach.[22] The association of "rational" prose with masculinity and "emotional" poetry with femininity corresponds to common, nineteenth-century gender stereotypes. Yet Briusov's "hermaphrodite," unlike Baudelaire's androgynous thyrsus, is hardly meant to provide an appealing model. It rather looks like a freak of nature, provoking revulsion instead of admiration.

Briusov's attitude toward Turgenev's prose poems appears ambivalent. He does not name Turgenev in his list of successful prose poets, which makes one wonder whether he figures among the providers of the "insupportable" existing models. The last sentence, however, seems partially to rehabilitate Turgenev. We learn that his prose poems are indeed in prose. Presumably, this means that they lack the rhythmical "smoothing over" which turns other examples of this genre into insupportable "hermaphrodites." Briusov does not elaborate on how Turgenev achieves an artistic effect of beauty. It is certainly noteworthy that of the three authors who, according to Briusov, wrote prose poems "such as they ought to be," none is Russian. The existing Russian models seem mainly responsible for Briusov's irritation with the genre. Unfortunately, the fragmentary form of Briusov's text (which is itself a prose miniature!) precludes any extensive theoretical discussion. One would like to know in particular how Briusov defines the "principle" of the prose poem. We can draw at least one conclusion: for Briusov, the prose poem is *not* a form of "poetic," rhythmically upgraded prose. He makes clear that the poeticity of the prose poem cannot be achieved by such "external" means. This is in itself quite a remarkable insight, which clearly sets Briusov apart from his colleague Bal'mont.

In Briusov's own poetic oeuvre, the prose poem occupies a rather insignificant place. The second and third volumes of the notorious anthology *Russkie simvolisty,* which catapulted Briusov to scandalous fame in the mid-1890s, contain Russian translations of two prose poems by Mallarmé as well as an original prose poem by Briusov's colleague and collaborator, A. L. Miropol'skii (i.e., Aleksandr Lang, 1872–1917), which carries a quatrain by Briusov as an epigraph.[23] Miropol'skii's prose poem is a study in decadent necrophilia, featuring the obligatory display of ghosts, skeletons, and decaying corpses. The first paragraph, with its metaphorically saturated apocalyptic imagery, will give a sufficient impression of the whole text:

> Darkness. The black fingers of the sky have moved together, and only for a moment are they separating to pour out fiery snakes over the earth and to close again with a thunder. The breast of the earth shudders in premortal convulsions. The heavy bolts of the burial vaults break with a clinking sound, and in the general darkness walk slowly and sadly the long deceased. The people moan, pray, call for salvation. Somebody's guffaw answers them.

Briusov never published any of his own prose poems, but one of them was included in a posthumous edition of his writings in 1931.[24] "Otdalennye dni"

("Distant Days"), written in 1898, relies for its exotic effect not on geographical, but on historical remoteness. The text evokes the life of prehistoric lake-dwellers, which is rendered with a fascination for primitive savagery reminiscent of European travelers' accounts of African cannibals. A group of warriors are "boasting with their enemies' skulls," with their "wolf-eyes burning under the low forehead" and their "sharpened teeth gleaming," while the women, "naked, with enormous bellies, with hanging breasts, with bulging cheekbones," prepare the evening meal. One wounded warrior lies alone under a tree. In his feverish delirium, he begins to despise his primitive surroundings and has visions of another, more civilized life; of clothing which "captivates the eyes with its colors"; and a "varied, delicate, quick, and charming" form of human speech. He has a "great foreboding of the fullness of life" and realizes that he alone will be able to bring it about. The shouts and laughter of the tribe huddling around the fire awake him from his dream. In the guise of a Stone-Age ethnographic sketch, Briusov provides a variant of the familiar romantic theme of the poet's alienation from his mundane surroundings.

Briusov did not himself designate this text as a prose poem. It received this generic label from the editors who retrieved it from Briusov's notebooks. Whether the author would have concurred with this designation must remain an open question. In any event, Briusov did not deem it a text worthy of publication. Briusov's unpublished notebooks of the 1890s contain many more sketches, which, for lack of a better term, one might call prose poems.[25] However, the tentative nature of these texts makes it difficult to decide whether they were intended as self-sufficient prose miniatures, or whether they are the abandoned fragments of planned longer works. Given Briusov's francophile leanings and his interest in the latest French poetry, it may appear somewhat surprising that the prose poem did not play a greater role in his own poetic oeuvre. His development from a decadent provocateur in the 1890s to a sober neo-classicist in the first decade of the twentieth century provides a partial explanation. With its fluid contours and uncertain structure, the prose poem ill-fitted the Parnassian poetics of Briusov's later years. It is not surprising that Briusov, preoccupied with his effort of achieving an effect of marmoreal monumentality with his verse, came to regard the "hermaphrodite" of the prose poem as a "most insupportable form of literature."[26]

The other great francophile among the Russian symbolists was Innokentii Annenskii (1856–1909). Like Bal'mont and Briusov, Annenskii also experimented with forms of prose poetry. His unpublished manuscripts contain an undated cycle of twenty-six prose miniatures with the title "Autopsia."[27] Eight of these pieces were published in 1979 under the title "prose poems."[28] In the meantime, it has become clear that these texts are not original creations, but Annenskii's translation of rhymed verse poems

from the volume *Fatalitá* (published in 1892) by the Italian poet Ada Negri.
It is curious that Annenskii gave his translations the form of prose miniatures
rather than resorting to the traditional verse-for-verse rendition that he followed in all his other translated poetry. A. V. Fedorov has suggested that
Annenskii adopted this solution under the influence of Turgenev's prose poems.[29] One could add that the prosaic translation of verse poems, although
unusual in Russia, is a more common practice in French literature.

Thematically, the "Autopsia" cycle bears a certain resemblance to the
socially engaged, neo-realist prose poems that became popular at the turn
of the century. The female first-person narrator, a "Doch' naroda" ("Daughter of the People"), engages in a posthumous lament about the misery and
tribulations of the working class. Annenskii's interest in these topics may
have been influenced by the populist views of his elder brother Nikolai.
Although the theme of urban poverty is not absent from Annenskii's later
poetry, these pieces differ significantly in style and tone. The naive allegorization of populist optimism and unquestioning celebration of modern
technology at the end of "Ne trevozh' menia" ("Don't disturb me"), for example, would be unthinkable in Annenskii's own poetic work. The lyric
praise of machines anticipates Aleksei Gastev's *Poetry of the Worker's Blow:*

> The steam-engine smokes, the plow tears into the fertile breast of the earth,
> the machines howl and hammer, the hearths blaze, and over this wild howl of
> the earth, in this fermentation, Freedom has unfolded its white wings, and
> their rumble proudly resounds in the wind.[30]

Annenskii's own four prose poems, which his son, V. Krivich, included in
the 1923 edition of his posthumous poetry, are radically different from this
model.[31] Melancholic in tone, they constitute a self-exploration of the
poetic persona in its interaction with the external world. The first piece,
"Mysli-igly" ("Thought-Needles"), gives an allegoric self-portrait of the poet
as a dying fir-tree. Its needles, which correspond to the poet's thoughts, tear
themselves off the branches in "pain and torment" and fall to the ground to
form a humus from which a "tall and proud tree" will eventually grow. This
future poet will be unaware that his predecessor spent "the last blood of his
heart" for his sake. The second piece, titled "Andante," provides an impressionist rendition of a carriage ride on a windy and cloudy evening in July.
This aesthetic experience produces a rapprochement of the lyrical persona
with the external world (literally, "all that which is *not-us*"), but fails to bring
him together with his companion. He hopes to achieve this reunion in a
protracted moment of silence and immobility: "We will be together, but
separate. And may in other, roundabout ways our shadows, melted in the
July fog, come close, flow together and become one shadow. . . ." "Sentimental'noe vospominanie" ("Sentimental Reminiscence"), the third prose
poem, evokes the distant memory of a rainbow seen in the evening, which

at the time prompted the poet to write some "bad verse" full of "banal rhymes" and "pitiful metaphors." He was interrupted by the sound of an old Italian street organ playing an aria from Verdi's *Trovatore,* moving him to tears despite its questionable qualities—"contrived feeling, false notes, the smug music of the still young Verdi. . . . " This leads to a general meditation on beauty and art, leaving the question open whether their secret lies in the "conscious, inspired victory over torment, or in the unconscious longing of the human spirit, who sees no exit from the circle of vulgarity, mediocrity and thoughtlessness (*nedomyslie*) and is tragically condemned to seem smug or hopelessly false." In "Moia dusha" ("My Soul"), the final piece, the narrator evokes three different allegoric dream visions of his own soul which appear to him during a boat trip on the Volga. First, the soul takes the form of an old Persian porter, dragging an enormous bale, then it appears as a "dishonored, pregnant old maid," and finally as an old, worn-out canvas bag, which, after being filled with various loads and pushed around, will be shredded and turned into paper.

On the surface, Annenskii's texts seem reminiscent of the decadent world of Bal'mont's prose miniatures. We find a similar impressionistic style saturated with colors and atmospheric descriptions, a similar concern with creating a musical prose, and a similar sense of melancholy and elegiac self-involvement. A closer look, however, reveals significant differences. While Bal'mont engages in a rather naive display of neo-romantic clichés, Annenskii manipulates these elements in a self-conscious way. Rather than examples of unmediated lyric effusion, his prose poems are highly complex, self-reflective metatexts concerned with their own production and nature as works of art. Essentially, they all deal with the problematic status of poetry in a "prosaic" world. The alienation of the poet from his mundane surroundings is of course an old romantic and decadent commonplace (as we have seen in Briusov's Stone-Age parable), but it takes a different turn in Annenskii's work, where the integrity of the poetic self is called into question. As Lidiia Ginzburg has put it: "The affirmation of the absolute value of one's own personality [. . .] was an immutable source of romantic pathos and tragedy, whereas the modern conflict represented by Annenskii takes place in a consciousness that does not believe any more in its own value."[32] The autonomy of the poetic voice becomes impossible in a world where the "*I* cannot escape from the *Non-I*," as Annenskii phrased it in his programmatic poem "Poetu" ("To the Poet").[33] The three allegories of the poet's soul in "Moia dusha" all demonstrate this phenomenon: the old Persian is called *ne svoi* (not "his own man"), the pregnant woman is "dominated by the still nonexistent person who fatally was growing in her," and the bag is "condemned to live with all kind of rubbish and junk with which life thievishly stuffed him."[34]

The intrusion of the prosaic into the lyric world is a defining feature of both Annenskii's verse and prose poetry. The description of the pregnant woman in "Moia dusha," for example, is rendered in a coarsely naturalistic style: "Her swollen face was strangely marked by the yellow stains of a mustache, and among her chance acquaintances smelling of fish and train-oil, the girl carried awkwardly and haughtily her plump belly." The hybrid nature of the prose poem provides a generic locus for the clash between beauty and *byt* (a Russian term loosely translatable as the "daily grind" and a key element in Annenskii's poetics). The blurring of boundaries becomes evident in the atmospheric settings of Annenskii's prose poems, such as the incongruously foggy July evening. In its refusal to conform to the strictures and expectations of verse poetry, the prose poem represents a form of "bad" writing akin to the bad poetry alluded to in "Sentimental'noe vospominanie:" "These were bad verses, completely bad verses, this was not even a poetic rhetoric, but something even more pitiful." The question of what exactly constitutes "good" or "bad" art remains unresolved or, as Annenskii puts it, assuming the tone of a mock-address to his audience, "all this is complicated, gentlemen." He is unsure what earthly music a heavenly creature would find preferable, "a Bach chorale in the Cathedral of Milan, or the 'Valse des roses' played by a two-year-old child, who is ruthlessly turning the handle of his much-suffering street organ in the wrong direction."

In a world where traditional notions of poetic beauty have become problematic, the exalted status of the poet as a purveyor of eternal truths is equally called into question. At best, his usefulness may consist in forming with his decaying "thought-needles" a humus for the growth of a future poetic genius, "who will give to people all the happiness that their hearts can accommodate." However, one has to wonder how serious Annenskii is about this prediction of utopian bliss, especially since the motif of the usefulness of the poet reoccurs in "Moia dusha," but this time in a clearly parodistic mode. After the old bag is worn out from its duties, it will not find peace in a state of nonbeing. Instead, its material will be recycled into stationery for the composition of *billets doux*. Addressing his female readers, the poet predicts that "sticking out your little finger with the dark sapphire, you will use me to write a note to your lover . . . O, curse it!" Rather than being in control of the writing process, the poet turns into the passive receptacle of someone else's writing—a writing, one might add, of dubious literary quality. In addition, the story of the poet's life will serve as grist for moralizing pulp fiction: "My fate will be touchingly described in an edifying little book costing three silver kopecks. They will describe the fate of the poor bag of pliant canvas, worn out from serving the people." Both the practical usefulness of the love note and the moral usefulness of the edifying tale is something that Annenskii can well do without. As he notes at the end of his programmatic "Mysli-igly": "Fall down on the all-receiving black lap, you thoughts, unnecessary to the people! Fall down, because you too were beautiful sometimes, if only because you did not gladden anybody. . . ."

It becomes clear that Annenskii's "decadence" is of a quite different, and much more modern nature than that of Bal'mont or Briusov. Both Bal'mont's and Briusov's stars began to fade after 1910, whereas the older Annenskii, who had spent his entire life outside the limelight, gained posthumous fame among the newly emerging, postsymbolist avant-garde. In this sense, the image of the "thought-needles" preparing the humus for the growth of future poetry was indeed prophetic. In the wider European context, Annenskii's prose poems seem closer to the French model than those of his Russian symbolist contemporaries. Given Annenskii's expert knowledge of French literature and interest in the latest French poetry, this is of course hardly surprising.[35] "Mysli-igly" opens with a French epigraph, "Je suis le roi d'une ténébreuse vallée," taken from a prose poem by the Franco-American poet Stuart Merrill.[36] Although no direct thematic overlap exists with Baudelaire's *Petits poèmes en prose*, Annenskii's prose poems display a similarly self-conscious and self-critical poetic stance. At the same time, however, they use only a narrow range of possibilities exemplified in the Baudelairean model. All of them follow the mode of the first-person lyric confession without exploiting the potential for the citation and subversion of other narrative genres. We must remember, of course, that Annenskii only wrote a total of four prose poems. In fact, given his affinities for French literature, one wonders why he did not write *more* of these texts, and why he never published any of them, with the exception of "Mysli-igly." One suspects that, as in the case of Briusov, the fluidity of the prose poem ultimately failed to satisfy Annenskii's intense quest for form, exemplified both in his carefully crafted verse and in the complex architecture of his poetic cycles.

Bal'mont, Briusov, and Annenskii were not the only Russian poets of the decadent generation who experimented with prose miniatures. At least passing mention should be made of two more authors, Ivan Konevskoi (i.e., Ivan Ivanovich Oreus, 1877–1901) and Aleksandr Dobroliubov (1876–1944?). Konevskoi's volume of poetry *Mechty i dumy* (*Dreams and Thoughts*, 1900), contains a cycle of prose miniatures rendering his travel impressions from Switzerland.[37] In content and style, they fit into the long tradition of enthusiastic descriptions of the Alpine landscape penned by Russian travelers as far back as Karamzin. Unlike Turgenev's dialogue between the Jungfrau and Finsteraarhorn, Konevskoi's evocation of the majestic peaks of the Berner Oberland do not serve any didactic purpose. Neither do they indulge in Bal'mont's aesthetic celebration of death. They present the rather traditionally romantic monologue of a subject enthralled with the spectacle of the sublime.[38]

Konevskoi's friend Aleksandr Dobroliubov, who evolved from an 1890s' "arch-decadent" to a holy wanderer and leader of a religious sect, wrote prose poetry of a more unusual nature. His first published volume, *Natura Naturans. Natura Naturata* (1895) contains a total of ten lyrical prose fragments, interspersed with eighteen poems written in traditional and free verse. Do-broliubov's experimentation with form was clearly influenced by the French decadents and symbolists, whom he had studied "cover to cover," as we know from Briusov's memoirs.[39] Heterogeneous in nature, Dobroliubov's prose poems include lyrical monologues written from the point of view of different subjects (a young woman, an old man, Dobroliubov himself) and short, hallucinatory narratives. Perhaps in an attempt to take literally Ver-laine's famous injunction, "De la musique avant toute chose"—and antici-pating by several years Andrei Belyi's "Symphonies"—many of the pieces, both in prose and verse, are provided with musical notations of tempo and dynamics ("Adagio maestoso," "Presto," "Andante con moto," "Pianissimo," and so on). One piece bears the oxymoronic label "Andante con fuoco." Two fragments, marked "Allegro con moto" and "Moderato," simply consist of a dotted line—a literal realization, as it were, of the concept of Verlaine's "Romances sans paroles." Dobroliubov's formal eccentricities, resulting from a wish to "express the incomprehensible incomprehensibly," make him look at times like a forerunner of the later futurist avant-garde.

The prevalent theme of *Natura Naturans. Natura Naturata* is death. This has less to do with modish decadent necrophilia than with the passing away of Dobroliubov's beloved father in 1892, which caused an existential crisis in his then sixteen-year-old son. Many pieces are laments over irre-trievable loss. The common focus on death allows comparisons with Tur-genev's prose poems. Both authors allegorize death as a threatening old woman who is pursuing the narrator in a dream vision.[40] In Dobroliubov's version, the allegoric figure, presented as the feverish hallucination of a patient on his sickbed, takes on crudely naturalistic features: "She came close. He felt the entreating hands of the old woman seize his neck, her wrinkled cheeks bend down to him, a putrid smell envelop his whole being, her sweaty breath mix with his own—and a feeling of disgust was growing slowly. . . ."[41]

Several years after he took up his new life as a religious wanderer, Do-broliubov published a cycle of ten prose miniatures in Briusov's almanac *Severnye tsvety* (*Northern Flowers*).[42] The title "Obrazy" ("Images") points to a shift from music to painting as the underlying referential system. The word "obraz" (with a different plural form) can also signify an icon. As he declares in one of these texts, Dobroliubov sees his verbal art as akin to the spiritual task of icon painting: "I want to transmit not words—but a picture, the truth."[43] In spite of this overtly religious orientation, many features of these "Images" are reminiscent of the former decadent manner, including the reliance on complicated imagery and narcissist preoccupation with the self. The two prose miniatures published the following year in *Severnye tsvety*, however, are quite different. Presented as realist "Sketches from a Madhouse" (Dobroliubov indeed had several stints in psychiatric hospitals), they draw the portrait of two simple mental patients who in their madness are "wiser than many of the wise."[44] Dobroliubov's last published work was the book *Iz knigi nevidimoi* (*From the Invisible Book,* 1905), a large compilation of religious writings of a confessional and exhortatory nature. As in *Natura Naturans. Natura Naturata,* verse and prose mix freely. The former obsession with death is now replaced by a joyful praise of nature and life reminiscent of St. Francis of Assisi. In his final address to the reader, Dobroliubov renounces literature altogether, declaring that "on visible paper one will never express the Chief Truth and Mystery. Enter into the book of Life!"[45]

Dobroliubov's development from provocative decadence to religious "life-building" is representative of the shift between the first and second generation of Russian symbolism, when the earlier decadent spirit gave way to a search for a transcendent noumenon, and the task of the poet was seen as revealing the mystic core and unity of being. Among the most important members of this "younger" generation of Russian symbolists who gained prominence after 1900—Andrei Belyi (1880–1934), Aleksandr Blok (1880–1921), and Viacheslav Ivanov (1866–1949)—only Belyi worked in the genre of the prose poem in a more than cursory manner. In Blok's oeuvre, the prose miniature occupies an extremely marginal place, and Ivanov shunned the genre (and any kind of prose fiction) altogether. This neglect may be partially explained by the French origin of the *poème en prose* and its association with the spirit of decadence, which made it a somewhat tainted form of literature for the members of the younger generation of Russian symbolists.[46] The connotation of the prose poem with a period of cultural crisis and the breakdown of established order went against the grain of Ivanov's "theurgic" concept of literature, whose goal was not the creation of a subversive counterdiscourse, but the establishment of a regenerative religious art of lofty solemnity. Perhaps more important, the *stikhotvorenie v proze,* as we remember, was a genre practiced, with mixed success, by the realist writers of Gor'kii's entourage—a school of writing with which the symbolists had no desire to be associated.

Andrei Belyi's experiments with prose poetry mark the very beginning of his poetic career. Belyi's unpublished notebooks contain twenty-six so-called "lyrical fragments in prose," written between 1897 and 1900, when Belyi was seventeen to twenty years old. Six of these pieces, in a reworked form, were included in the volume *Zoloto v lazuri* (*Gold in Azure,* 1904), but not in any later edition of Belyi's works.[47] Belyi himself sometimes referred to these texts as "*stikhotvoreniia v proze.*" His later attitude toward them was utter irony and scorn. In his autobiographical letter of 1927 to R. V. Ivanov-Razumnik, he called them a "mixture of Turgenev and Edgar Poe with everything arch-left and arch-unintelligible" ("pomes' Turgeneva, Edgara Po so vsem naileveishim, naineponiatneishim"). Quoting some excerpts from memory, he added: "The lyricism of these fragments is unbelievable, it's a pity they disappeared, otherwise we could have a good laugh" ("mozhno bylo by pokhokhotat'").[48]

The Belyi scholar A. V. Lavrov concurs with this dismissive judgment, calling Belyi's lyrical prose fragments "entirely adolescent works."[49] This assessment seems indeed rather appropriate when we look at the texts, which could be characterized as sophomoric samples of decadent prose—impressionist mood pieces shot through with streaks of exoticism and mysticism. As Ronald Peterson has noted in his monograph on Belyi's short prose, "there is room for a vision of Christ at the dawn of a new day, but most of the attention is focused on hairy creatures and accounts of their actions at twilight."[50] These texts do deserve attention, however, as Belyi's first attempts at prose writing, which would later evolve into "symphonies," novels, and essays. The relation to the symphonies is particularly close: we find the same insistence on musical elements (supposedly Belyi wrote both his prose poems and symphonies while improvising on the piano—one fragment is based on a motif by Edvard Grieg), and some of the later fragments consist of numbered sentences like the first two symphonies.

In many ways, Belyi's lyrical fragments are reminiscent of Bal'mont's and Briusov's decadent prose of the 1890s. As in Bal'mont's prose poems, we are placed in a twilight zone between waking and hallucination—"half dream, half reality" ("ne to son, ne to deistvitel'nost'")[51]—rendered in a musical style saturated with impressionistic color and replete with ubiquitous omission points. This is how Belyi conveys an evening near Moscow, for example:

> In the sky and on the water a soft sunset . . . yellow and pink through a light, invisible steam . . . the pink in the sky covered by a suffused patina of blue-grey clouds . . . the haze, while not weakening the yellow and pink shine, gave to both of them a soft nuance: the dissonance between yellow and pink was resolved in an elegant harmony . . . the water seemed heavy, satiated with steam. . . .[52]

Like Bal'mont and Briusov, Belyi likes to indulge in exotic reveries. One of his fragments evokes a "night of strange, morbid dreams" in the "gardens of the Maharaja."[53] Frequently, the exotic effect relies on time as well as space travel. The fact that some of the characters are dressed in togas points to the Roman Empire as a backdrop.[54] In some cases, Belyi goes back to an even more distant past. "Ssora" ("A Quarrel"), like Briusov's "Otdalennye dni," is located in the prehistoric age. It shows a primordial man killing an orangutan with his bow and arrow while a "shaggy mammoth" comes out to the watering place.[55] "Etiud" ("Etude") is written in a similar vein. It evokes the post-Edenic old age of Adam and Eve, who live as savages in a shabby hovel amidst a landscape populated by flamingos and antelopes. Adam is longing for his first-born son Cain, who seems to appear before him in the grass: "The thick lips of the wild fratricide broke into a pitiful smile, his wolf teeth gleamed like pearls in the moonlight." However, it turns out that Adam, perhaps in a variant of Isaac's misplaced fatherly blessing in Genesis 1:27, unwittingly gives his blessing not to Cain, but to a bewildered goat.[56] Some pieces are located in an entirely fantastic atmosphere of legends and fairy tales. In "Volosatik," a cheerful crowd of revelers on a marble terrace is threatened by a huge, hairy spider hiding in an abyss covered with roses. "Revun" ("The Howler") features another terrace next to an abyss, where the narrator encounters an old man who turns out to be the "king of the mountain winds." We learn that this character has the capability of "illuminating all the graves," making them burn with a "yellow light amid the foggy chaos."[57]

Besides their undeniable entertainment value, Belyi's fantastic ministories present an untapped resource for psychoanalytically minded critics. In this respect, the unpublished fragment No. 4, dated May 1898, deserves particular attention as a projection of Belyi's Oedipal family drama (and anticipation of the conflict between Ableukhov junior and senior in the novel *Petersburg*). With more than ten manuscript pages, it is the longest text in Belyi's notebook. On a midnight stroll through a moonlit landscape of sad birch trees and willows, the narrator encounters a "pale woman" with whom he immediately falls in love. She tells him that she is cursed for her sins and asks him whether he can atone her guilt. The two of them fly through the air to a distant place near a pond, where the narrator's old father lives (Belyi's father was in fact twenty years older than his mother). It turns out that the pale woman is the narrator's mother, who has drowned herself in the pond. The old man comes to the shore, asking for her forgiveness. She embraces him. When the son approaches the couple, a conflict between father and son erupts: "The old man began to howl. . . . And the old man stood up to his full size, threatening me, cursing me—his son. . . . He was terrible (*grozen*) and severe in the flaming of his ecstasy." The story culminates with the corpse of the drowned father floating on the surface of the pond, while the mother whispers lovingly, "My son, my son. . . ." The text ends with the exclamation ". . . Mother!!. . . ."[58]

The decadent nature of Belyi's prose fragments, despite their similarity with Bal'mont's and Briusov's writings of the 1890s, is not the result of a direct borrowing. Belyi discovered the elder symbolists only at the turn of the century. Rather, these features need to be explained by what Lavrov calls Belyi's "more intuitive than borrowed or imitative" brand of symbolism.[59] In addition, there is an undeniable influence of Nietzsche, with whom Belyi became enamored in 1899.[60] Two of his later fragments are dedicated "To the memory of Fr. Nietzsche."[61] In the first piece, Belyi assumes the oracular, Zarathustra-like voice of a prophet addressing his disciples: "My friends,

do not ask, what is the matter with me . . . is it not true that lightning is reflected on my face?. . . ." In the second, significantly longer text, the speaker
is shrouded in crimson, addressing an audience of "corpses," while Nietzsche
himself makes a cameo appearance as a centaur.

As Belyi himself indicated in his letter to Ivanov-Razumnik, Turgenev's prose poems constitute an additional source for his lyrical fragments.
Besides generic similarities, some parallels exist on the level of plot. In both
authors, we find a dream-vision of the end of the world witnessed by the
first-person narrator.[62] Some of the details of Belyi's narrative are borrowed
from Turgenev, but adapted to his own style. For example, Turgenev describes the uncanny quietness before the apocalyptic storm in the following
terms: "This sky is like a shroud. And there is no wind . . . Has the air died,
perhaps?" Belyi expands this vision into an expressive tableau: "Northern
reflections in the banks of clouds . . . Despair in the turbid silhouettes . . .
Despair in the sky . . . Despair in the leaden gleam of the waters . . . And
no wind . . . And nothing like wind on the horizon. . . ." While Turgenev describes the end of the world as the coming of a gigantic flood wave which
destroys everything in its path, in Belyi's version the world ends not with a
bang, but with a whimper: "I saw somebody's pale face, confused, covered
with tears and grief, somebody's feverish shout, somebody's senseless call . . .
And it began to rain, incessantly and sadly . . . Everything became mixed up
in the dense chaos of tears."

Just like Turgenev, Belyi also included a beggar story among his prose
poems.[63] His encounter between almsgiver and beggar, reported in a series
of numbered sentences, presents yet another variant of the plot used by
Baudelaire, Turgenev, and Bunin. The narrator, clothed in a "snow-white
toga" fastened with an amethyst, wearing golden sandals and a laurel wreath
on his head, encounters an old beggar on crutches, with stinking rugs covering his wounds and scabs. In a dry, hoarse voice, the beggar praises the
"Lord Jesus." When the narrator approaches him, the beggar stretches out
his long hand and ask for alms, fastening his "dull pig eyes" on the frightened narrator, who complies with the request, "trembling as in fever." The
beggar, however, continues to stretch out his hand and to stare. The narrator finally breaks free, but at the corner of the street he turns around and,
to his horror, sees the old beggar still staring at him with an "immobile, dia-
bolic glance," stretching out his "long, dry hand." We learn that, many years
later, the narrator has two more encounters with the mysterious beggar.
Once he sees him during a sumptuous banquet in Egypt. Wearing a blue
toga and a wreath of red roses on his head, the narrator hears the familiar
voice singing the Psalms of King David. When he steps to the window, the
beggar stares at him with his dull pig eyes. The narrator freezes with horror as the rose petals on his toga seem to turn into stains of blood. The
final encounter happens when the narrator has himself become an old man,

wandering through the country dressed in sackcloth. On a moonlit night, he comes across a funeral procession. A group of ghastly old men, singing the Psalms of King David, are carrying the old beggar in an open coffin. His pointed beard is sticking out provocatively, and it seems that he is stretching out "his dry hand, asking for peace and justice." In an upsurge of grief, the narrator wants to stretch out his hand toward his "brother in mutilation" (*svoemu sobratu po uvech'iu*), but the gravediggers carry him quickly away.

The realist setting of Turgenev's beggar story mutates in Belyi's version into the dark romanticism of a fantastic, orientalist horror tale. The gesture of the handshake, Turgenev's ultimate token of brotherhood, is alluded to, but remains unrealized. Unlike all the other beggar stories discussed thus far, no satisfactory transaction takes place between narrator and beggar. They merely stare at each other in mutual horror (*uzhasaias' drug drugom*). The allegoric significance of the half-saintly, half-diabolical beggar remains vague. His sightings represent for the narrator a sort of initiation ritual. The descriptions of the first two encounters end with the identical formula: "Many things appeared dimly to me at that time, and I learned of many things for the first time." The impression that some secret wisdom was being imparted is underlined by the portentous, "biblical" style of Belyi's narrative. With its repeated formulas and numbered sentences, the text seeks to imitate the psalms to which it twice alludes.

The hieratic, prophetic style of Belyi's later prose fragments foreshadows the manner of his "Symphonies" and verse poetry after the turn of the century. "Videnie" ("A Vision"), the opening piece of the collection published in *Zoloto v lazuri,* is also written in numbered sentences.[64] It prophesies the coming of a king clothed in blood-red garments studded with precious stones. In a syncretic mixture of Dionysian and Christian emblems, he is described as holding in one hand a staff overgrown with lilies and narcissi; and in the other a golden cup filled with the "blood of the just."[65] Standing on the "blue dome of the cloud" amid thunder and lightning, he speaks with the voice of a "righteous storm." As in his poetry of that period, Belyi's apocalyptic foreboding is still a source of optimistic enthusiasm rather than an anticipation of catastrophic doom. The six prose fragments published in *Zoloto v lazuri* are followed by a longer text, written in 1904, which evokes in glowing terms the utopian vision of future space travel to the sun carried out by the "Order of Argonauts."[66]

Belyi's four symphonies, although an outgrowth of his "lyrical fragments in prose," present a qualitatively new phase in his experimentation with genre. With their vast dimensions, they differ significantly from the prose fragments of the 1890s. Although sometimes referred to as "prose poems" in the critical literature, they do not conform to the generic paradigm of the *stikhotvorenie v proze* (*poema v proze* would be a more appropriate term). It is true that the musical title "Symphony," applied to a literary text, points to the typical blurring of generic boundaries, which is a hallmark of the prose poem, as we have seen with the musical designations given to Aleksandr Dobroliubov's prose miniatures. But the very concept of a "symphony" implies a quest for harmonious complexity and vast overarching structure that is incompatible with the miniaturism of the *stikhotvorenie v proze.*

In the work of Belyi's fellow symbolist poet and coeval Aleksandr Blok, the prose poem occupies the opposite position: rather than the beginning, it marks the end of his career. In 1921, the year of his death, Blok published a few prose miniatures under the title "Ni sny, ni iav'" ("Neither Dream nor Reality") in the journal *Zapiski mechtatelei* (*Dreamers' Notes*).[67] The plans for such a work go as far back as 1902, as we know from Blok's diaries. In their published form, the sketches relate to events of 1908 and 1909 and also to the postrevolutionary period of January 1919. The tone of Blok's prose miniatures is wistful and melancholic:

> Всю жизнь мы прождали счастья, как люди в сумерки долгие часы ждут поезда на открытой, занесенной снегом платформе. Ослепли от снега, а всё ждут, когда появится на повороте три огня.
>
> Вот наконец высокий узкий паровоз; но уже не на радость: все так устали, так холодно, что нельзя согреться даже в теплом вагоне.[68]

All our lives we waited for happiness, as people in the twilight wait long hours for a train on an open platform covered with snow. They have been blinded by the snow, and they are still waiting, when three lights appear at the turn.

Here is finally the high narrow steam engine; but it brings no more joy: all are so tired, it is so cold, that it is impossible to get warm even in the heated carriage.

The mood of utter physical exhaustion, coupled with disillusionment over the shattered utopia of the Russian Revolution, contrasts sharply with Belyi's earlier, euphoric, apocalyptic expectations. In their foreboding of impending death, Blok's miniatures resemble Turgenev's "Senilia." They also seem a mark of creative impotence: if for Turgenev, the prose poem indicates the death of the novel, for Blok it is connected with the loss of his poetic capabilities. By 1921, only disjointed fragments remain of his former world of symbolist idealism. It is perhaps no accident that some of these pieces seem to anticipate the black miniatures of Daniil Kharms.[69]

The relative unimportance of the prose miniature in the oeuvre of the major Russian symbolists does not mean that no prose poems were produced in the first decade of the twentieth century. The symbolist almanacs of the period featured a variety of lyrical prose pieces, most of them written by now long-forgotten authors such as A. L. Miropol'skii (i.e., Aleksandr Lang), N. Stal', N. Iarkov, Odinokii (i.e., Aleksandr Tiniakov), Nikolai Tabetskii, A. Kursinskii, and others.[70] In style and content, most of these prose miniatures evoke the decadent spirit of the 1890s, combining a mannered "musical" prose with vague mysticism. The cliché-ridden fin de siècle character of these prose poems makes them look like involuntary, symbolist self-parodies. One is reminded most of all of Chekhov's lampoon of a symbolist play in "The Seagull." Hardly qualifying as masterpieces of literature, these texts deserve attention at best as examples of turn-of-the-century kitsch. In fairness, it has to be said that they are no better and no worse than the juvenile prose poetry of more famous authors, such as Bal'mont and Belyi.

In their lyricism, their emphasis on subjective (and frequently morose) feelings, and their interest in dreams, these miniatures can be considered descendents of Turgenev's "Senilia." Very few of them, however, follow Turgenev's example of aphoristic laconicity. Among the few exceptions are the texts published by Lidiia Zinov'eva-Annibal (1866–1907) under the title "Teni sna" ("Shadows of Sleep").[71] This cycle of eighteen short pieces is focused on the theme of death, centered around the drowning of a little girl in a river. In a spirit of compassion with all creatures of nature reminiscent of Dobroliubov's *Invisible Book*, the author laments the death of a mole killed by a gardener and a little rabbit killed by her cat, the death of butterflies, may-bugs, and of young birds falling from their nest. The cycle ends with a flaming hymn to a cosmic fire which will come to "awake the dreamer."

Evgenii Lundberg's six prose fragments published in 1907 follow an even more compact minimalism.[72] In their aphoristic laconicity, they display a sense of formal restraint that is diametrically opposed to the decadent effusions of other prose poets of this time. The guiding principle of Lundberg's prose miniatures is negation and rejection. The lyric persona displays a hostile attitude toward the surrounding world, preferring to dwell in a self-imposed blindness. The title of the final fragment, "Zver' protiv zveria" ("Animal against Animal") recalls the Hobbesian "homo homini lupus," or Ivan Karamazov's famous dictum "pust' gad est gad" ("let one reptile devour the other"). Lundberg's text presents a sort of "anti-fairy tale." His minimalist story is reminiscent of both Fedor Sologub's "Little Fairy Tales" and Aleksei Remizov's dreams, which will be discussed in the following chapters. The narrator is attacked by a wild animal from the "cursed wood," which is about to pose him a riddle and to devour him, "all according to custom." However, the narrator refuses to follow the fairy-tale script. He declares that he has no interest in solving any riddles and proposes to fight instead, since "might is right" (*ch'ia sila—togo i pravda*). The confused animal runs back into the wood.

In a self-reflective prose miniature, Lundberg justifies his rejection of romantic fantasies and Dionysiac frenzy with a "lack of words," which leads to the ultimate vanishing point of minimalism: silence. His text becomes a self-parody of the symbolist prose poem, illustrating its own impossibility:

Когда нахлынут

Когда нахлынут ночные видения, нужно лететь и нет крыльев—мне мало слов, презираю слова.

Крикну: В пляске разорвите меня. Упейтесь мною—в пляске.

Исступленный упаду на постель: пляска забыта в веках, а петь не умею.[73]

When They Gush

When nightly visions gush, one needs to fly and there are no wings—I don't have enough words, I despise words.

I shout: In dancing tear me to pieces. Get drunk on me—in dancing.

Frenzied I fall down on the bed: the dance is forgotten in centuries, and I don't know how to sing.

Lundberg's miniature anticipates the impending crisis of symbolism. His skepticism is particularly damaging for the idea of a "poetic" prose breaking free from the strictures of verse on the wings of its own transcendental lyricism. Overall, the symbolist prose miniature came to be perceived as an artistic dead end, a form that most serious authors did not deem worthy of pursuing.

This can be illustrated with the miniature "Mimoletnoe" ("Fleeting Things") by Vasilii Rozanov (1856–1919), published in 1903 in *Severnye Tsvety*. While the topic—an elegiac lament over old age—fits perfectly both with the model of Turgenev's "Senilia" and decadent *taedium vitae*, Rozanov's radical nihilism and self-denial strike a new chord:

«Да, я вышел весь. Выдохся, как выдыхается табак, как выдыхаются духи. Были духи, а через тридцать лет при открытом горлышке остается просто дрянная, не чистая, но отнюдь не душистая вода. Пить ее нельзя, душиться ею нельзя. Можно только выплеснуть. И меня нужно выплеснуть.»[74]

Yes, I am all used up. I have gone flat, like tobacco goes flat, or perfume goes flat. There was perfume, and thirty years later, with an open bottleneck, there remains only worthless water, not clean, but not fragrant. One can't drink it, one can't perfume oneself with it. One can only throw it out. And I too need to be thrown out.

One wonders whether the process of going stale could not be read also as Rozanov's comment on contemporary literature in general, and the symbolist prose miniature in particular. In his later writings, *Uedinennoe* (*Solitaria*, 1911) and *Opavshie list'ia* (*Fallen Leaves*, 1913 and 1915), Rozanov developed a radically innovative genre hovering on the margins of aesthetic literary discourse. Mixing philosophical aphorisms and literary criticism with gossip, personal confessions, and sheer buffoonery, Rozanov created a kind of "polyphonic metaliterature" that parodies a host of traditional genres.[75]

Like Rozanov, those writers who had originally shown an interest in the genre of the symbolist prose miniature resorted to various "exit strategies." One solution consisted simply in abandoning prose for verse. That was the path taken by Bal'mont, who introduced line breaks into his two metric prose miniatures, and discarded the rest of them. Briusov's solution consisted of upholding a strict separation between poetic and narrative genres. In a review essay written in 1908, he voiced his skepticism over the "lyric prose" practiced by the neo-realists:

> Among young Russian writers of fiction there is a whole group which thinks that in a "story" it is precisely the story element that should be absent, and the most eminent of these is Boris Zaitsev, who does all he can to turn his stories into lyric poetry. In his works by and large nothing happens, nothing is narrated, and the short story form is for him only a pretext for stringing together a series of images, of pictures, unified only by their general mood. There is no reason to be hostile to this form of art, to deny this "prose lyricism," and it may be that such work is capable of attaining high perfection. [. . .] But, of course, this *lirika v proze* can never replace or displace the genuine short story, where the strength of the impression made on the reader depends on the logic of events as they develop and on the vividness of the characters depicted.[76]

In his own prose fiction, Briusov relied on traditional narrative techniques without resorting to formal experiments. Among the authors discussed in this chapter, only Andrei Belyi continued to experiment with unconventional forms of narrative prose, as evidenced by his symphonies and novels. Yet as we have seen, he shunned his earlier genre of the "lyrical prose fragment." The fact that he later reworked three of these texts as verse poems demonstrates that, like Briusov, he evolved toward a stricter conceptual separation between prose and verse. Belyi's later prose writings, apart from their larger dimensions, differ in two other respects from his earlier lyrical prose fragments. They contain a larger amount of plot, as opposed to being mere subjective lyrical effusions, and they introduce a dose of "lower reality" into the stylized world of the prose poem. In Belyi's "Second Symphony" in particular, the symbolist discourse is infused with elements of grotesque humor. The prose genre recuperates, as it were, its narrative function, but in a grotesque rather than in a realist key. An intrusion of "lower reality" and grotesque buffoonery also occurs in the minimalist fairy tales and dreams of Fedor Sologub and Aleksei Remizov, who, besides Belyi, are the only other important Russian symbolist writers of prose fiction. By giving their prose miniatures the form of absurdist mini-stories rather than impressionist mood pieces or lyric fantasies, they revitalized the obsolete, decadent prose poem and gave it a new and more fruitful direction, as the following two chapters will show.

What are we to make then of Merezhkovskii's prophecy mentioned at the beginning of this chapter? As we remember, Merezhkovskii predicted a great future to the genre of the prose poem. As far as Russian symbolism is concerned, this certainly turned out to be an exaggerated claim. It is noteworthy to mention that Merezhkovskii himself did not practice what he preached. Aside from the translations of Baudelaire that he wrote when aged nineteen, he never wrote any prose poems of his own. Nevertheless, Merezhkovskii deserves credit for discovering an aspect in Turgenev's oeuvre that had eluded previous critics. He was the first commentator who noticed the kinship between Turgenev's prose poems and the nascent Russian decadence. Both thematically, with his stress on old age, sickness, and death, and formally, with the breakdown of the novelistic form, Turgenev anticipated the coming literature of the fin de siècle. In this sense, the genre of the prose poem embodies a general spirit of crisis and a turning away from what Merezhkovskii dubbed "utilitarian vulgar realism."

The fact that most symbolist prose miniatures remained a marginal phenomenon does not mean that they are devoid of interest for the literary historian and theoretician, who might want to study these texts if only to find out "what went wrong." One could speculate that the symbolists did not go far enough in exploring the negative potential of the form. While correctly identifying the value of the prose poem as an antidote to conventional realism, they failed to follow through with some of the genre's more radical implications. Bal'mont's attempt to create a synthetic form of poeticized prose, for example, resulted in a "hermaphrodite" (to quote Briusov's term) of dubious aesthetic validity. On the other hand, Annenskii's conscious focus on the "prosaic" pointed the way toward a more radically anti-aesthetic concept of the genre. Dobroliubov's dotted line marks the outer limit of this potential minimalism. In this sense, the decadent prose miniature, despite its inclination toward aestheticist preciosity, was the first step on the road toward the modernist dismantling of traditional literariness.

Chapter Five

Fedor Sologub's "Little Fairy Tales"

FEDOR SOLOGUB (Fedor Teternikov, 1863–1927) belongs to the more prolific writers of the Russian Silver Age. Known most of all for his poetry and his best-selling novel *Melkii bes* (*The Petty Demon*, 1907), Sologub also left a voluminous legacy of short stories. His *Skazochki* ("Little Fairy Tales") are among the least known and least explored of his narrative works. They have never been republished since they appeared in the 1913 edition of Sologub's works,[1] and unlike his novels, they have not attracted thus far much critical attention.[2] One puzzling feature of Sologub's *Skazochki* is that they do not fit easily into any kind of recognizable generic category. The title suggests a form of folktale, to be sure, but the texts only partially live up to this expectation. We do find the typical opening formula "zhil(i)-byl(i) . . ." ("once upon a time . . ."), the signal marker of the Russian fairy tale, and the style is at times folksy and colloquial, with a preponderance of diminutives and a proclivity toward puns and verbal games. The nonrealistic content of the stories and the fact that they are populated by "flat" characters also point to the realm of fairy tales.

In many respects, however, Sologub's *Skazochki* deviate from the generic tradition that they seemingly evoke. In the majority of texts, the acting characters are children rather than the customary fairy tale heroes. In a strange twist, the implicit audience of fairy tales assumes here the role of the literary protagonist (originally, of course, fairy tales were not a genre specifically intended for children, but they had become associated with children's literature by Sologub's time). One wonders who constitutes the implicit audience of Sologub's texts. The qualifier "*politicheskie* skazochki," which Sologub attached to some of his stories, seems to point to an adult rather than a juvenile readership. However, someone who expects straightforward political satire in the manner of Saltykov-Shchedrin's *Skazki* will be disappointed. In many cases, it seems hard to distill any kind of transparent political agenda from Sologub's *Skazochki*. In fact, the stories originally marked as "political" were republished in the *Sobranie sochinenii* edition without such a qualification and mingle with "nonpolitical" tales on a random basis.

It is not surprising then that Sologub's little fairy tales evoked consternation among contemporary critics, especially those who expected literary texts to express a progressive humanitarian message. The realist writer and critic V. G. Korolenko, in his review of the first edition of fairy tales, quoted two of Sologub's stories in extenso to demonstrate their absurdity.[3] Perhaps it will be useful to follow Korolenko's example and to quote the same two texts. This can all the more easily be done as they are very short. The first example is the opening story of the 1904 collection reviewed by Korolenko:

Ворона

Летела ворона. Видит мужика, и спрашивает:

—Мужик, а мужик?

—Чего тебе?—говорит мужик.

—Ворон считать умеешь?

—Ишь ты, какая затейная, чего захотела,—проваливай по добру по здорову.

Полетела ворона, встретила купца, спросила:

—Купец, ворон считать умеешь?

А купец говорит:

—Нам такими пустяками не приходится заниматься,—наше дело торговое.

Полетела ворона, встретила гимназиста, самого маленького из всей гимназии, и спрашивает:

—Гимназист, ворон считать умеешь?

А он и говорит:

—Я все считать умею, я до миллиона умею считать, и даже больше. Я Малинина и Буренина учил.

А ворона ему в ответ:

—А вот ворон не сосчитаешь.

—А нет, сосчитаю,—говорит гимназист.

И стал считать:

—Одна, две, три . . .

А ворона тут влетела ему в рот, и укусила его за язык. Заплакал гимназист, и говорит:

—Никогда вперед не буду вас, ворон, считать,—коли кусаетесь, как и живите так, несчитанные. (SS 31–32)

The Crow

A crow was flying. It saw a peasant and asked:

"Hey you, peasant?"

"What?"

"Can you count crows?"

"How d'you like that! What a joker you are. Make yourself scarce!"

The crow flew off, came to a merchant, and asked:

"Merchant, can you count crows?" The merchant said:

"We do not occupy ourselves with such nonsense—we are in the trading business."

The crow flew off and came to a high school student, the smallest one of the entire school, and asked:

"Student, can you count crows?"

He said:

"I can count everything. I can count to a million and even more. I taught Malinin and Burenin."

And the crow answered him:

"But crows you can't count."

"Yes I can," said the student.

And he began to count:

"One, two, three . . ."

But the crow flew in his mouth and bit him in the tongue.

The student began to cry and said:

"Never again will I count you crows. If you want to bite, you may as well live the way you do—uncounted."

At first sight, this little story seems to belong to the generic realm of the animal fable. Its concise form, folksy style, and reliance on dialogue are reminiscent of Ivan Krylov's classic models of the genre. Another traditional folktale element is provided by the formulaic repetition of episodes, introduced each time by the crow's encounter with a new character and the phrase "Can you count crows?" After the first two characters fail to perform the required task, we expect the third one to succeed. Characteristically, he is described as "the smallest one," akin to the youngest of three brothers in the folktale who usually is the one who, against all odds, ends up marrying the princess and winning the kingdom. However, in this case, all expectations prove deceptive. If this story is a fable, it lacks an essential ingredient of the genre: a clearly discernible moral message. Is this a tale of transgression and punishment? The boy appears to be somewhat of a nerd, to be sure, and one could perhaps conclude that he is paying the price for his boasting. But his behavior is not particularly egregious. The attack of the bird seems rather uncalled for. It looks like a sudden, unmotivated infliction of pain for no intelligible reason. Did the boy perhaps break some secret taboo by trying to count the birds? If so, he violated a rule known to no one except the crow. In any event, the bird provoked the outcome. Significantly, it is the child, rather than the two grown-ups, who becomes its victim. The ending of the text mimics the rhetoric of an etiological myth, suggesting an explanation for why the crows have to live "uncounted." But then again, why should they be counted? Many other things are not counted either, after all. As a result, the reader remains confused about what the "deeper meaning" of this fable could possibly amount to.

After quoting this story at the beginning of his review, Korolenko writes: "This is Mr. Sologub's first 'fairy tale.' And here, if you like, is number thirty-one:

Веселая девчонка

Жила такая веселая девчонка,—ей что хочешь сделай, а она смеется.

Вот отняли у нее куклу подруги, а она бежит за ними, заливается-смеется и кричит:

—Наплевать на нее! Не надо мне ее.

Вот мальчики ее прибили, а она хохочет:

—Наплевать!—кричит,—где наше не пропадало!

Говорит ее мать:

— Чего, дура, смеешься,—вот возьму веник.

Девчонка хохочет.

—Бери,—говорит,—веник,—вот то не заплачу,—наплевать на все!

Веселая такая девчонка! (SS 13)

The Cheerful Little Girl

There once lived a cheerful little girl—you could do to her whatever you wanted, and she would laugh.

Her companions took away her doll, and she would run after them, break into laughter and shout:

"I don't give a damn! [literally: I spit on it] I don't need it."

The boys beat her up, and she would guffaw:

"I don't give a damn!" she would shout, "what have we not lost!"

The mother tells her:

"What are you laughing at, you fool—I am getting the birch whip."

The little girl guffaws.

"Get your whip," she says, "I am not going to cry—I don't give a damn about anything! [literally: I spit on everything]

Such a cheerful little girl!

This story again deceives the reader's expectations triggered by the heading "fairy tale." At first sight, the text appears to provide the moral edification associated with the genre of children's literature. One could argue that it illustrates the ideal of cheerful equanimity in the face of adversity, the renunciation of worldly possessions, the "turning of the other cheek," and so on; that is, it seems to give a positive example in the venerable Russian tradition of Christian meekness and humility. However, it becomes clear that Sologub's heroine hardly qualifies as a positive role model for young readers. The expression "naplevat'," which is repeated three times in the text and functions like a structuring leitmotiv, does not belong in the stylistic register of fairy tale language. Its somewhat aggressive vulgarity culminates in the final exclamation "naplevat' na vse!" which seems more an expression of decadent world-weariness and cynicism than of charming, childlike simplicity. The last sentence of the story repeats the words of the title, but the sense of closure that this device seems to convey remains deceptive, as the reader in the meantime has become thoroughly confused about the meaning of this title. Besides the absence of a moral message, the text also lacks another essential feature of fairy tales: there is no *story* to speak of, only an accumulation of repeated actions. Repetition, to be sure, is a standard feature of folk narrative, but what is missing here is a sense of denouement. The typical fairy tale pattern of quest, adversity, and fulfillment described by Vladimir Propp is nowhere in sight. The various events reported by the narrator do not constitute a sequential development leading to some qualitative change, but rather a senseless going around in circles. One could easily imagine the story to continue ad libitum.

After quoting his two text samples in full, Korolenko comments: "That's all! Of such fairy tales Mr. Sologub wrote thirty-nine. In two or three of them, with a certain effort of imagination, one can find glimpses of meaning, in the overwhelming majority, there is nothing but pure perplexity (*sploshnoe nedoumenie*)." The critic goes on to compare Sologub's stories with the oeuvre of Kozma Prutkov, the fictitious, nineteenth-century bureaucrat and author of pretentious inanities created by the poet A. K. Tolstoi and his two cousins. In light of the comical nature of Prutkov's writings, Korolenko speculates whether the inventors of Prutkov did not provide with their spoof an unwitting, parodistic anticipation of Sologub's fairy tales: "[They] wanted to allude to some writers who have such an inflated self-image that every single verbal outburst (*vnezapnost'*) seems to them worthy of publication to the general public, regardless of meaning." It did not seem to occur to Korolenko that Sologub's fairy tales might be of a parodistic nature as well, in which case the comparison with Kozma Prutkov would indeed be of some relevance.

If Sologub's "Skazochki" are not really fairy tales, can we find another generic category in which they fit more comfortably? Stanley Rabinowitz described the stylistic locus of these stories as "midway between poetry and prose." He based this argument on the observation that the texts feature the colloquialisms and folksy oral style of prose narrative, yet at the same time display the "compactness, intensity and imaginativeness" of poetic language.[4] Rabinowitz argues that two of Sologub's fairy tales, "Budushchie" ("The Future Ones") and "Oni" ("They") are in fact prose poems (*stikhotvoreniia v proze*) in the Turgenevan tradition.[5] The German scholar Ulrich Steltner mentions Baudelaire's and Turgenev's prose poems as a possible generic model for Sologub, and he concurs with Rabinowitz's assessment of "Oni," calling it a "typical prose poem."[6] Ulrich Schmid, the author of a recent monograph on Sologub, also suggests that some of Sologub's fairy tales should be classified as prose poems.[7] He justifies this designation with the musical quality of Sologub's language, as demonstrated, for example, in the opening sentence of the story "Guli" ("Pigeons"), where the sound effect takes precedence over semantic meaning: "Zhili Guli, lili puli, eli duli" (SS 98). The literal meaning of this sentence, "There lived Pigeons, they cast bullets [or, if understood idiomatically, "they told lies"], they ate pears," is not much more than a pretext for a virtuoso display of internal assonances and rhymes. In its instrumentation dominated by the liquid "l"-sound, this line resembles a much-quoted stanza from a poem that Sologub wrote in 1901: "Lila, lila, lila, kachala / Dva tel'no-alye stekla. / Belei lilei, alee lala / Bela byla ty I ala" ("[You] poured, poured, poured, and swung two flesh-colored red glasses. Whiter than a lily, redder than a ruby, white were you and red").[8]

Such an identification of Sologub's "Skazochki" with the realm of the prose poem relies on the alleged "poetic" qualities, the lyricism and musicality of their language. However, as we have seen earlier, such an equation of the prose poem with poetic prose does not really capture the essence of this genre. In addition, lyrical pieces of this kind make up a rather small minority of Sologub's texts. "Oni," the evocation of a fleeting encounter with some unfathomable, unearthly being, singled out by both Rabinowitz and Steltner as a typical prose poem, is quite unique within the corpus of Sologub's fairy tales, since it constitutes the only first-person narrative in the entire collection. The lyricism of "Budushchie," vaunted by Rabinowitz for its poetic qualities, seems undermined by the ending of the text. The story begins with the poetic evocation of yet-to-be-born souls living in a state of bliss and dreaming of their future life. Four souls express their longing for the earthly elements, which they describe in a highly lyrical style. The first soul declares to love "the earth, soft, warm, and firm," the second loves "the water, eternally falling, cool and transparent," the third loves "the fire, cheerful, bright and cleansing," and the fourth loves "the air, rushing broad and high, the light air of life." "And this is what happened," the story continues. "The first one became a miner—and when he was at work, the mine collapsed and buried him. And the second one shed tears like water, and ended up drowning. And the third one burnt alive in a blazing house. And the fourth one was hanged" (SS 72–73). This laconic enumeration of catastrophic deaths in rapid succession contradicts the lyricism of the opening image. Rather than presenting a sustained example of poetic prose, this story illustrates the destructive intrusion of "prosaic" reality into a lyrical dream world. If this text recalls Turgenev's "Senilia," as Rabinowitz claims, it is mostly in the Schopenhauerian pessimism of its final exclamation: "O, comforting place of nonbeing, why does the Will drive us out from there!"

This is not to say that we cannot place Sologub's *Skazochki* into the category of the prose poem. But if we wish to retain this label, it is necessary to rely on something else than the poetic nature of their style. In this respect, the connection of Sologub's texts with the tradition of the folktale proves to be a pertinent factor. Among the generic models utilized or parodied by the French authors of prose poems, the folktale has played a prominent role. Several of Baudelaire's *Petits poèmes en prose* make use of supernatural and fairy tale elements. Such prose poems as "Les dons des Fées," "Les tentations," "Le joueur généreux," or "Les bienfaits de la lune" all rely on traditional folktale models for their basic plot: Fairies are handing out gifts to newborn babies, demonic figures act as tempters, and so on. However, Baudelaire's intention hardly consists in telling a fairy tale for its own sake. The comic effect of these texts relies on the clash of the miraculous world of the folktale with the modern, "prosaic" reality of nineteenth-century France. We are told, for example, that before the crowd of supplicants, the beneficial fairies were "as bewildered as cabinet ministers on hearing days, or employees of a pawnshop when a national holiday allows free redemptions."[9] The Devil, in "Le joueur généreux," turns out to be a cigar-smoking, suave man of the world who declares that he is himself "the person most interested in the destruction of *superstition*."[10] The moralizing didacticism of fairy tales turns in Baudelaire's prose poems into a logic of the absurd. Thus the narrator, after having sold his soul, prays to God that the Devil may keep his promise to him. The fairies bestow their gifts to the most unsuitable people: money is given to those already rich and with no sense of charity, while the gift of poetry is bestowed to those who have no use for it. This points, as J. A. Hiddleston has observed, "not to providence but to moral anarchy at the heart of the universe."[11]

In his discussion of the relationship between fairy tale and prose poem, Yves Vadé has noted that "the miraculous characters and motives which the prose poem can use as ingredients are not only, as in the modern literary tale, detached from their traditional structure—they are, in all meanings of this term, displaced."[12] This becomes most evident in Arthur Rimbaud's "Illuminations," where the fairy tale model is subverted even more radically than in Baudelaire's prose poems. Rimbaud's "Conte" ("Fairy Tale"), a prose poem that carries a generic label as its title, disposes altogether with the notion of a logically coherent plot. Some traditional elements of the oriental folktale, such as a prince, a spirit (*génie*), women referred to as a "garden of beauty," luxurious beasts, and a palace with golden roofs, only serve as the building blocks of an absurd minimalist story. The prince, acting like a Nero or Caligula, goes on a destructive rampage, killing his women and animals and setting fire to his palace. Yet in a strange twist, all his acts of destruction seem to be canceled as soon as they happen. One evening, the prince encounters a spirit whose looks and behavior suggest "an unspeakable, even unbearable happiness." The prince and the spirit annihilate each other and die. This denouement is followed by a second ending that seems at odds with the first one: "But this Prince died in his palace at an ordinary age. The Prince was the Spirit. The Spirit was the Prince. Our desire lacks erudite music" ("la musique savante manque à notre désir").[13]

The "strangeness" of the events depicted in "Conte" goes far beyond the miraculous or fantastic. No supernatural explanation resolves the blatant contradictions in the text, where each subsequent statement cancels out the validity of the previous assertion. As Barbara Johnson has observed, by declaring the two main characters of the story to be one and the same, Rimbaud reveals their existence to be an illusion of language, and by giving two endings to the story, he is subverting the very notion of an ending.[14] Anticipating certain twentieth-century trends, Rimbaud's "Conte" not only parodies a traditional genre, but undermines any form of narrative discourse by questioning the referential function of language itself.

Sologub was well acquainted with Baudelaire's and Rimbaud's prose poems, as we know from the fact that he translated Baudelaire's "Chacun sa chimère"[15] and most of Rimbaud's "Illuminations," including "Conte."[16] His interest in this genre is further documented by his translation of Mallarmé's "Divagations"[17] and Oscar Wilde's prose poems.[18] Sologub never succeeded in publishing his strangely literal renditions of Mallarmé, which at times violate the syntax of the Russian language in an effort to stay faithful to the French original. A few of his similarly literalist renditions of Rimbaud's "Illuminations" appeared, long after they were written, in the futurist collection *Strelets* (*The Archer*) in 1915 and 1916 (which demonstrates to what extent Sologub was ahead of his time). It does not seem far-fetched to conclude then that Sologub's "Little Fairy Tales" hark back to the subversive potential of the French originators of the *poème en prose* rather than to Turgenev's generic model.[19] In Vsevolod Bagno's judgment, Sologub translated Rimbaud's and Mallarmé's prose poems with the intention to "enrich his own literature with the Russian equivalent of such a bright and fruitful genre as the French prose poem."[20] Although Sologub did not write any text labeled as *stikhotvoreniia v proze*, his fairy tales can be interpreted as an attempt to realize the creative impulse of the French prose poems in his own manner. Similar to Baudelaire's and Rimbaud's undermining of traditional folktale narratives, Sologub's fairy tales constitute a sort of anti-stories that thwart basic expectations of linear plot-development and logical narrative cohesiveness. In some ways, they anticipate later twentieth-century examples of what has become known as the "literature of the absurd."

One of the most salient features of Sologub's "Skazochki" that sets them apart from the fairy tales of other Russian authors is their minimalist form. This is underlined by the diminutive which Sologub attached to the generic designation of the stories published in the 1913 edition. By calling them *"skazochki"* rather than *"skazki,"* Sologub imitated the rhetoric of Baudelaire's title *"Petits* poèmes en prose." Instead of the customary fabulistic expansion of the folktale, Sologub offers extremely condensed miniatures. Many of them take up less than a page. This laconicity is a major contributing factor to the general "strangeness" of these stories. Sologub's shortest text occupies only a few lines:

Капля и пылинка

Капля падала в дожде, пылинка лежала на земле.

Капля хотела соединиться с существом твердым,—надоело ей свободно плавать.

С пылинкою соединилась она,—и легла на землю комком грязи. (SS 53)

The Raindrop and the Speck of Dust

A drop fell down in the rain, a speck of dust was lying on the earth.

The drop wanted to unite with a solid being,—it was tired of floating freely.

It united with the speck of dust—and lay on the earth as a lump of dirt.

Despite its minimalist form, this "fairy tale" is not devoid of meaning. In fact, it has a more transparent allegoric significance than some of Sologub's longer stories. As in "Budushchie," the underlying message is directed against the idea of incarnation, which is presented here quite literally as the story of a "fall." With its Manichean condemnation of the union of matter and spirit, this parable contradicts the fashionable attempts to "sanctify the flesh" which were pursued by other Russian symbolists of that time. Faithful to his relentlessly dualist view of the world, Sologub can find no attractive or redeeming qualities in material reality, which amounts to nothing but "dirt." Beauty is only possible in the realm of the unincarnated, free-moving spirit.[21]

In another philosophical micro-story, Sologub targets the idea of teleological existentialism:

Три плевка

Шел человек, и плюнул трижды.

Он ушел, плевки остались.

И сказал один плевок:

—Мы здесь, а человека нет.

И другой сказал:

—Он ушел.

И третий:

—Он только затем и приходил, чтобы нас посадить здесь. Мы—цель жизни человека. Он ушел, а мы остались. (SS 64)

The Three Spittles

A man came and spat three times.

He went away, the spittles remained.

And one spittle said:

"We are here, and the man is gone."

And the other said:

"He has left."

And the third:

"He only came to put us here. We are the goal of man's life. He went away, and we remained."

Using a somewhat unsavory image, Sologub's parable anticipates Heidegger's *Geworfenheit,* as it were, in the form of *Gespucktheit.* The beginning of the story anticipates one of Daniil Kharms' miniatures, "Sinfoniia No. 2" ("Symphony No. 2," 1941), which opens with the same image:

Антон Михайлович плюнул, сказал «эх», опять плюнул, опять сказал «эх», опять плюнул, опять сказал «эх» и ушел. И Бог с ним. Расскажу лучше про Илью Павловича.[22]

Anton Mikhailovich spat, said "Ugh," spat again, said "Ugh" again, spat again, said "Ugh" again, and went out. The hell with him. I'd better tell you about Ilya Pavlovich.[23]

In Kharms' reworking, the three-fold act of spitting has turned into an extended slapstick scenario. At the same time, Sologub's tale of the three spittles provides the conclusion to Kharms' aborted narrative.

The lampooning of self-importance is a frequent theme in Sologub's *Skazochki.* In some instances, there is a rather obvious political connotation, which is not surprising if we remember that some of the stories were published as "politicheskie skazochki." "Razduvshaiasia liagushka" ("The Inflated Frog") is presented as the "correction" of the well-known fable of the frog and the ox. The narrator begins by asserting that no ox was involved in the story at all—how could there be an ox in a swamp? Rather than in competition with another animal, the frog conceived on his own the idea of inflating himself, and he did not do it all at once, but in small increments over a period of many days. Once he reached his gigantic size, the frog turned into a dictator of the swamp, terrorizing and bullying the other animals. The frog's skin was very thin, however. That was no problem as long as he kept sitting in the same place, but one day, having become over-confident, he made a jump and was punctured by a little leaf of dry grass. With a hissing sound, all the air came out, the frog croaked, and everybody saw that he was really small. Sologub ends his story with a parodistic stab at Krylov: "That's how it really was. And he dragged in the ox for no good reason. But perhaps he told this about some other frog" (SS 110).

The playful intertextual game with the tradition of the fable cannot detract from the poignancy of the historical and political allegory. Significantly, Sologub was able to publish his collection of "political fairy tales" only after censorship restrictions had been eased in the wake of the 1905 revolution. Images of oppression and bullying occur throughout Sologub's tales. In a variant of another well-known fairy tale, Andersen's "The Emperor with no Clothes," Sologub tells the story of a mushroom (*mukhomor*)[24] who makes a career in the government service. "People knew that he was not a human being, but only an old mushroom, and a nonedible one at that, but they had to obey him. The mushroom growled, grumbled, got angry, slobbered saliva and ruined all the papers." But one day, a barefoot little boy sees the mushroom emerging from his carriage. He shouts "What a big mushroom, and what a disgusting one!" The boy seizes him and smashes him against a wall. The mushroom splatters into pieces. The little boy gets thrashed, but the people of the town are very relieved, and "one stupid man even gave the barefoot little boy a gingerbread." It is probably stories like these that Evgenii Zamiatin had in mind when he praised Sologub's fairy tales in an essay of 1924, at a time when a new set of "mushrooms" were solidifying their power in Russia:

> The whip has not yet been given its full due as an instrument of human progress. I know of no more potent means than the whip for raising men from all fours, for making him stop kneeling down before anything or anyone. I am not speaking, of course, of whips woven of leather thongs; I am speaking of whips woven of words, the whips of the Gogols, Swifts, Molières, Frances, the whips of irony, sarcasm, satire. And Sologub wields such a whip perhaps even more skillfully than the stiletto of misericordia. Read the two books of his fairy tales and you will see that they are still as sharp as they were twenty years ago.[25]

Sologub's parodistic citation of the fairy tale tradition refers not only to literary models (Krylov, Andersen), but also to the Russian folktale, as a consultation of A. N. Afanas'ev's standard collection will confirm. In addition to certain stylistic markers, Sologub borrowed from this source a few concrete motifs. In light of the minimalist and absurdist character of Sologub's *Skazochki,* Afanas'ev's series of so-called *Dokuchnye skazki* ("Tiresome Tales") deserves particular attention. In their extreme laconicity, some of these texts seem to anticipate the minimalism of the later Russian avant-garde, as the following example demonstrates:

> Жил-был старик, у старика был колодец, а в колодце-то елец; тут и сказке конец.[26]

> There once lived an old man, the old man had a well, in the well there was a dace: here the story ends [or, to capture the rhyme, we could translate: "there was a dace in the well; there is nothing else to tell"].

This "story" begins with a traditional fairy tale opening, only to short-circuit the narrative by directly cutting to a closing formula. As in the opening of Sologub's "Guli" quoted earlier, plot development is abandoned in favor of a lyrical device—the consonance of internal rhyme. By withholding the promised narration, the text highlights the act of storytelling itself. One of

Afanas'ev's *dokuchnye skazki* served as the inspiration for Sologub's fairy tale "Pro belogo bychka" ("About the White Bull"),[27] a story that again thematizes the impossibility of storytelling. The opening question of the folktale, "Skazat' li tebe skazku pro belogo bychka?" ("Shall I tell you the story of the white bull?") functions as a sort of narrative tease, since the promised story never materializes. Instead, the narrator reverts continuously to the initial announcement, creating a series of circular loops. In Sologub's reworking of Afanas'ev's text, the girl Lenochka senses that the storytelling nanny engages in this form of verbiage only to conceal the fact that she does not really know anything about the white bull. Lenochka decides therefore to go to sleep and dream about this creature herself. But when, after almost a whole night of dreamless sleep, she finally succeeds in this attempt, the annoying nanny comes to wake her up, thus thwarting again the quest for narrative fulfillment. The white bull remains as elusive as ever.

In one story, it is the child character who assumes the role of the narrative teaser, only to suffer grievous consequences:

Что будет?

Один мальчик спросил:
  —Что будет?
Мама сказала:
  —Не знаю.
Мальчик сказал:
  —А я знаю.
Мама спросила:
  —А что?
Мальчик засмеялся и сказал:
  —А вот не скажу.
Мама рассердилась. Пожаловалась папе. Папа закричал:
  —Ты как это смеешь?
Мальчик спросил:
  —А что?
Папа опять закричал:
  —Дерзости говорить! Ты что такое знаешь?
А мальчик испугался и сказал:
  —Я ничего не знаю. Я пошутил.
Папа еще больше рассердился. Он думал, что мальчик знает что-то,—и закричал страшным голосом:
  —Говори, что ты знаешь! Говори, что будет!
Мальчик заплакал, и не мог сказать, что будет. И ему досталось.
Такое ведь вышло недоразумение!

What Will Be?

A boy asked:
  "What will be?"
The mother said:

"I don't know."
The boy said:
"And I know."
The mother said:
"What?"
The boy laughed and said:
"I won't tell you."
The mother got angry. She complained to the father. The father shouted:
"How dare you?"
The boy asked:
"What?"
The father shouted again:
"To be impertinent! What is it you know?"
The boy got scared and said:
"I don't know anything. I was kidding."
The father got even angrier. He thought that the boy knew something—and began to shout in a terrible voice:
"Say what you know! Say what will be!"
The boy began to cry, and he couldn't say what will be. And he got punished.
What a misunderstanding that was!

What begins like a harmless child's prank reported in a sort of slapstick dialogue escalates into a serious, albeit absurd, confrontation. The word "misunderstanding" indeed captures the unsuccessful communication between parent and child. Neither mother nor father are able to relate to the playful nature of the boy's boasting and insist on a serious interpretation of his words. In this sense, they resemble critics like Korolenko, who was equally unappreciative of the parodistic and ironic character of Sologub's fairy tales, demanding an unequivocal meaning. The predicament of meaninglessness is real, of course, since nobody knows "what will be." Sologub implies that children are better equipped to deal with this epistemological void because of their vivid imagination. Unlike adults who are confined to a world of stifling dullness, they can construct for themselves an enchanted counterreality. The story also shows, however, how the character endowed with imagination gets bullied and crushed by an insensitive surrounding world, represented by a humorless mother acting as an informer and an authoritarian father whose choleric frenzy seems out of control. The tension between child and parent anticipates Kafka in its sudden explosion of aggressive energy. In accordance with the narrative poetics of the absurd, the final statement mimics the gesture of a conclusion, but does not resolve anything.[28]

The fairy tale is in itself part of the project of building a counterreality to a stultifying "prosaic" world. This becomes evident in a story called "Skazki na griadkakh i skazki vo dvortse" ("Fairy Tales in Flowerbeds and Fairy Tales in the Palace," SS 61). The text begins with the evocation of a garden where fairy tales grow in flowerbeds. They come in all different colors, some of them smell sweetly, others are beautiful to look at. The gardener's little son tells his companions about them, who report it to their parents, who tell other people, until the empress herself hears about the fairy tales allegedly growing in her garden. She wishes to see them, and one morning the gardener cuts a bouquet and sends it to her, not listening to the protests of his son, who cries over the fact that the fairy tales are cut down. The empress does not find anything remarkable in the flowers. "What kind of fairy tales are these?" she says in amazement. "They are most ordinary flowers." The poor fairy tales are thrown out, and the little boy gets thrashed "so that he would tell no more stupidities." Again we are confronted with an unbridgeable gap between a literally minded, unimaginative adult mentality and a child's fantasy world. It is interesting to note that the narrator of the story assumes the child's perspective throughout, referring to the plants in the imperial garden as fairy tales rather than flowers. In this sense, Sologub's tale could be read as a meta-fictional comment on the genre of the prose poem. An ordinary flower becomes a "fairy tale" in the same manner as a prose text becomes "poetry"—through an act of renaming.

Perhaps the ultimate meta-text in Sologub's collection is a brief story called "Palochka" ("The Wand"):

Палочка

Есть такая чудесная палочка на свете,—к чему ею ни коснись, все тотчас делается сном, и пропадет.

Вот если тебе не нравится твоя жизнь, возьми палочку, прижми ее концом к своей голове,—и вдруг увидишь, что все было сон, и станешь опять жить сначала и совсем по-новому.

А что было раньше, в этом сне, про все вовсе забудешь.

Вот какая есть чудесная на свете палочка. (SS 43)

The Wand

There exists a miraculous wand in this world—whatever you touch with it, everything instantly turns into a dream and disappears.

If you don't like your life, take the wand, press its end against your head—and suddenly you will see that all was a dream, and you will again begin to live all anew.

And what was before, in this dream, you will all forget altogether.

Such a miraculous wand exists in this world.

Like "Veselaia devchonka," this text presents an example of a minimalist nonstory. Both pieces have a circular structure, ending with a laconic, sententious statement that refers back to the title world and suggests a deceptive sense of closure. These recapitulative sentences ring hollow, since in both stories, *nothing has happened.* The device of the magic wand is introduced in "Palochka" as a value in itself without serving as the prop for any kind of narrative action. Rather than telling a story, this text belongs in the generic category of the "user's manual" (*Gebrauchsanweisung*), as Ulrich Steltner has suggested.[29] Stanley Rabinowitz has pointed to the metapoetic nature of this piece: for Sologub, the genre of the fairy tale functions itself like a magic wand, having "the power to turn even harsh reality into something beautiful and uplifting."[30] While the self-reflective character of this story is indeed evident, one could quibble over its alleged uplifting message, however. The proposed counterreality seems rather ambivalent. One can find in this text the expression of a typically decadent worldview, celebrating the escape from the prosaic world of daily life into a (drug-generated?) "artificial paradise" of dream-like oblivion. Through this process, the real world is obliterated and turns into nothingness (presumably, this is what really happens to one's head when it is touched by the magic wand!). Forgetting everything becomes the functional equivalent of "not giving a damn about anything"—the motto of Sologub's "cheerful little girl."

It is no accident that the theme of dreams surfaces at this point. As we will see in the following chapter, dreams play an important role in the poetics of the prose poem, starting with Turgenev's *Stikhotvoreniia v proze*. Sologub's fairy tales frequently evoke dreams, both as a theme (as seen in the story of the white bull, for example) and in their narrative technique. In a handwritten note preserved in his archive, Sologub linked the world of fairy tales to that of "sny i grezy" (dreams and reveries).[31] In the *Sobranie sochinenii* edition, the fairy tales are followed by two actual dreams (*Sny*, SS 123–26). In their laconic depiction of a dehumanized world of cruelty and destruction, Sologub's dreams are closer to nightmares than to escapist fantasies of bliss. In the first dream, people are burnt in a stove as fire logs, whereas in the second dream, the narrator is only able to walk with straight legs after he has crushed a baby.

One wonders whether the ultimate escape offered by the "magic wand" is not simply death. The celebration of death as a welcome liberation from a dreary and vulgar world is a common theme both in Sologub's poetry and narrative fiction. The motif also appears in his *Skazochki*. In one of the earliest fairy tales, "Plenennaia smert'" ("The Captive Death," SS 40–41),[32] Sologub tells the story of a knight who captures death and imprisons her (death being feminine in Russian) in his castle. As a result, nobody dies anymore. The knight decides to kill death once and for all by beheading her, but asks her first what she has to say in her defense. Death declares that she has nothing to say, but suggests that life should speak for her. Life turns out to be a big woman (*babishcha*), "plump," "ruddy," and "ugly," who begins to say such "nasty and profane words" that the horrified knight rushes to free death instantly. In consequence, people die again, including the knight himself.

Sologub's *Skazochki* reflect in many ways the decadent spirit of their age. The preoccupation with a world of magic enchantment as a foil to the banality of daily life was a favorite theme of romantics and decadents, and fairy tale motifs of this kind play an important role in much of Sologub's narrative oeuvre.[33] The child as the embodiment of a more "poetic" reality figures as a central character not only in the fairy tales, but also in Sologub's novels and short stories. Stanley Rabinowitz, in his monograph on Sologub's "literary children," has shown that "by allowing the free play of their imaginations, children, as it were, provide air to the closed, stultifying world of routine as they suggest an escape from an existence which is ruled exclusively by the laws of necessity."[34] It seems questionable, however, whether Sologub's fairy tales can really be interpreted as the expression of "an undeniably optimistic shift in his world view," as Rabinowitz has claimed.[35] The escape into the enchanted realm of the fairy tale is constantly undermined by Sologub's radical skepticism which makes the success of such an operation seem tenuous. Even the very act of narration, as we have seen, is exposed to be a problematic endeavor, which means that the longed-for fantastic world remains elusive. What we can hope for at best are miniature fragments, glimpses of an ideal realm rendered problematic through a series of constantly disintegrating narratives.

While fairy tale motifs occur in much of Sologub's oeuvre, it is only in the *Skazochki* that this interest in folklore crystallized into a qualitatively new form: the playful minimalist tale. Sologub's concern with the creative potential of minimalist prose becomes evident in other contemporaneous writings, for example, in his recently published collection of aphorisms.[36] Just like the metafictional fairy tales growing in flowerbeds, Sologub's *Skazochki* are heterogeneous in nature and come, as it were, in all shapes, colors, and fragrances. As Steltner has noted, the generic label "fairy tale" becomes the mere pretext for an "experimentation with the different possibilities of the short prose form."[37] Lyrical pieces mingle with grotesque ones, political satire alternates with philosophical miniatures and childish pranks. In some cases, an allegorical deciphering is possible, other texts seem opaque and absurd. Narrative conventions are alluded to only in order to be parodistically subverted.

All of the foregoing sounds like a description of a familiar genre: the modern prose poem. The minimalist form and experimental nature of Sologub's *Skazochki* certainly places them in the tradition of this genre. The dualist tension between opposed poles, an important feature of both Baudelaire's and Turgenev's prose poems, also underlies the poetics of Sologub's fairy tales. The texts are shot through with contrasts like "good" vs. "bad," "dark" vs. "bright," "Moon" vs. "Sun," "quiet" vs. "loud," "pale" vs. "colorful," "dream" vs. "life," and so on, an outgrowth of the general

Manichean dualism of Sologub's worldview.[38] Unlike his symbolist contemporaries, who concentrated on only a small segment of the possibilities offered by the form of the prose poem, Sologub reverted with his *Skazochki* to the wide thematic spectrum contained in Baudelaire's, and to a lesser extent, Turgenev's generic model. The "poeticity" of these texts is of a radically modern nature. Traditional lyricism in the form of confessional, elegiac effusions has evaporated from Sologub's texts. Their poetic character relies on linguistic and structural features. The play of fantasy creates an irrational counterreality that is sharply opposed to the "prosaic" realm of quotidian banality, even though it uses elements of this prosaic world as building blocks for the construction of a novel type of fairy tale.

The perplexity that Sologub's *Skazochki* caused in critics like Korolenko shows how radically they were breaking with a traditional "horizon of expectation." This does not mean that nobody was able to appreciate their novelty. In his review of the 1904 edition, Briusov praised the author for his fusion of realism and symbolism. He claimed that the "abusive words of everyday reality" successfully combine in Sologub's stories with the "otherwordly" in a new kind of literary discourse, where "reality and dream are not mixed up, but totally fused." As a particular quality of Sologub's fairy tales, Briusov praised their "laughter," which sets them apart from the pretentious rhetoric of much contemporary literature (and also, one could add, from many of Sologub's other writings). Briusov asserts that "in Sologub's fairy tales there are all forms of laughter—from bitter sarcasm to good-natured guffawing, from cruel irony to a sly smile over the reader's bewilderment."[39]

The humor of Sologub's *Skazochki* is indeed of a unique kind. One could call it a Gogolian "laughter through tears," a defense mechanism against a world of grotesque absurdity. The cover illustration of the 1904 edition of fairy tales depicts a curtain, on which a house, a bush, and a boy are drawn in a clumsily childish style. A hand lifts the curtain a bit to reveal an empty darkness lurking behind. In his review of the book, Korolenko interpreted this picture as Sologub's involuntary admission that his stories make no sense whatsoever. Yet one could object that the absence of meaning is an inherent feature of the material world depicted by Sologub rather than a deficiency of his writing. In this sense, the illustration revives the familiar romantic idea of the work of art as a "veil thrown over the abyss," a temporary illusion of beauty in a world of darkness. At the same time, it reveals the highly self-conscious nature of Sologub's verbal art. What the picture seems to illustrate is the fact that, rather than providing a mimetic reflection of the visible world in a "realist" style, Sologub's miniature stories create their own independent reality through an innovative and imaginative use of language.

Chapter Six

Aleksei Remizov's Dreams

ALEKSEI REMIZOV (1877–1957) belongs together with Fedor Sologub and Andrei Belyi to the most gifted and prolific writers of prose fiction during the Russian Silver Age. Like his contemporary Sologub, Remizov experimented in his literary oeuvre with the creative possibilities of fairy tales and dreams. In his opinion, the two genres were intimately linked. As he stated in a letter to Natal'ia Kodrianskaia, "Fairy tale and dream are brother and sister. The fairy tale is a literary form, and the dream can also be a literary form. Certain fairy tales and legends originate in a dream."[1] As a manifestation of the collective unconscious, as it were, the fairy tale merges with the private myth of the author expressed in his dreams. Both genres allow the writer to suspend the laws of logical causality by evoking the irruption of irrational and fantastic forces into the world of day-to-day reality. The common symbolist heritage of Sologub and Remizov explains their interest in such nonrealist forms of writing. However, "pure dreams" constitute only a very minor part of Sologub's oeuvre,[2] whereas they proliferate in the works of Remizov. Like no other writer, he made the dream his own literary form.

According to Sona Aronian's count, Remizov's published work contains no fewer than 340 different dreams.[3] In addition to his fictional dreams incorporated in novels and short stories, Remizov throughout his long life published a series of *"sny"* (dreams) which he claimed to be unadorned transcriptions of his own dreams.[4] He always kept notepaper and pen at his bedside in order to write down his dreams immediately after awakening. *Nulla nox sine somnio* could have served as his motto. He declared, "a night without a dream for me is like a day lost."[5] Besides recording his own dreams, Remizov also analyzed the dreams contained in the works of other writers. The volume *Ogon' veshchei* (*The Fire of Things*), published in Paris in 1954, contains Remizov's comments about the dreams of Pushkin, Gogol', Lermontov, Turgenev, and Dostoevskii.

In their minimalism and absurd logic, Remizov's dreams have a certain similarity with Sologub's "Little Fairy Tales." Interestingly enough, Sologub himself makes an appearance in one of Remizov's dreams. Remizov frequently populated his *sny* with fellow writers, who were not always flattered by this honor.[6] The dream about Sologub reads as follows:

Чорт и слезы

Я не дома, а где-то у моря и не один, а со мной Федор Сологуб, автор «Мелкого беса». Всякий день мы купаемся в море: сперва он, потом я.

Нянька Карасьевна рассказывает:

«После них я выловила маленьких чертенят, а после вас вот такого чорта».

Карасьевна руки растопырила, показывает какого такого чорта она выловила. Я не знаю, что ей ответить, и отвожу глаза: как раз против окна береза.

У березы белый конь стоит. Смотрю на лошадь. Воробей пролетел, пархнул на коня, стал коню глаза клевать. И выклевал—кровь потекла.

И я чувствую как во мне подымаются слезы.[7]

The Devil and the Tears

I am not at home, but somewhere by the sea and not alone, but with Fedor Sologub, the author of *A Petty Demon.* Every day we swim in the sea: first he, then I.

Nian'ka Karas'evna says:

"After them I fished out some tiny little devils, but after you, look what a big devil."

Karas'evna spread her arms wide to show what a big devil she fished out. I don't know what to answer her and avert my eyes: there is a birch tree just opposite the windows.

By the birch tree stands a white horse. I am looking at the horse. A sparrow flew by, fluttered to the horse and began to peck its eyes. And it pecked them out—blood began to flow.

And I feel tears welling up in me.

The laws of narrative logic are even more radically suspended in this text than in Sologub's "Vorona," which also features an aggressive bird. As is to be expected in a dream, there are no clear parameters of space and time. The focus of narration shifts from one scene to the next without regard to an overarching plot. A certain "poetic" coherence is provided at best by the water imagery, connecting the sea with the flow of blood and tears. The deadpan narration looks like an open invitation to search for more than what is presented on the surface. One could try to read the text as an allegory of its own purported deciphering. Are there any "devils" lurking in the murky waters of this story, waiting to be "fished out"? The afterword to Remizov's book of dreams, *Martyn Zadeka,* is entitled "Ton' nochi" ("The Fishing Ground of the Night"), suggesting an analogy between the recording of dreams and the catching of fish. The image of the devils seems to be inspired by the title of Sologub's novel, to be sure, and the fact that Remizov swims in the same water as Sologub, but *after* him, points to an intertextual genealogy.[8] Nevertheless, much remains unclear. Who are the people who leave little devils in their wake? In what ways is the big devil connected to Sologub and Remizov? In any event, the narrator seems to want to avoid a confrontation with an uncomfortable truth. The woman's tale about the size of the devil she caught, sounding like the stereotypical fisherman's yarn, appears to hit a raw nerve. By averting his eyes, the narrator witnesses an attack on someone else's eyes. The white horse by the birch tree is an image of purity defiled. Is it inspired by Raskolnikov's famous dream about a tortured horse in *Crime and Punishment*?

It becomes clear that this story cannot be reduced to an unambiguous allegorical message. Rather, it presents a highly condensed, semantically overdetermined blend of various sources. Remizov himself described his dreams as a mixture of "memories, reaction to books, events of the day, word play, and prophetic riddles."[9] While some of these elements are open to deciphering, others, given their entirely private nature, have to remain necessarily below the surface. Even a trained psychoanalyst would be hard pressed to come up with a diagnosis in view of the absence of any circumstantial data. In any event, it was hardly Remizov's intention to open up his subconscious to the preening eyes of psychiatrists. Why then, one wonders, did he decide to publish these texts?

Dreams have of course always played a prominent role in literature, from the *Epic of Gilgamesh* and Homer all the way up to the novels of Dostoevskii and Tolstoi. Traditionally, authors have used them for such purposes as foreshadowing, illuminating the workings of divine providence, or providing insights into a character's psyche. In realist fiction of the nineteenth century, dreams served as a convenient motivation for elements of the fantastic in plots, allowing even the most bizarre flights of fancy to remain grounded in an empirical reality. This situation changed with the emergence of modernism, when dreams began to break loose from their fictional frame and to acquire an independent reality of their own. Rather than serving as an ancillary part of a larger work of narrative fiction, dreams could now become self-sufficient entities able to stand on their own as literary texts. This phenomenon is commonly associated with the French surrealist movement and with its attempt to abolish traditional, authored literature through the process of automatic writing. For the surrealists, literary creation, at least in theory, consisted in transcribing the data of the unconscious mind without the interference or control of an aesthetic or moral super-ego. It has been largely overlooked, however, that the textual emancipation of dreams is a process that began much earlier than the surrealist "revolution" of the 1920s. Remizov's first dream recordings antedate the surrealists by two decades. This raises the question whether we should consider him as a surrealist *avant la lettre*.

What is the source of Remizov's fascination with dreams? The most detailed explanation can be found in the preface to his book of dreams, *Martyn Zadeka*. One has to keep in mind, however, that this preface is a rather idiosyncratic document, which seems to deliberately shun any notion of argumentative clarity or logical cohesiveness. This comes as less of a surprise if we are aware that the main function of dreams for Remizov is their challenge to rationality. "The genuine dream," he writes, "is always folly, nonsense, twaddle, subversion and disorder (*bezobrazie*)."[10] A similar assessment could be made of Remizov's explanatory preface, which seems to mock and subvert the genre of expository prose that it seemingly embraces. The startled reader who expects an explanation is instead confronted with a series of elliptic and cryptic pronouncements and non sequiturs.

Most notable is Remizov's lack of interest in two major schools of dream interpretation, the psychoanalytic and the occult. Nowhere does he mention Sigmund Freud or Carl Gustav Jung in his treatise on dreams.[11] Remizov's approach has been characterized as more "magical" than "medicinal."[12] At first sight, several points raised in Remizov's preface seem indeed connected with the traditional occult lore of dreams. Among the benefits of dreaming, Remizov mentions communication with the dead, telepathy, and prophecy. However, Remizov's treatment of these topics is decidedly unconventional. For example, he conceives of life after death as an uninterrupted dream whose content corresponds to the ideas the dreamer had about the afterlife while still alive. Once this faith is exhausted, "the human soul flies like a spark into the ocean. And those who are not connected in any way with 'heaven' continue to 'darn stockings' or to organize words (*raskladyvat' slova*), in general they carry on with their life's business."[13] Remizov claims that through the medium of dreams, the living can communicate with the dead and even "influence their fate," although he does not explain how this is done.

Communication with the "beyond," to be sure, was a favorite idea of Remizov's symbolist contemporaries. The merging of the spark of the human soul with the ocean of being is reminiscent of Hindu beliefs and may be attributed to the general interest in Eastern religions in Russian intellectual circles at the beginning of the twentieth century. But Remizov's approach seems strangely eclectic and whimsical. The darning of socks, for example, does not usually figure in the mystical contemplation of the afterlife. By introducing such prosaic realia of everyday life into his picture of nirvana, Remizov seems to deflate and parody the symbolist discourse on other worlds.

The same observation can be made about Remizov's treatment of another stock element of occult dream lore, the prophetic revelation. Remizov declares that dreams have frequently foretold him the future. As an example, he mentions a dream about two unknown girls, twin sisters, which seemed to him an omen announcing some important event. The day after he saw this dream, as he was riding the Parisian metro, the door to his car opened, and a mother with twin girls stepped in, the exact ones he had seen in his dream. But, as it turns out, this is already the end of the story. Remizov continues: "But that day, nothing happened, so it seems my dream was good for nothing (*ni k chemu*), it simply showed me the coming day."[14] Prophecy, which is usually associated with the foreshadowing of fateful, momentous developments, is here reduced to the foretelling of a trivial, daily-life occurrence. This outcome contradicts a tenet of both occult and psychoanalytical dream interpretation: the belief that the seemingly insignificant dream detail contains encoded messages hinting at a much larger meaning. In Remizov's example, the trivial dream detail is simply an accurate, un-encoded foretelling of a trivial daytime event. It seems no accident then that perhaps the most pedestrian of daily-life prophecies, the weather forecast, also surfaces in Remizov's discussion of prophetic dreams. He claims that he has a sure means of predicting the next day's weather. Each time he dreams of the literary scholar Konstantin Mochul'skii, this indicates that it is going to rain: "As with a barometer I say: according to Mochul'skii—rain."[15] The juxtaposition of Mochul'skii with rain is probably based on a pun (*mochit'* = to wet, to soak), and it also provides an indication of Remizov's not very high opinion of Mochul'skii's literary criticism.[16] One wonders also whether Remizov is not simply pulling the reader's leg.

The suspicion that Remizov may be mocking his audience and occasionally pursuing an agenda different from the one he asserts is nourished by a story reported in the afterword of his dream collection. Remizov mentions a couch in his former apartment in St. Petersburg which had a miraculous quality: as soon as he lay down on this particular piece of furniture, he saw the most vivid dreams. Remizov reports that he urged all of his numerous daytime visitors to take a nap on this couch in order to find out whether it had the same effect on them. Many visitors consented after some initial protest—to no avail, as none of them ever experienced any dream. The experiment did have one benefit, however. While his guests were safely tucked away in bed, Remizov reports that "taking advantage of the sleep-generated silence, I continued my interrupted work."[17] One wonders whether this was not the real purpose of this dream experiment all along.

Since everything Remizov says about his dreams has to be taken *cum grano salis*, we can hardly trust him fully when he asserts that his *sny* are simple, un-invented transcriptions of actual dreams. Despite Natal'ia Kodrianskaia's assertion that Remizov never invented a dream,[18] there is evidence that sheds at least some doubt on this claim. Remizov published many of his dreams more than once. Twenty-nine of the fifty dreams contained in "Bedovaia Dolia" reappear in the collection *Martyn Zadeka,* but in an altered form. A comparison of the earlier and later publication of the same texts reveals considerable revisions in style and content. No text has been left untouched. While in some cases the revisions amount to only minor changes, other dreams were very extensively rewritten.

As an example, one could mention the dream "Chut' bylo ne s'eli" ("They almost ate me") from the collection "Bedovaia dolia," which reappears half a century later under the title "Pylesos" ("The Vacuum Cleaner") in *Martyn Zadeka*.[19] There can be no doubt that the two versions are variants of the same dream. The beginning and ending are identical in both texts: the narrator is deprived of his keys to twelve underground closets and of the rags that he was collecting in a courtyard, and he is betrayed and abandoned by his companion. At the end of the dream, the companion unexpectedly reappears and returns the keys and rags together with "rye flour for the brewing of thick paste." In both variants the narrator goes through an unsettling experience of being robbed and is threatened with death. At the same time, the story has undergone major changes in its second version. The fear of "being eaten with bread" (a mock reenactment of the Eucharist?) seems to have abated and is replaced with references to death by freezing—perhaps a realistic reflection of Remizov's living condition during the war years in Paris. The second version also contains some metaliterary statements that are absent in the first version: the narrator points to the manuscripts of his "unfinished books." Corresponding to Remizov's own dislocation from St. Petersburg to Paris, the geographic setting of the dream has shifted as well, with the Russian *shveitsar* (porter) replaced by a French concierge. The second version features a modern household item, the vacuum cleaner. In addition, the treacherous companion has changed his name from Vlasov to Solonchuk.[20]

In general, the second version is more compact and laconic than the first (this is true for the majority of Remizov's rewritings). By leaving out much of the information provided in the original text, the second dream becomes even more enigmatic and opaque. For example, the last paragraph of the second version contains a reference to an "announcement" which remains unexplained. The reader has to turn to the earlier text to find out that the announcement concerns the taking-off of galoshes.

Unless we assume that Remizov was haunted by a large number of recurring dreams which became updated and altered (in fact, he never mentions anything of the sort), we must conclude that the second dream is not the protocol of an actual dream experience, but the revision of a previously existing text.[21] The second dream constitutes a sort of palimpsest of the first. Remizov's vast collection of dreams is best described not as an inventory of fixed entities, but as an ongoing project of rewriting an ever-shifting corpus of elusive texts. With a single-mindedness verging on graphomania, Remizov altered almost every sentence in his dreams as he revised them for republication, with changes ranging from major additions and omissions to minuscule alterations in punctuation and syntax. T. V. Tsiv'ian has speculated that Remizov's graphomania could explain his interest in recording his dreams in the first place: with his hyperactive temperament, Remizov simply did not want to stop producing literature even while asleep.[22]

This concern with writing raises the question of the "literariness" of Remizov's dreams. Should one not consider Remizov's *sny* first and foremost as literary texts, rather than as factual recordings? Remizov touches on the theme of literature at the end of his preface to *Martyn Zadeka,* when he asserts that "with writers dreams assume a *literary form.*"[23] As Natal'ia Kodrianskaia reports, Remizov was very attentive to the problem of how to convey a dream experience by verbal means: "Dreams have form and color, and sound, and smell. Dreams are musical. A particular rhythmicality distinguishes dream events from daytime, waking events. No unconscious recording is able to convey a dream—verbal work on the recording is necessary. To give the dream a voice (*ogolosit' son*) is a great art."[24] In particular, Remizov associates dreams with poetry. He claims that even people with no literary interests can have poetic dreams, and he raises the question, in his afterword to *Martyn Zadeka,* whether "it is possible to compose dreams as one composes verses." Metric verse, still the norm in Russian poetry, seems less than ideal for the recording of dreams: "In the composition of verses, the measure sways the imagination and calls forth the image, but the formlessness of dreams is unmeasurable."[25]

The ideal generic medium for the evocation of dreams, it would appear then, is a form of poetry without the constrictions of regular verse or line breaks—in other words, a poem in prose. Remizov was interested in the creative possibilities of this form, as we know from the fact that he translated Stanislaw Przybyszewski's prose poems from Polish into Russian.[26] Some of Remizov's own early miniatures, including his dreams, have been described by literary critics as prose poems.[27] Much of Remizov's early oeuvre is in fact an experimentation with poetic prose and occasional free verse.[28] Remizov's literary début, "Plach devushki pered zamuzhestvom" ("A Maiden's Lament before Marriage"), published in 1902, was an attempt at stylized folklore written in a rhythmic prose that approaches free verse in its typographical presentation. Remizov's imprisonment and exile in the far north for political reasons inspired a series of lyric mood pieces in rhythmic prose, which appeared in collected form under the title "Belaia bashnia" ("The White Tower") in 1908[29] and in a reworked version as part of the story "V plenu" ("In Captivity").[30] The boundaries between poetry and prose become porous in many of these texts. In some instances, the typographical presentation alters from one edition to another, betraying an uncertain generic status. The poem "Severnye tsvety" ("Northern Flowers"),

for example, which first appeared in Briusov's almanac of the same name, became later "depoetized" and was included in "V plenu" as a prose fragment.

In many ways, these early lyrical prose pieces correspond to the decadent and symbolist aesthetics of the time. Three of Remizov's miniatures
appeared in the symbolist *Grif* almanac in 1904.[31] The first two texts evoke
a world of decadent doom and gloom. "Molitva" ("Prayer") expresses in a
lyrical, rhythmic prose the nostalgic religious longing for a distant mother
figure, uttered by a speaker trapped in an empty universe, alone on a "grain
of sand senselessly flying around the sun." "Poslednii chas" ("The Last
Hour") takes up the fashionable topic of the end of the world.[32] The text
opens with a sequence of verbless sentences conveying an impressionistic
evocation of a cataclysm, followed by eleven lines in regular iambic meter,
and ends with the allegoric personification of death, shown as a woman in
whose "hands the flowers were blackened from hardened blood." Over the
bones of the deceased are wafting the sounds of somebody's song, "slow and
saturated with forgetting." The third and longest piece, "Ivan-Kupal" ("St.
John Baptist's Day"), belongs to Remizov's folkloric northern sketches and
was later republished in *Chortov Log* and "V plenu."

It is important to stress that Remizov's dream narratives are very different from these early symbolist miniatures. In a development comparable
to that of Bunin, the sprawling fin de siècle impressionism of the earlier
prose miniatures gives way to an extremely condensed, laconic form. Although replete with "strange" events that contradict empirical realism,
Remizov's dreams cannot be called poetic or lyrical in any conventional
sense: they feature no romantic flights of fancy, grandiose vistas, or elaborately crafted rhetorical flourish. With their prosaic style and frequent focus on daily life trivialia, they seem more anti-poetic than poetic. However,
this is exactly what allows us to place these texts in the "subversive" tradition of the prose poem. With its uncertain ontological status, the prose
poem appears to be the ideal vehicle for the evocation of an oneiric vision
that straddles the fence between trance and awareness, fantasy and reality,
the presence and absence of meaning. Greta Slobin has pointed to Remizov's subversive challenge to binary oppositions, such as the dichotomies
between "old and new, sacred and profane, literary and nonliterary, oral and
written, written and visual, and fiction and life."[33]

Turgenev's *Stikhotvoreniia v proze*, the first example of prose poems
in Russian literature, present not only a possible generic model for Remizov's *sny*, but they also constitute an early example of Russian dream-texts.
Several of Turgenev's prose poems are explicitly presented as dreams. Two
of them bear the generic subtitle "son."[34] In several other texts, the framing
narrative presents the story as the narrator's dream, using formulas like "I
dreamt that . . . ," or "I saw in a dream. . . ."[35] Many more prose poems, although not specifically marked as dreams, exude a dreamlike atmosphere.

As mentioned earlier, Turgenev's rough drafts reveal that he was planning to include an entire cycle of dreams in his collection of prose poems.[36] In the original manuscript sent to Stasiulevich, five more prose poems were marked with the explicit subtitle "son" ("Starukha," "Nasekomoe," "Lazurnoe tsarstvo," "Khristos," and "Priroda"), but Turgenev, following the advice of his friend P. V. Annenkov, removed these subheadings in the published version.[37]

Turgenev's oneiric prose poems deserve attention as an early example of a new genre in Russian literature. To be sure, literary dreams had existed before in Russia, but dreams as independent literary texts had only figured thus far as lyric poems in verse, whereas prose dreams were integrated into larger narrative structures. Turgenev's innovation consists in using dream narratives as independent prose miniatures. In his investigation of Russian nineteenth-century literary dreams, Remizov came to a somewhat mixed conclusion about the dreams contained in Turgenev's prose poems. He states that some of Turgenev's texts, although explicitly marked as dreams, have nothing dream-like about them, whereas others, while not designated as such, clearly are dreams nevertheless. As an example of the first kind, he names "Priroda" ("Nature"), and of the second, "Starukha" ("The Old Woman").[38]

An analysis of these two pieces will suggest certain insights about the relationship of Remizov's dreams to Turgenev's. "Priroda" is placed in a narrative frame which clearly identifies the text as a dream. The story begins with the words "I dreamt that . . ." and ends with the closing formula "and then I woke up."[39] The main body of the text consists of the narrator's encounter with an allegorical representation of nature, which is shown as a woman dressed in green. To his amazement, the narrator discovers that this woman, contrary to his expectations, shows very little interest in the destiny of humans. It turns out that her main concern at this moment is to strengthen the leg muscles of fleas in order to restore what she calls "the balance of attack and repulse." She brushes aside the concepts of goodness, reason, and justice raised by the narrator as mere "human words," having no relevance in a world where there is no essential difference between humans and worms. Remizov does not specify why he considers this story undreamlike, but one can surmise his reasons: the dream simply makes too much sense. It is a straightforward didactic exposition of the sort of Darwinian worldview to which Turgenev was drawn in his more pessimistic moments. Although the concept of reason is questioned in the story, the text itself does not in any way defy reason. On the contrary, it lays out its message in an entirely coherent and intelligible fashion.

The second prose poem mentioned by Remizov, "Starukha," also exhibits an allegorical nature.[40] The narrator is followed by a grotesque old woman, who turns out to be a representation of "fate." His attempts to escape her pursuit are utterly in vain. Although the message of this dream is rather obvious as well (the woman drives the narrator to the grave), it found more favor with Remizov, probably because the dream is a genuine nightmare with all the trappings of this genre. For example, the narrator experiences vague feelings of unease and fear which later develop into a sense of horror, his attempts to flee are futile, and so on. Furthermore, the text contains narrative details that are not immediately decipherable (unlike the green dress of Mother Nature in "Priroda"). For example, the old woman's eyes are covered with a sort of white membrane reminiscent of certain species of birds. This attribute makes for a striking image, although it does not seem to serve any transparent allegorical purpose.[41]

One of Remizov's own dreams to some extent resembles Turgenev's "Starukha."[42] In Remizov's version, the narrator also is persecuted by a frightening old woman, who chases him through a suite of rooms and finally corners him behind a piece of furniture as he tries to hide. "What are you afraid of?" the woman asks, "I am your mother!" The narrator is startled by this revelation. He protests that his mother does not look like this woman at all, but at the same time thinks to himself: "Could it really be that my mother has become like that?" Meanwhile, the old woman has already jumped at his throat. Although thematically linked to Turgenev's prose poem, Remizov's text reads more like a parody of Turgenev's dream. The old woman seems more vile and aggressive, while the narrator appears slightly ridiculous and childish. Remizov's story certainly defies any easy allegorical decoding. The situation becomes even stranger in the reworked version published in 1954, where the narrator, instead of wondering whether his mother has really become like that, utters the cryptic words: "Is she one of my mothers?"

Remizov's collection of dreams, like the prose poems of Baudelaire, Turgenev, Belyi, and Bunin, also features a beggar story. The encounter between narrator and beggar takes up the first half of the dream "U khvosta" ("At the Tail"):

У хвоста

Магазин «Hôtel de Ville». Почтовую бумагу взял, а пакет с конвертами забыл. А у нас ни жеванного, а писать письма надо и не «описания природы», а все о деньгах. Придется вернуться.

Подходит нищий: голова тыква, голая, ни волоска, а уши—тоненькие красные ручки. А у меня нечего подать, все ухлопал на бумагу и конверты, только что на метро. И я скорее назад в «Hôtel de Ville». Да никак не могу найти, пропал из глаз. А этот нищий оборвал себе уши и сует мне в руку красные ручки.

«Да на что они мне, говорю, мне надо конверты».

«А как же, отвечает нищий, ходить с ручкой». [. . .][43]

At the Tail

The store "Hôtel de Ville." I took the writing paper, and forgot the packet of envelopes. And we have nothing to chew, it is necessary to write letters and not "descriptions of nature," and all about money. I have to go back.

A beggar approaches: his head is a pumpkin, naked, not a hair, and the ears are delicate red handles [or pens]. And I have nothing to give, I squandered all on paper and envelopes, and just now on the metro. And I am rushing back to the "Hôtel de Ville." But I can't find it in any way, it has dropped from view. And this beggar broke off his ears and slips the red handles in my hand.

"But what good are they to me," I say, "I need envelopes."

"And how," answers the beggar, "can one walk with a handle."

The equality between beggar and narrator emphasized in Turgenev's "Nishchii" takes a new twist here: the narrator himself is a pauper who has to beg for money. Unlike the well-off Turgenev, he cannot indulge in "descriptions of nature" (an allusion to "Priroda"?), and he certainly has no change to spare. The beggar seems to sense this and, reversing the usual scenario of almsgiving, makes a donation to the narrator which looks like a grotesque parody of Turgenev's solemn handshake. Mimicking a gesture of self-sacrifice, the beggar hands over his own ears, which are really *"ruchki."* The word *"ruchka"* is semantically overdetermined. It literally means "little hand," which could refer to Turgenev's handshake, but it can also be translated as "handle" (a metaphorical literalization of the beggar's protruding ears?), and as "pen," a reference to the theme of writing which plays such a prominent role in this dream. In order to write his planned letters, the narrator obviously will need a pen, although his mind seems set exclusively on the lost envelopes. Remizov's beggar is neither as pitiful as Turgenev's, nor as majestic as Bunin's, nor as demonic as Belyi's. With his pumpkin head he looks more like a grotesque character from a children's story. In his afterword to *Martyn Zadeka*, Remizov explains that the expression *"khodit' s ruchkoi"* means "to beg." In other words, the dream image of the beggar is generated by the literalization of a colloquial expression. Mocking the explanatory rhetoric of popular "Dream Books," Remizov adds that having such a dream is a sure sign of the dreamer's straitened financial means.[44]

It becomes evident that Remizov does not simply follow in Turgenev's footsteps. The main difference between the two authors lies in the role of allegory. Very much in keeping with the traditional function and interpretation of dreams, Turgenev's oneiric narratives serve as the vehicle for the convocation of a symbolic message. In Remizov's dreams, this process has become scrambled as the reader searches in vain for allegoric cues that would allow for deciphering the dream text. Remizov thus challenges a tenet shared by both occultists and Freudians: the assumption that dreams ultimately make sense. For the traditional interpreter of dreams, the manifest content only leads to the latent content. Once the real meaning has been established, the literal level of the text fades into insignificance.[45] In Remizov's case, the manifest content remains the primary point of reference. The strangeness and opaqueness of dreams, for the traditional interpreter only a temporary obstacle on the road to meaning, become for Remizov something that is to be savored for its own sake. Dreams constitute, so to speak, our own nightly private theatre of the absurd.

The genuine dream, according to Remizov, is always characterized by a semantic "disruption" (*sryv*). This phenomenon can manifest itself in an uncalled-for causal relationship, or an unexpected and inappropriate modifier, for example, "planetary meat" (*planetnoe miaso*).[46] In the expert handling of these "disruptions," Remizov claims, lies the whole art of dream-writing.[47] With his emphasis on semantic dislocation and estrangement, Remizov emerges as the proponent of an eminently modern poetics. If we equate his term *sryv* with the semantically related *sdvig* of the futurists,[48] Remizov begins to sound like a member of the Russian avant-garde (with many of whom he did indeed have friendly relations). He appears particularly close to Elena Guro, sharing with her an interest in folklore and fairy tales, the combined practice of literature and visual arts, as well as the habit of writing prose miniatures.[49]

In their alogism and deliberate lack of allegorical depth, Remizov's dreams differ from those of his symbolist contemporaries, such as Fedor Sologub's two *sny*. It is not surprising that many contemporary critics reacted to Remizov's dream accounts with incomprehension, consternation or hostility. The poet Mikhail Kuzmin, the advocate of "beautiful clarity," likened them to the nonsensical babbling of an old woman who had lost possession of her faculties.[50] Others reacted more positively, however. Aleksandr Blok, for one, was impressed. Although he questioned Remizov's claim that his *sny* were transcriptions of real dreams, he praised them for their capacity for showing "a very real piece of our soul, where everything is turned topsy-turvy."[51] Another admirer of Remizov's dreams was the painter Vasilii Kandinskii, who illustrated three of them, and whose own prose poems bear a certain similarity to Remizov's dream texts.[52] The critic D. V. Filosofov compared Remizov's incongruous juxtaposition of trivialia with the mixture of unrelated events reported on the typical page of an illustrated journal. According to Filosofov, Remizov's collage in itself becomes an illustration of the meaningless emptiness of modern reality, prompting in its turn a longing for a "more real" reality à la Viacheslav Ivanov.[53] It is worth pointing out, however, that such a world of *realiora* never appears in Remizov's dreams. Rather than establishing Remizov's credentials as a symbolist, Filosofov's comparison of his dreams to the incongruous page layout of a modern illustrated journal in fact underscores, perhaps unwittingly, Remizov's affinity to the postsymbolist avant-garde and its technique of montage.

96

While having many points of contact with both classic Russian literature and twentieth-century avant-garde movements, Remizov's dream-project ultimately remains a sui generis phenomenon. The narrative persona of Remizov's dreams falls into the larger context of his literary self-fashioning. As Andrei Siniavskii has observed, the creation of a series of grotesque masks of the authorial self is a hallmark of Remizov's writing in general.[54] The advantage of the dream for such a project is obvious: it is a medium which allows for a seemingly autobiographical stance, yet also provides a motivation for distancing and estrangement. To some extent, this observation is valid for Turgenev's dreams as well. The declaration of a text as a dream allows the author to avoid personal "liability" for his writings by removing the element of intentionality.[55]

Kuzmin's verdict of "nonsense," if we leave out its derogatory connotations, indeed seems to capture the essence of Remizov's dream narratives. In his exploration of nonsense as a literary genre, the Dutch scholar Wim Tigges defined it as "a genre of narrative literature which balances a multiplicity of meaning with a simultaneous absence of meaning. [. . .] In order to be successful, nonsense must at the same time invite the reader to interpretation and avoid the suggestion that there is a deeper meaning which can be obtained by considering connotations or associations, because these lead to nothing." Tigges adds that "the material may come from the unconscious (indeed, it is very likely in many instances to do so)."[56] He also asserts that nonsense, by its very nature, excludes allegory and satire, and he stresses its lack of emotional attachment.[57]

In the context of Russian literature, the closest forerunner of Remizov in the genre of nonsense is Nikolai Gogol'. More than half of Remizov's book *Ogon' veshchei* is devoted to Gogol' alone—both to his fiction in general, and his dreams in particular. Even when talking about other authors, Remizov keeps coming back to Gogol', whom he considers the fountainhead of Russian literary dream-writing. As he put it: "Dostoevskii, Tolstoi, Turgenev all had dreams, but they all involuntarily remembered the Gogolian dream: literature is contagious."[58] Among Gogol''s fictional works, "The Nose" in particular functions in a similar manner as Remizov's dreams: it teases the reader with possible allegorical decodings only to frustrate the expectation of a meaningful interpretation.[59] It is worth noting that Gogol' originally considered presenting his story of the missing nose as a dream (the title *nos* may be read as an anagram of *son*). Gogol' considered dreams as quintessentially meaningless collages. In a letter to his mother, he described them as "simply incoherent excerpts, which have no sense, taken from what we have thought and then pasted together to make up a kind of salad."[60] In the final version of his story, Gogol' decided to dispense with any kind of direct oneiric motivation for his sequence of nonsensical events. Remizov's *sny* come close to the Gogolian model inasmuch as they also do away with the traditional framing devices of dreams that we still find in Turgenev—formulas such as "I dreamt that . . ." or "And then I woke up."[61] Only the subtitle of Remizov's dream collections preserves a tenuous link with the world of sleep. The reader is likely to lose sight of this fact, however, as Remizov's texts appear more like a collection of raw nonsense without any external motivation.

In the larger context of European literature, an obvious question that arises is the connection between Remizov's dream-writings and the verbal experiments of the French surrealists.[62] Remizov lived in Paris during the heyday of surrealism and was personally acquainted with some of its leading representatives—in fact, he had *dreams* about them. He also contributed to André Breton's dream anthology *Trajectoire du rêve* with a presentation and discussion of Pushkin's dreams, illustrated by two of his drawings.[63] Remizov's friend during his Parisian exile, Iurii Annenkov, reports in his memoirs that "in French literary circles Remizov was considered a 'surrealist.'"[64]

In some respects, Remizov's position indeed seems reminiscent of surrealist pronouncements. Like the surrealists, Remizov understood dreams less as a nightly escape into a realm of fantasy than as an integral part of day-to-day reality.[65] In the afterword to *Martyn Zadeka,* he asserts that "what we call 'fantastic' is not at all a spectral, not a 'deformed' reality, but a reality that exists independently and acts together with palpable reality. [. . .] Life is not limited to daytime occurrences of three-dimensional reality, but continues in the multi-dimensionality of dreams, which are equally existing and equally valid as the waking world."[66] In his Surrealist Manifesto of 1924, André Breton asserted something similar when he declared: "I believe in the future resolution of these two states, dream and reality, which are seemingly so contradictory, into a kind of absolute reality, a *surreality*, if one may so speak."[67] The "encyclopedia entry" on surrealism which Breton included in his manifesto states that "Surrealism is based on the belief in the superior reality of previously neglected associations, in the *omnipotence of dreams*, in the disinterested play of thought. It tends to ruin once and for all all other psychic mechanisms and to substitute itself for them in solving all the principal problems of life."[68]

It is worth pointing out, however, that Remizov, although he must have been familiar with the work of the French surrealists,[69] never claimed the surrealist label for himself. A closer look reveals some significant discrepancies between his approach and that of the surrealists. Remizov explicitly rejected the method of *écriture automatique*. As we have seen earlier, he stresses the importance of conscious verbal labor on his dream material. In his Surrealist Manifesto, André Breton had described the surrealist method as a "psychic automatism" and "dictation by the mind, unhampered by conscious control." Remizov, on the contrary, asserts that the writer has to be in charge of language when he records his dreams. The conscious mind has to "control the word, rather than the word controling speech. One has to take from the stream of words according to one's will, and not what comes automatically (*chto lezet na iazyk*)."[70]

Remizov's dream accounts also differ in style from the dreams of the French surrealists. Dream recordings were a favorite genre during the early years of the surrealist movement. Inspired by Freudian dream analysis, André Breton began writing down his dreams in 1920.[71] The best sampling of French surrealist dreams can be found on the pages of the journal *La Révolution Surréaliste,* which appeared from 1924 to 1929 in twelve volumes. With the exception of volumes 6, 8, and 11, all issues of the journal contain a section devoted to dreams (*rêves*), with contributions by André Breton, Michel Leiris, Antonin Artaud, Paul Eluard, and others. In general, the dreams of the French surrealists are longer than Remizov's, and they appear written in a more elaborate, "literary" style. Herbert Gershman described them as "a potpourri of scenes presumably dreamed [which] give every indication of careful reconstruction."[72] Sarane Alexandrian came to a similar conclusion, asserting that "these dreams are sometimes a little too long, a little too complex and coherent to be always immediate notations."[73] The beginning of Michel Leiris' "Le Pays de mes Rêves" ("The Land of my Dreams") may serve as an example:

> On the steps which lead to the view of emptiness, I am holding myself upright, my hands resting on a blade of steel. My body is penetrated by a bundle of invisible lines which connect every point of intersection of the building's roof-tree with the center of the sun. I am taking a walk without being hurt through all these threads that penetrate me, and every place in the universe breathes into me a new soul.[74]

This solemn evocation of a quasi-mystic cosmic experience seems rather far removed from the anxiety-ridden prosaic world of Remizov's dreams. Interestingly enough, the dreams in *La Révolution Surréaliste* that come closest to Remizov's style are those dreamt by children. In their laconic, deadpan manner, they are reminiscent of some of Remizov's *sny.* As an example, here is the dream of an eleven-year-old:

> One day I dreamt that a dog came to see me in order to kill rats. I took a clog (*sabot*) and hit a rat which was killed. Then the dog took the rat and buried it in the ground and he put yellow flowers and withered roses there and he watered it by doing his business (il l'arrosait avec le besoin qu'il avait).[75]

While the infantile world plays a rather marginal role in French surrealism[76] (among the dozens of dreams in *La Révolution Surréaliste,* only three are by children), the realm of fairy tales, nursery rhymes, and the specific worldview of preadolescents informs a substantial part of Remizov's oeuvre.

As was mentioned at the beginning of this chapter, Remizov compares the functioning of dreams to fairy tales. In his afterword to *Martyn Zadeka,* he asserts that fairy tales emerge from dreams, and, like dreams, fall into two categories: "There are fairy tales with a plot (*siuzhetnye skazki*), based on material, and pure fairy tales (*skazki chistoi skazochnosti*), which emerge by themselves out of nothing, made of air."[77] He claims that the dreams in his collection are of this second sort, "dreams of pure imagination." Some of Remizov's dreams indeed have a kind of aerial lightness about them. They seem inspired by a *haiku*-like minimalist aesthetic, constituting brief epiphanies of absolute verbal art and verbal play, as in the following example:

Кошка

Ловили кошку. И поймали. Поставили на стол, как ставят цветы. Кошка постояла немного, съела цветы и ушла.[78]

The Cat

They were chasing a cat. And caught it. They placed it on the table as one places flowers. The cat stood for a while, ate the flowers, and went away.

In its laconic simplicity, this text has much in common with the children's dreams reported in *La Révolution Surréaliste,* but much less with surrealist "adult" dreams. Ultimately, Remizov's dreams are more akin to nonsense literature than to surrealism (it is true, of course, that the two categories may overlap to some extent).[79] According to Wim Tigges, a dream only qualifies as nonsense if it is "stripped of all its symbolism—not a wish-dream, nor a day-dream or a nightmare."[80] Remizov's dream of the cat provides an illustration of this principle. What Remizov lacked altogether was the surrealist belief in dreams as interpretable revelations of a subconscious reality accessible through Freudian dream-analysis. Remizov never psychoanalyzed his own dreams as Breton did.[81] Furthermore, he lacked the revolutionary fervor of the surrealists. He did not believe that it was his mission to transform the world, or as Breton put it in his Surrealist Manifesto, "to solve the principal problems of life." Even less, of course, did Remizov share the French surrealists' naive embrace of Soviet Communism, having witnessed the reality of Lenin's revolutionary regime with his own eyes.[82]

It is not surprising then that Remizov kept his distance from the French surrealists. Not only did he not claim the surrealist label for his work, he never even mentioned the existence of the surrealist movement in his writings—at least not in his critical, metaliterary statements. As mentioned earlier, however, the French surrealists do make a cameo appearance in his dreams. *Martyn Zadeka* contains two texts involving the leading French surrealists, Paul Eluard and André Breton. Eluard appears briefly in the dream "Ne v tu dver'" ("The Wrong Door").[83] The narrator believes to have entered a café, but finds himself instead in a shoemaker's shop. As he grudgingly serves him a cup of coffee, the shoemaker announces to the narrator that Eluard has killed his dog. This provokes the astonishment of the narrator, who declares that he does not own a dog. The shoemaker does not respond to this objection. Instead, he breaks into a grandiose declamation "with the sentimentality of Sterne," and, without forewarning, he finishes drinking the narrator's cup of cold coffee.

André Breton, the founder and leading spirit of surrealism, appears in a more elaborate dream entitled "Podkop i zatychka" ("Underground Passage and Plug").[84] Again, the narrator seems to have entered the wrong door. Believing to have purchased a ticket to a movie theater, he lands instead in an art gallery where Breton is showing his paintings. The narrator wants to question Breton about Mexico and its inhabitants. Breton responds: "I am like Ulysses, I forgot everything under the song of the Sirens." He hands the narrator a stone which he declares to be a cornerstone from an underground passage. The narrator returns aboveground and finds himself in a building resembling a monastery or prison. On top of the building, a "Committee of guaranty" (*Komitet ruchatel'stva*) is handing out matches. The narrator is tempted to go there, since he is a smoker and likes the perspective of obtaining matches without standing in line. He decides otherwise, however, because the head of this committee is a "lover of domestic spectacles," a man of many words and few thoughts. Nobody ever dares to enter his office, since he is surrounded by a swarm of bats, his bodyguards. The narrator now decides to make some tea. He is interrupted by a knock at the door: Breton is there with a rifle and a Mexican scythe. The narrator refuses to let him in—it is too early. Yet it turns out that the visitor is not really Breton, but the Russian writer Mikhail Prishvin. He declares that "in Russia, many things happened and happen that don't and won't happen on earth," and begins to bang at the door.

It is tempting to read these dreams as Remizov's indirect comment on the surrealist movement. While it would be a mistake, in light of our earlier discussion of Remizov's dreams, to try to distill any kind of unequivocal message from these texts, some pertinent observations can nevertheless be made. The dream about Breton is especially striking for its evocation of realia that are reminiscent of the Soviet experience. Certain goods are hard to come by and people are standing in line. The atmosphere of a "monastery or prison" evokes Stalin's militarized, pseudo-religious despotism. Things are run by a (Central?) "Committee," and the person ultimately in charge is a shady, demonic leader, a lover of "spectacles" (show trials? orchestrated public adulations?). Breton's Mexican garb could hint at third-world revolutionary romanticism, and perhaps also at Trotskii, whom Breton admired. Significantly, the dream shows Breton having succumbed to "Siren songs."

The end of the text makes clear that this dream is as much about Russia as it is about Breton, as the French surrealist metamorphoses into the Soviet writer Prishvin.

Mikhail Prishvin was one of Remizov's friends during the years he lived in St. Petersburg. It is interesting to note that Prishvin makes numerous appearances in the dreams of *Vzvikhrennaia Rus'* (*Russia in the Whirlwind*), Remizov's idiosyncratic chronicle of the revolutionary period. In one scene, for example, we see Prishvin grotesquely disfigured with wisps of hair sprouting out of his nostrils and ears. In another, he appears with a trumpet in hand and commands the band to play the *Internationale*, claiming to be a "Wetterprophet."[85] We know that Remizov held Prishvin's writings in high esteem, especially his depictions of Russian nature. In his Parisian exile, he regarded them as a precious link with his Russian homeland (*"vest' iz Rossii"*),[86] but he also had mixed feelings about Prishvin's accommodation with the Soviet regime.[87] The seemingly very incongruous juxtaposition of Breton and Prishvin thus follows a certain logic: both of them are gifted writers who, in Remizov's judgment, have succumbed to political blindness.

Remizov's dreams about the French surrealists not only illustrate his political disagreements. In various ways, these dreams also document the surrealists' ultimate irrelevance for Remizov as an artist. The threat of Eluard having killed his dog (a reference to the film *Un chien andalou*?) proves unfounded, since he doesn't own a dog in the first place. The surrealist coffee shop owner/shoemaker ends up mouthing traditional literary phrases while he drinks his own stale coffee. The "cornerstone" solemnly handed to the narrator by Breton doesn't amount to anything of value either. The promised (Freudian?) "underground passage" only leads to the Soviet prison house. Remizov prefaces his dream about Breton by quoting and commenting on a Russian proverb: "'The head doesn't wait for the tail!' but the opposite happens too: the tail is dashing off (*ulepetyvaet*), and the head is dangling (*boltaetsia*)." Perhaps this image of the "tail wagging the head" could be read as Remizov's comment on the proclaimed poetics of surrealism: automatic writing without input from the conscious mind results at best in empty chatter, at worst in subjugation to totalitarian brainwashing.

Ultimately, Remizov's disagreement with the surrealists may also stem from the fact that the surrealists didn't take their dreams *seriously enough*. Essentially a genre of early surrealism, dream reports ceased to play a role in the later development of the movement.[88] By contrast, Remizov continued to record and publish his dreams until the end of his long life. Rather than an attempt to overcome literature under the influence of dadaist *épatage* and Freudian psychoanalysis, dream-writing constituted for Remizov, as we have seen, a specific form of literary production that remained an essential part of his creative endeavor. Rather than a fellow traveler of the surrealists, Remizov was in a certain sense their antipode—or, if we want to look ahead, perhaps he could be seen as a forerunner of the later absurdist writings of Ionesco or Beckett. As we will see, a similarity also exists with the prose miniatures of Daniil Kharms. In the writings of the surrealists, a noisily declared revolutionary intention, announcing a radical break with tradition, was frequently carried out with elaborate rhetorical means reminiscent of the conventions of the most classical French literary style. Conversely, Remizov's dreams make no claim to revolutionary innovation, and they are presented with deceptive understatement as mere factual recordings. Yet they appear much more radically unsettling in their laconic depiction of an absurd world that ultimately frustrates any attempt at rational explanation.

Chapter Seven

Ut Pictura Poesis: Futurist Prose Miniatures

DESPITE THEIR DIVERSITY, all the prose minia-
tures discussed thus far share a common trait. Although they may mix up
generic taxonomies and violate the laws of narrative logic, they are nevertheless bound by the rules of the Russian language. Their vocabulary can be
looked up in a dictionary, and their grammar and syntax correspond more
or less to established practice. This situation began to change with the ar-
rival of the futurist avant-garde around 1910, when, similar to the emancipation of color and shape in contemporary painting, language itself became
the raw material for artistic experimentation. If music had been the primary
inspiration for the symbolists, painting now assumed the role of the most
important extra-literary model orienting literary creation. Many of the Russian futurists were in fact active both as poets and painters.

This painterly orientation has always been an important factor in the
poetics of the prose poem. Aloysius Bertrand gave his *Gaspard de la Nuit*
the subtitle "Fantaisies à la manière de Rembrandt et de Callot." In the
preface to his prose poems, Baudelaire declared that his project was analogous to that of Bertrand, namely "to apply to the description of modern life
. . . the process that he had applied to the painting of ancient life, so
strangely picturesque."[1] One of Baudelaire's prose poems bears the charac-
teristic title "Le désir de peindre." The parallel with the visual arts is a frequently invoked element in the history and practice of the prose poem in
France and elsewhere.[2] As we remember, the first anthology of prose poems in English appeared under the title *Pastels in Prose.* Michel Beaujour
has noted that "in a sense, the prose poem remained faithful to the old apo-
dictic injunction, *ut pictura poesis:* the prose poem is 'like a picture' (see
Rimbaud's *Illuminations,* Butor's *Illustrations*), and this interchangeability
or 'correspondence' is particularly evident in the context of the luxury art
book displaying text and print on facing pages."[3] A tendency toward description and ekphrasis is noticeable also in Turgenev's prose poems. Some
of his texts dispose entirely with narrative and are purely descriptive, such
as "Kamen'" ("The Stone," PSS 10:162–63), where an old stone lying on the
seashore is presented as the allegorical image of the poet's heart. The prose

poem "Necessitas, Vis, Libertas" (PSS 10:149) establishes a direct connection with the visual arts through its subtitle "Barel'ef" ("bas-relief"), declaring the text to be an ekphrastic description of a (probably) imaginary piece of sculpture.

The turning away of the visual arts from mimetic representation in the early twentieth century changed the dynamics of this correspondence between text and image. Like the modernist painting, the futurist prose poem refuses to give a transparent, "realist" copy of a visible reality. At the same time, it also rejects the symbolist referral to a transcendent noumenon. As Suzanne Bernard put it in her discussion of literary cubism:

> It is undeniable that the reaction of the painters against impressionism and of the poets against symbolism went in the same direction and took on identical forms. United in a same will to return to the real, to the *object,* as a protest against the world of reflections, fleeting appearances and symbols that had enchanted their predecessors, painters and poets, rather paradoxically, ended up with creations that were completely independent from external reality. Their "object-paintings" and "object-poems" tend not to represent the real anymore, but to become artistic creations existing in themselves, expressing nothing else but their creators.[4]

An important model for this "cubist" concept of the prose poem was provided by Rimbaud's *Illuminations.* The title itself, as noted by Beaujour, contains an allusion to the visual arts. In addition, Rimbaud incorporates pictorial expressions such as "tableau" and "gravure," and at one point uses the plural "ciels" (rather than "cieux"), a form reserved for art criticism.[5] At the same time, it becomes extremely difficult to construct any coherent, realistic "picture" from Rimbaud's texts, given their disruptive, illogical, and even ungrammatical character. Tzvetan Todorov has argued that Rimbaud's *Illuminations* do not represent anything at all, but constitute an example of "presentative" literature. As he puts it, "Rimbaud's text rejects representation, and therein lies its poeticity."[6] It is no accident that Rimbaud was one of the favorite poets of the Russian cubo-futurist Benedikt Livshits (1881–1939), and that it was the futurists, rather than the symbolists, who published Sologub's translations of *Illuminations.*

The Russian cubo-futurists made their boisterous entrance into the literary arena with the 1912 manifesto *A Slap in the Face of Public Taste,* signed by David Burliuk, Aleksei Kruchenykh, Vladimir Maiakovskii, and Velimir Khlebnikov. They famously advocated to "throw Pushkin, Dostoevskii, Tolstoi, et al., et al., overboard from the Ship of modernity" and denounced their symbolist and realist colleagues as a bunch of hacks aspiring to nothing more than owning a *dacha* on a river. At the same time, they claimed the poets' right to "enlarge vocabulary in its scope with arbitrary and derivative words" and "to feel insurmountable hatred for the language

105

existing before them."[7] This manifesto served as the opening piece of a miscellany containing poetry and prose by Khlebnikov, Livshits, Nikolai and David Burliuk, Vasilii Kandinskii, Kruchenykh, and Maiakovskii.

The prose pieces by Khlebnikov, Livshits, Nikolai Burliuk, and Kandinskii in *A Slap* give a representative sample of the various manifestations of what we could call the Russian futurist prose poem. It is true that few futurist writers used this generic term. The only exceptions are Kandinskii and Elena Guro, but Kandinskii was included in *A Slap* rather accidentally, as we will see, and Guro hardly qualifies as a mainstream futurist (characteristically, her work was not featured in *A Slap*). Nevertheless, given the futurist interest in Rimbaud, there exists an undeniable connection between the tradition of the French prose poem and the Russian futurist prose miniature. Despite the proclaimed hostility of the futurists toward their symbolist predecessors, their break with the poetics of the symbolists was not absolute. We find a similar attempt to create a "poeticized" prose, although by different means. At the same time, the futurist rejection of conventional aesthetics and interest in primitivism led at times to an extremely condensed, minimalist form that anticipates the miniatures of Daniil Kharms.

What becomes evident immediately when we look at the prose miniatures included in *A Slap* is the wide diversity within the futurist movement. Not all authors live up to the militant spirit of the opening manifesto. The most conventional pieces are those written by Nikolai Burliuk, entitled "Smert' legkomyslennogo molodogo cheloveka" ("Death of a Frivolous Young Man"), "Tishina Ellady" ("The Stillness of Hellas"), and "Solnechnyi dom" ("A Sunny House"). As Vladimir Markov has observed, these pieces are "neither cubistic nor primitivistic, but rather impressionistic."[8] The first story relates the passage of the narrator to the netherworld after he has died from poisoning. Similar to some of Baudelaire's prose poems, the author creates an effect of grotesque humor by confronting mythological set-pieces (Charon, the River Lethe, Hades, and so forth) with modern-day reality. It turns out that Hades is completely deserted, since all souls have been forgiven and released by Zeus, Hermes has "gone commercial," and Cerberus died of old age. The only person who keeps Hades company is Eve, who turns out to be a rather ordinary old woman occupied with mending cloths and growing vegetables. The second piece is quite different in style. Rather then poking fun at Greek mythology, it extols the world of Ancient Greece in a hymnic tone, using the Black Sea shore as a scenic backdrop. "Hylaea," the Greek name of the landscape around Kherson, served as the designation for the association of futurists who published *A Slap in the Face of Public Taste*. Burliuk's third piece, written in a dreamlike, impressionist manner, evokes the gradual encroachment of mysterious forces on a country estate. None of these three texts features any linguistic or formal experimentation. The style corresponds to the parameters of conventional narrative prose, despite the fact that this type of literature had been allegedly "thrown overboard from the ship of modernity."

Khlebnikov's contribution, "Pesn' miriazia" ("The Song of the Worldling"), is a much more radical attempt to transcend established language use. It illustrates the injunction of the manifesto to enlarge the poet's vocabulary with derivative words. The title itself contains a neologism, combining the word "mir" (world) with a derivative suffix.[9] The creation of new words was more than a literary game for Khlebnikov. It reflected his concern to access a deeper layer of meaning through the etymological analysis and creative combination of Slavic roots. Khlebnikov's interest in the Russian past and the traditions of folklore are comparable most of all to Remizov's pursuits. "Pesn' miriazia" bears a certain resemblance to Remizov's poetic prose sketches of the Russian north. It also resembles Aleksandr Blok's cycle "Puzyri zemli" ("Bubbles of the Earth"), an evocation of a swamp teeming with goblins and ghosts. Written in an incantatory, melodic prose that verges at times on free verse, Khlebnikov's prose poem evokes a primordial landscape populated by all kinds of animals and fantastic fairytale creatures. The demigods and spirits of Russian folklore mingle freely with figures of Khlebnikov's own invention. Remizov's tendency toward nonstandard folk vocabulary is surpassed by Khlebnikov's pervasive use of neologisms, as the following excerpt will demonstrate:

> Когда же воды приходили в буйство и голубые водяные ноги начинали приходить в пляску, вдруг брызнув и бросив черными с белыми косицами копытами, тогда звучал хохот и кивали миряными верхушками осоки и слетались мирязи звучать в трубу и под звон м实яных гусель и на неких нижних струнах рокот мерный выходил из голубых вод негей нежить щеки и ноги под взорами хорошеющих краснея хорошеек, подымающих резвые лица над синим озером, среди тусклых облак лебяжьего пуха и вселеннеющих росинок росянок.[10]

Khlebnikov's innovative prose poses a particular challenge to the translator. Here is Paul Schmidt's version of this passage:

> When power came over the waters and watery blue feet began to move in the dance, a sudden splashing and tossing of black hooves with white curlylocks, then a ha-ha resounded and lotuses nodded their worldform flowers and worldlings flocked together to trumpet to the music of worldovering gleemen, and from a few low strings came a rhythmic racket, and from the blue waters of languor the watersprites arose, faces and limbs and eyes of belleblush femfolk, their pranky faces floating over the dark blue lake amid thick dark clouds, swansdown clouds and dewdrops universalized on flytraps.[11]

While this translation manages to convey to some extent the word-forming energy of the original, it misses what we could call "the music of the signifier." Khlebnikov's text abounds in sound effects based on the repetition of phonemes in subsequent words, such as "bryznuv i brosiv," "kositsami kopy-tami," "khorosheiushchikh krasneia khorosheek," and the final pun, "rosinok rosianok." Striving to achieve a correspondence between content and form, Khlebnikov's poetic prose turns into an iconic depiction of the whirling dance that it represents.

"Pesn' miriazia" is a fairly typical example of Khlebnikov's early prose. It resembles in style and content his first published work, "Iskushenie gresh-nika" ("A Sinner's Temptation," 1907). Possibly a fragment from a longer lost work, this piece contains neither a sinner nor a temptation, but evokes again a kind of proto-Slavic pastoral replete with creative neologisms.[12] The inde-terminacy between prose and poetry is representative for Khlebnikov's ten-dency to abolish generic boundaries. Perhaps Khlebnikov's most successful work in this genre is the prose poem "Zverinets" ("Zoo," 1909), a text that has been classified at various times as a poem or as a prose piece.[13] Already Khleb-nikov's earliest known literary texts, dating from 1905 but not published un-til 1940, were experiments in poetic prose that still resemble symbolist prose miniatures in their impressionist style and somewhat derivative allegorism.[14]

Khlebnikov's later prose works are quite different from these begin-nings, however. In a development that parallels to some extent that of Bunin or Remizov, the earlier "poetic" prose with its ornamental, lyric, and rhythmic character gives way to a "prosaic" diction of almost classic sim-plicity. Iurii Tynianov went as far as to claim that Khlebnikov's later stories are written in a "prose as semantically clear as Pushkin's,"[15] which is some-what of an overstatement. It is true, however, that these texts lack one fea-ture that for many readers has become Khlebnikov's trademark par excellence: the reliance on neologisms. Given their length, most of these pieces fall outside the realm of the prose poem, but in a few cases, the au-thor follows a minimalist aesthetic. As an example of such a text, one could mention "Vykhod iz kurgana umershego syna" ("The dead son leaves his burial mound"),[16] a surrealist evocation of a couple of corpses visiting a wedding party. The topic itself is reminiscent of baroque allegorizations of death and could also have been inspired by Blok's "Pliaski smerti" ("Dances of Death"). The style resembles Bunin's miniatures in its deadpan laconic-ity, reliance on short sentences, and exclusive use of the present tense. The fantastic content of the piece is contradicted by a completely dry, matter-of-fact style of narration. Khlebnikov's minimalist style is also evident in "Okhota" ("The Hunt"), a short fable reminiscent of Kafka that relates the deadly encounter between a rabbit and a hunter, seen from the rabbit's point of view.[17] The rabbit first mistakes the hunter's gun for a black stick and the hunter's eyes for those of the "Great Rabbit," who has "come to de-liver his little cousins from the awful scourge of Man." Wanting to perform a sacred ritual for this deity, the rabbit runs out into the snowy clearing.

When he sees "a pair of horrible blue eyes" he realizes his error, freezes with terror and is shot. Khlebnikov wrote this text at the request of a psychiatrist while he was undergoing observation at a hospital near Kharkov in 1919, hoping to avoid being drafted into the White Army. It reflects in condensed form the experience of the Civil War with its deadly brutality and difficulty of distinguishing between friend and foe.

With his Slavophile leanings, Khlebnikov displayed little interest in Western culture. Neither the poetry nor the painting of the contemporary Western avant-garde was of much importance to him (although, like all of his fellow futurists, he did show an interest in the visual arts). In this sense, Benedikt Livshits could be called Khlebnikov's antipode. In his memoirs, Livshits wrote that "French painting of the first decade [of the twentieth century] meant more to me than anything else. Of course, I did not know and could not know how to make use of this new experience and these still untried methods of work in Russian poetry, but I was firmly convinced that the light came from over there, from the banks of the Seine, from the happy country of liberated painting."[18] In addition to French painting, Livshits was also captivated by French poetry, Rimbaud in particular. He declared himself to be "a pupil of the *poètes maudits*" and always carried a volume of Rimbaud in his pocket.[19]

Livshits' contribution to *A Slap in the Face of Public Taste* consisted in the prose poem "Liudi v peizazhe" ("People in a Landscape"). Given the importance of this text as an example of literary cubism, it merits to be quoted in extenso:

Люди в пейзаже

Александре Экстер

I.

Долгие о грусти ступаем стрелой. Желудеют по канаусовым яблоням, в пепел оливковых запятых, узкие совы. Черным об опочивших поцелуях медом пуст восьмигранник, и коричневыми газетные астры. Но тихие. Ах, милый поэт, здесь любятся не безвременьем, а к развеянным облакам. Это правда: я уже сказал. И еще более долгие, опепленные былым, гиазинтофоры декабря.

II.

Уже изогнувшись, павлиньими по елочному звездами, теряясь хрустящие в ширь. По иному бледные, залегшие спины—в ряды! в ряды! в ряды!—ощериваясь умерщвленным виноградом. Поэтам и не провинциальным голубое. Все плечо в мелу и двух пуговиц. Лайковым щитом—и о тонких и легких пальцах на веки, на клавиши. Ну, смотри: голубые о холоде стога и—спинами! спинами! спинами!—лунной плевой оголубевшие тополя. Я не знал: тяжело голубое на клавишах век!

III.

Глазами, заплеванными верблюжьим морем собственных хижин—правоверное о цвете и даже известковых лебедях единодушие моря, стен и глаз. Слишком быстро зимующий рыбак Белерофонтом. И не надо. И овальными—о гимназический орнамент!—веерами по мутно-серебряному ветлы, и вдоль нас короткий усердный уродец, пиками вникающий по льду, и другой, удлиняющий нос в безплодную прорубь. Полутороглазый по реке, будем сегодня шептунами гилейских камышей![20]

People in a Landscape

For Alexandra Ekster

I.

Long with sadness we tread as an arrow. Acorn-colored in the silky apple trees, in the ash of olive commas, are narrow owls. Of honey black from kisses gone to rest is empty the octahedron, and brown the newspaper asters. But quiet. Oh, dear poet, here one is not loved in hard times, but to scattered clouds. This is the truth: I already said it. And still longer, incinerated from the past, the hyacinth-bearers of December.

II.

Already bent, like peacock stars in the manner of fir-trees, vanishing crackling in the distance. Differently pale, the backs lying low—in rows! in rows! in rows!—gnashing their teeth like a killed vine. To the poets and the non-provincials, blue. The whole shoulder in chalk and of two buttons. As a kid-skin shield—and with delicate and light fingers on the eyelids, on the keys. Well, look: blue with cold the stacks and—with backs! with backs! with backs!—turned blue from the lunar membrane the poplars. I did not know: heavy is the blue on the keys of the eyelids!

III.

With eyes, spat on by the camel sea of their own shacks—orthodox with the color and even lime swans, the unanimity of the sea, the walls and eyes. Too quickly wintering a fisherman as Bellerophon. And unnecessary. And as oval fans—oh high-school ornament!—dull-silvery the white willows, and along us the short zealous little monster, poking with pikes in the ice, and the other one, lengthening the nose into the sterile ice-hole. The one-and-a-half eyed one on the river, today we will be the whisperers of the Hylaean reeds!

The connection between Livshits' prose poem and the visual arts is quite explicit. As Livshits later said, the piece was "100% Cubism transferred to the sphere of organized speech; it was not for nothing that, having appropriated the title of this work from one of Léger's paintings, I dedicated it to Alexandra Exter."[21] As we know from Livshits' memoirs, *The One and a Half-Eyed Archer,* he composed this prose poem in Chernianka, the estate of the Burliuks in Southern Russia. Inspired by the photograph of a Picasso painting that they had obtained from Paris, the Burliuk brothers were engaged in turning out one cubist canvas after the other. Livshits, who to his chagrin lacked any talent for painting, tried to do something analogous in poetry. As he later explained, his challenge consisted in creating a correlation between visual and verbal art without falling into the trap of symbolist synaesthesia. Rimbaud's famous sonnet about the color of vowels, in Livshits' opinion, "was a brilliant but unsuccessful example of the subjective approach to the question. It was essential to move into the opposite direction. First and foremost, this meant throwing overboard any sort of specific detail. No concrete colors, no concrete sounds! None of those metaphors which are used with such disgusting flippancy to establish correlations between music and architecture, poetry and music, etc.!"[22]

Livshits understood his poetic venture as a pioneering effort that would help to usher in a new epoch in the history of literature: "The virgin soil had to be dynamited, trails had to be blazed through the dense jungle, while support was mobilized in the visual arts (above all in painting): it was in the visual arts that the banner of the emancipation of material had been raised over forty years ago. It was a path of the most dangerous analogies, of continual disruptions, but there was no choice and I embarked on it."[23] The essence of the new painting consisted for Livshits in a "renewed perception of the world: displaced construction, multiplicity of perspective, seas of black (the Impressionists had rejected black), pandemonium of planes and unprecedented treatment of texture."[24] How then was this new art to be transposed into literature? Livshits gives the following brief summary of the creative principles that were at work in the composition of "Liudi v peizazhe":

> I wanted to displace the visual planes by the unusual use of prepositions and adverbs. The resulting fracture of syntax gave the narrative new direction and, as a whole, formed a complex system of mutually intersecting axes. All metaphors aside, *People in a Landscape* was an experiment in authentic Cubist construction from a verbal mass, one in which the *objective parallelism* of the visual media of two independent art forms was taken to the absolute limit.[25]

Despite its seemingly objective and scientific tone, Livshits' recipe for verbal cubism leaves much unclear. Surely, a "verbal mass" is not quite the same as raw paint on a canvas, given the inherently signifying function of language. Nevertheless, at least on a superficial level the analogy works quite satisfactorily. Just like a cubist painting eschews mimeticism by giving a displaced, fractured representation of visual reality, Livshits' prose poem avoids any superficially coherent linguistic utterance. It becomes clear, however, that Livshits follows a different method from Khlebnikov's word-creation. As he himself acknowledged, "for me the path chosen by Khlebnikov was a forbidden one."[26] Rather than expanding the lexical boundaries of the Russian language, Livshits' concern is what he calls the "fracture of syntax," exemplified by an "unusual use of prepositions." The preposition "o" plays a prominent role in this project, appearing five times in the text. Usually, "o" indicates the reference or point of an utterance or action and is translated as "about," "of," or "concerning." Less commonly, it can be used to describe the properties of something, as in "a table with three legs." None of these translations works well in Livshits' text. If anything, "o" seems to point to some kind of causal relation, demonstrated by the opening statement, "dolgie o grusti" ("long with sadness") or "golubye o kholode" ("blue with cold") in the second stanza. While "o" is not used in a syntactically incorrect way (it is followed by the required prepositional case), it becomes semantically displaced. A similar effect of semantic "scrambling" is achieved through the widespread use of the instrumental case, which creates a kind of free-floating syntactic indeterminacy. Again, Livshits' syntax is not, strictly speaking, ungrammatical, but it stretches the rules of Russian grammar close to the breaking point. In this respect, one could add, he follows the practice of his French models Rimbaud and Mallarmé.

Livshits' use of the instrumental case demonstrates his willingness to rely on the specific resources of the Russian language for achieving his effect of verbal cubism. The same observation can be made about the almost complete absence of conjugated verbs in the text. One could argue that the resulting elliptic, nominal style mimics the fractured lines in a cubist painting. It is true also that such constructions are less unusual in Russian, a language with no articles and where the copula in a predicative sentence is left out in the present tense. In this sense, one might as well connect Livshits' prose poem to the Russian tradition of impressionist "verbless" poetry, as exemplified by the nineteenth-century poet Afanasii Fet. It becomes clear that Livshits' "fractured syntax" is far from being taken to an "absolute limit." The text still preserves the outward trappings of a coherent sentence structure, disposing neither with grammatical concordance nor with punctuation.

Any attempt of crossing over from painting to poetry raises the question of spatial and temporal parameters. How can a work of art that is based on the simultaneous presence of visual elements be translated into the chronological sequence of a verbal utterance? The most radical solution would be a text where, as Suzanne Bernard put it, "the words or members of the phrase are not joined together like musical notes, but rather juxtaposed like spots of color in a painting."[27] As we have seen, Livshits is far from even attempting such a thing. Nevertheless, issues of time and space do arise in his text. The very first word, "dolgie" (long), an adjective only applicable to temporal events, is used here to characterize the first-person agents ("we"), and later the "hyacinth-bearers of December." As a result, the categories of space and time are mixed up, perhaps leading toward something like a fourth dimension. As one of the objectives of cubism, Livshits mentioned the project "to discover the key to the first three dimensions in the fourth."[28]

Faithful to his stated intention of avoiding any kind of cheap metaphorical analogy between painting and poetry, Livshits refrains from indulging in the excessive coloration that was so typical for the prose poems of the fin de siècle. Nevertheless, some colors do appear in his text. Black is one of them, and we remember that Livshits called it an essential ingredient of cubism. More important, light blue (*goluboe*) dominates the second stanza. The author recommends it to "poets and non-provincials" (an allusion to the "provincials" at Chernianka who are already in its possession?). Volkmar Dietsch has detected in this stanza a metaphorical allusion to one of Livshits' aesthetic postulates.[29] In his contribution to the manifesto "My i zapad" ("We and the West," 1914) he demanded a "differentiation of the [verbal] masses according to their various degrees of rarefaction: lithoidal, fluid and phosphenoidal."[30] "Phosphen" was the term used in nineteenth-century physiology for the (mental) image created through pressure on the eyeball. The passage about the heavy blue on the eyelids can thus be understood as an allusion to the highest degree of poetic abstraction. At the same time, the color blue relates to Livshits' vision of cubist primitivism. As he explains, "in the Neanderthal night the retina of the pitheanthropus vaguely reflected only those surfaces which were nearby. The heavy mounds of basalt could hardly be distinguished from the black background of the sky. When would the retina learn once again to react to blue light?" By attuning our eyes to this light, Livshits argues, "we will be able to perceive nature and see her once again with a purity of vision."[31] Livshits' theory of seeing the world as if for the first time resembles the famous de-automatized vision of the formalists, but it also contains overtones of the adamism of the acmeist school of poetry.

"Liudi v peizazhe" operates both as an illustration of verbal cubism and as a sort of manifesto. The metatextual dimension of the piece becomes evident in the various references to poets and poetry. The third stanza could be read as a polemic attack against poetic "orthodoxy," against Bellerophons who are unworthy to ride the futurist Pegasus, creators of "high school ornaments," or poetic pygmies fishing for profundities in sterile ice holes. It would no doubt be a mistake, however, to try to "decode" this text entirely to arrive at some underlying, clear-cut message. Livshits himself expressed his unwillingness to compose a "rebus" or "charade which could be solved piece by piece."[32] The meaning of this prose poem cannot be separated from its fractured syntax and semantics. Rather than a text "about" something, "Liudi v peizazhe" presents an example of a self-sufficient verbal artifact. The only clearly referential statement comes in the last sentence, which functions as a sort of group signature. The one-and-a-half-eyed archer, turning half an eye to the West, served as the emblem of the Hylaeans, who

113

derived their name from the Greek name of the landscape around Chernianka. Perhaps in an effort to counteract or downplay the Western influence
on his concept of art, Livshits turned this figure into an emblem of autoch-
thonous Russian Eurasianism:

> Atavistic strata, diluvian rhythms, confronting the West and sustained by the
> East, approached in a relentless cataclysm, flooded by the light of prehistory.
> And out in front, brandishing his spear, galloped a bold horseman in a cloud
> of rainbow dust, a Scythian warrior who had turned his face back and who
> squinted at the West with only half an eye—the one and a half-eyed archer![33]

Livshits' enthusiasm for verbal cubism gave way later to a more skeptical
attitude. In his memoirs, which were written twenty years after the composition of his prose poem, he described "Liudi v peizazhe" as a form of "mute
prose." He claims that the problem of creating a linguistic equivalent of cubist painting had so absorbed his attention that he "forgot about the other
elements of potential speech: the word, in coming so close to painting,
stopped sounding for me. [. . .] Later I managed to draw back from this
dangerous boundary and to return to the articulatory and melodic sources
of the word, and thence to its saturation with semantic content. I moved full
circle."[34] As we can see, "Liudi v peizazhe" was meant to be absorbed as a
kind of mental image without regard to the verbal signifier. In this sense,
Livshits neglected to pursue an analogy with an aspect of avant-garde painting that he himself had highlighted: the "unprecedented treatment of texture." Compared with the interest of the Hylaean artists in the materiality
of the paint on the canvas, or the preoccupation of the futurist poets with
sound, Livshits' concept of verbal art seems strangely Platonic in its privi-
leging of the signified over the signifier. Livshits' approach to the "verbal
mass" appears thus at the opposite end of the futurist attempt to liberate
the word from the chains of semantic meaning.

Interestingly enough, *A Slap in the Face of Public Taste* offered a further example of prose poetry inspired by analogy with avant-garde painting.
The author was none other than the painter Vasilii Kandinskii. The editors
included the Russian translation of four of Kandinskii's *Klänge* (*Sounds*), a
series of prose poems and woodcuts that had just been published in Munich.[35] Apparently, the Russian cubo-futurists printed these texts without
the author's knowledge or approval. When Kandinskii found out that
Burliuk had included four of his pieces in *A Slap*, he was clearly irritated
and distanced himself publicly from the cubo-futurists in a letter to the editor of the Moscow newspaper *Russkoe Slovo*.[36] Kandinskii composed his
prose poems between 1909 and 1912 during a crucial period in his creative
development marked by the transition from figurative to abstract art. He
originally intended to publish his album of prose poems and woodcuts
with Vladimir Izdebskii, a sculptor acquaintance in Odessa. We know from

114

Kandinskii's correspondence that Izdebskii visited him together with David Burliuk during his stay in Odessa in December 1910.[37] A maquette for the Russian edition is preserved in Kandinskii's estate in Munich. However, this edition, which was to contain seventeen prose poems, never materialized. Instead, the album was brought out by Piper Verlag in the fall of 1912 in a luxuriously produced edition of three hundred copies, containing thirty-eight German prose poems and fifty-six woodcuts.

The almost simultaneous publication of some of these texts in German and Russian raises the question as to which language should be considered the "original." Although Kandinskii wrote some of his prose poems in Russian and later translated them into German, there can be little doubt that the majority of *Klänge* were written directly in German. Some of them contain puns that work only in that language. In "Unverändert" ("Unchanged"), for example, "Banane" becomes "Bann! Ahne!" a polysemic expression that can be translated as either "banish! ancestor!" or "charm! foresee!"; and "Tinten" (inks) turns into "tin-ten," the onomatopoetic imitation of a bell. Even where a Russian version exists, it is not always clear whether it is the original form, or whether it is a self-translation from the German. Boris Sokolov, who undertook a detailed comparison of the German and Russian variants, came to the conclusion that of the twenty-six existing Russian texts, only twelve are probably Russian originals.[38] In other words, *Klänge*, or *Zvuki*, seems to have been a bilingual project from the start. It is noteworthy that Kandinskii used for his literary endeavors both his native Russian and a foreign language (of which he did have a solid command, of course, having learned German in childhood from his Baltic grandmother). As a painter engaging in verbal art, he was also crossing over from one medium to another, or, as Kandinskii later said in his 1938 essay "Mes gravures sur bois," changing instruments by putting the palette aside and using the typewriter in its place.[39] In this sense, *Klänge* represents an example of both artistic and linguistic border crossing, perhaps not unlike Samuel Beckett's switching back and forth between English and French. Interestingly enough, most of the few poems and prose poems that Kandinskii wrote later in his life when he was residing in Paris, are also written in German.[40]

The title *Klänge*, with its allusion to musical sounds, locates Kandinskii's prose poems at the opposite end of Livshits' "mute prose." His intention was not primarily to make language "painterly"—after all, as a painter he could always achieve visual effects in a more direct way—but to apply and test in another medium the creative urge that generated his painting. In addition to painting and poetry, music provided an important third element in this endeavor. In his book *Über das Geistige in der Kunst* (*Concerning the Spiritual in Art*), the writing of which roughly coincided with the composition of *Klänge,* Kandinskii calls music "the best teacher" for the contemporary artist. In his words, "a painter who finds no satisfaction in mere representation, however artistic, in his longing to express his internal life, cannot but envy the ease with which music, the least material of the arts today, achieves this end. He naturally seeks to apply the means of music to his own art. And from this results that modern desire for rhythm in painting, for mathematical, abstract construction, for repeated notes of color, for setting color in motion, and so on."[41]

Although Kandinskii's philosophical idealism, his longing to express an "inner life," differs sharply from the brazen attempt of the cubo-futurists to raise "the banner of the emancipation of material," the results parallel each other to some extent: both attitudes lead to a rejection of the mimetic representation of external reality. In this sense, it is not surprising that the editors of *A Slap in the Face of Public Taste* saw in Kandinskii a potential ally. Had they perused *Über das Geistige in der Kunst* more closely, however, they would have realized that there was a world of difference between Kandinskii's position and their own. Rather than an attempt to throw the art of the past overboard from the ship of modernity, Kandinskii understood his artistic method as the fulfillment of the spiritual mission that had always been the hallmark of great art. With its idealist, mystic, and even occult elements, and with its orientation toward music, Kandinskii's theory of art has much more in common with the symbolists than with the futurists.[42] By highlighting the mutual interdependence of different art forms and posing analogies between specific colors and instrumental sounds, Kandinskii subscribed precisely to the type of symbolist synaesthesia that Livshits derided. Inspired in part by Richard Wagner's idea of the *Gesamtkunstwerk*, Kandinskii dreamt of a future synthetic "monumental art" in which "each art will bring to this general tone its own special characteristics, thereby adding to it a richness and a power which no one art form could achieve."[43] With its beautifully crafted outlook, Kandinskii's bibliophile album of prose poems and woodcuts was diametrically opposed to the deliberately anti-aesthetic *Slap in the Face of Public Taste,* which was produced on gray and brown wrapping paper bound in a cover of coarse sackcloth.

From a literary point of view, Kandinskii's *Klänge* cannot be directly connected with any particular style or school. They combine elements of symbolism and German expressionism while anticipating certain features of Dada and concrete poetry. The fact that Kandinskii himself referred to his texts as prose poems (*Prosagedichte, poèmes en prose*)[44] raises the question to what extent he was working consciously in this generic tradition. It has to be assumed that he was familiar with Baudelaire's and Turgenev's models of the genre, although he never mentions either author. Sokolov has pointed out some common motifs with Baudelaire's *Petits poèmes en prose* and Turgenev's *Stikhotvoreniia v proze,* but they remain too vague to prove a concrete borrowing.[45] Within the German tradition, Kandinskii's style of prophetic aphorism certainly owes a debt to Nietzsche's *Zarathustra.* Regardless of the specific influence of preexisting models, it is obvious that the form of the prose poem corresponded ideally to Kandinskii's idea of a synthetic art and his project of crossing boundaries between different artistic media, languages, and genres.

The various *Klänge* are quite heterogeneous in nature and cannot easily be reduced to a common poetic formula. Lyric effusions mingle with absurdist minimalist tales, an abundance of colors in some pieces contrasts with a lack of color in others. The influence of music makes itself felt in frequent repetitive patterns, moving from a denotative to a purely suggestive form of language. At the same time, Kandinskii's syntax can be of an extremely laconic, almost childlike simplicity. In this respect, Kandinskii's colloquial prose style lies closer to the primitivism of the futurists than to the verbal refinement of symbolist poetics. "Kletka" ("Cage"), the first of the four prose poems printed in *A Slap,* will provide an example of Kandinskii's verbal art:

Клетка

Это было разорвано. Я взял за оба конца обеими руками и держал концы друг к другу. Вокруг что-то росло. Со всех сторон прямо-таки вокруг меня. Но ничего этого не было видно. Я и думал, ничего нет. А вперед я не мог. Я был как муха под стаканом. Т.е. ничего не видно, а не пройти. Было даже пусто. Совсем одиноким стояло передо мной дерево, скорее деревцо. Листья совсем, как медянка, зеленые. Крепкие, как железо, и твердые, как железо. Маленькие, кроваво-светящиеся яблочки висели на ветках.

Вот и все, что было.[46]

Cage

It was torn. I took both ends in both hands and held the ends together. Something grew around. From all sides directly around me. But nothing of it could be seen.

Indeed, I thought there was nothing there. And yet I could not move forward. I was like a fly under a glass. I. e., nothing visible, yet still you cannot pass through. It was even empty. Completely alone in front of me stood a tree, or rather a sapling. Its leaves completely green like verdigris. Strong like iron and hard like iron. Little bloodshimmering apples hung from its branches.

That was all.

With its paratactic laconicity and externally illogical narrative, Kandinskii's story resembles most of all Remizov's dream narratives. It is interesting to note that Kandinskii was in fact well acquainted with Remizov's dreams and even illustrated some of them.[47] The opening sentences establish an aura of semantic indeterminacy reminiscent of a nightmare. Something is torn in two, but we are not told what it is. Something grows, but we cannot see it, and something impedes the narrator's movements, although he thinks that nothing is there. This oscillation between visibility and invisibility, presence and absence, can be connected to Kandinskii's theory of art. As Elizabeth Napier pointed out, "in a world in which change has become a factor of relevance, man's capacity to adjust and understand his environment depends critically upon his ability to perceive. For Kandinsky, moments of impotence and confusion are typically moments of not seeing. [. . .] A similar dilemma is described in *Käfig*. Here, the narrator's inability to apprehend his surroundings has been reified as an invisible cage which arrests his forward movement."[48] The unexpected epiphany of the apple tree, with its explosion of colors, presents a possible resolution. Its artificial, metallic appearance blurs the line between nature and art. The fact that it is still a sapling points perhaps to the possibility of future growth. The image of the tree is a frequently occurring motif both in the prose poems and the woodcuts of *Klänge*. As Patrick McGrady has pointed out, these iconographic and textual references could be read as an allusion to the biblical Tree of Life.[49] As abruptly as the tree appears in the text, as suddenly is the story cut short. "That was all," declares the narrator in an ending that seems to anticipate the style of Daniil Kharms' miniatures.

Some of Kandinskii's *Klänge* are of an even more abstract nature. "Videt'" ("Seeing"), which was also included in *A Slap*, sounds like a verbal recreation of a nonfigurative painting. The programmatic nature of this text is underlined by the fact that Kandinskii later used it as the opening piece for the Russian version of his memoirs, entitled *V. V. Kandinskii. Tekst khudozhnika. Stupeni* (*V. V. Kandinskii. Text of the Artist. Steps*), which came out in Moscow in 1918. As Boris Sokolov has shown, this version of "Videt'" is based on the *Slap* publication rather than the original Russian text kept in the Munich archive.[50] A major difference concerns the typographical arrangement of the text on the page. Whereas the two later Russian versions follow the German translation (of which they are in fact a re-translation) by breaking up the text into a new paragraph with almost every sentence, the original Russian text has a much more compact, "prosaic" feel:

Видеть

Синее поднялось, поднялось и упало. Острое, тонкое свистнуло и вонзилось, но не проткнуло. Ухнуло по всем концам. Густокоричневое повисло будто навеки. Будто навеки повисло. Будто, будто, будто ... Будто. Шире разведи руками. Пошире, пошире. А красным платком закрой свое лицо. А, может быть, оно вовсе еще не сдвинулось, а сдвинулся только ты. Белый скачок за белым скачком. А за этим белым скачком еще один белый скачок. Вот нехорошо, что ты не видишь мути: в мути-то оно и есть. Отсюда все и начинается ....
Треснуло ....[51]

Seeing

Blue rose up, rose up and fell. Sharp, thin whistled and pressed in, but could not pierce through. There was a crying [or banging] in every corner. Dense brown hung seemingly for ever. Seemingly, seemingly, seemingly . . . Seemingly. Stretch your arms out wider. Wider. Wider.

And cover your face with red cloth. And maybe it has not shifted yet at all, but only you have shifted. White leap after white leap.[52]

And after this white leap another white leap. It is not good that you don't see the murk: in the murk is where it is.

From here is where it all starts ....
.... It crashed ....

The version published in *A Slap*, which closely follows the German text, differs not only in its typographic layout, but in some other important respects as well. Interestingly, the verbs in the opening sentences have switched from the perfective to the imperfective aspect. As a result, what had been the narrative of a one-time "event" turns into the description of an ongoing process. The capitalization of the color nouns prompted by the rules of German grammar gives the Russian text an aura of heightened allegorization. Given the fact that Kandinskii himself is the author of the German translation, it would be misguided to treat the (first) Russian text as the sacrosanct "original" and the German and subsequent Russian versions as merely imperfect copies. On the contrary, one could argue that the German translation constitutes Kandinskii's further development and hence more perfect realization of his initial creative design. This would explain why Kandinskii used for his 1918 Moscow publication not the original Russian text, but a Russian calque of the German translation.[53] Here is the text as it appeared in *A Slap:*

Видеть

Синее, Синее поднималось, поднималось и падало.

Острое, Тонкое свистело, вонзалось, но не протыкало.

По всем концам грохнуло. Толстокоричневое повисло будто на все времена.

Будто. Будто.

Шире расширь свои руки.

Шире. Шире.

А лицо свое покрой красным платком.

И может быть, еще ничего не сдвинулось: только ты сдвинулся.

За белым скачком белый скачок.

А за этим белым скачком еще белый скачок.

И в этим белом скачке белыи скачок. В каждом белом скачке белый скачок.

Вот то то и не хорошо, что ты не видишь Мутное: в Мутном то оно и сидит.

119

Отсюда-то все и начинается ....
........................Треснуло ....[54]

Seeing

Blue, Blue was rising up, rising up and falling.
   Sharp, Thin was whistling and pressing in, but could not pierce through.
   From every corner came a banging.
   Fat Brown hung seemingly for all eternity.
   Seemingly. Seemingly.
   Stretch your arms out wider.
   Wider. Wider.
   And cover your face with red cloth.
   And maybe nothing has shifted yet: only you have shifted.
   White leap after white leap.
And after this white leap another white leap. And in this white leap a white leap. In every white leap a white leap.
   But that's not good, that you don't see the Turbid: the Turbid is where it sits.
   From here is where it all starts ....
.... It crashed ....

One understands the enthusiasm of the Russian cubo-futurists for this text. With its radical abstractionism and rhetoric of "shifts," "leaps," and "crashes," Kandinskii seems to parallel here the verbal revolutions of the futurists. "Videt'," or rather its German version "Sehen," also became a favorite text of the Zurich dadaists. Hugo Ball included it in the proto-Dadaist magazine *Cabaret Voltaire* in 1916, and Jean Arp later praised *Klänge* in an essay of 1951 as "one of the extraordinary great books. . . . These works breathe the secrets of eternal and unexplored depths. Forms arise, as powerful as talking mountains. Sulphur and poppy stars blossom at the lips of the sky."[55] In a few cases, Kandinskii does indeed engage in verbal pyrotechnics that are reminiscent of futurism both in their reliance on neologisms and their fractured syntax.[56] However, *Klänge* is hardly an exercise in pure abstraction. The new seeing that "Videt'" announces has to be understood as a spiritual vision. Like many other pieces in the cycle, "Videt'" has apocalyptic overtones, describing a destructive cataclysm as the necessary condition for spiritual rebirth. In this sense, as Claudia Emmert has suggested, the title "Seeing" can be related to the frequently occurring formula "And I saw . . ." in the Book of Revelation.[57]

   The piece opens with the evocation of seemingly disembodied colors and shapes.[58] Kandinskii's theoretical writings on art shed some light on the use of colors in "Videt'." In *Über das Geistige in der Kunst*, he characterizes blue as the quintessential heavenly color, whereas white represents "a silence . . . pregnant with possibilities."[59] "Sharp" and "thin" are semantically related to a another color which is perhaps implied here, although it is not named in the text: yellow.[60] As in "Kletka," there is a sense of arrested movement and confinement: something is trying, at first unsuccessfully, to break through. The rising colors come to challenge the seeming permanence of brown, which Kandinskii describes as "unemotional, disinclined to movement."[61] This "murk" will be the starting point of the coming revolution. It is possible that the left-leaning Russian futurists read the toppling of brown, the overcoming of "bourgeois" inertia through the dynamic forces of primary colors, as at least in part a political allegory. In Kandinskii's understanding, however, it certainly points to the triumph of the spiritual over materialism. The admonition to open one's arms wider, that is to assume the position of the Crucifixion, seems to call for an *imitatio Christi.* As Patrick McGrady has observed, the same image occurs in the woodcut preceding the text, which represents the unleashing of apocalyptic chaos.[62] Claudia Emmert reads the triple repetition of "seemingly" as an allusion to the Trinity, and the twofold naming of "blue" as a reference to the Old and New Testaments.[63] But Kandinskii's syncretic concept of spirituality is only partially based on Christian beliefs. In her study on Kandinskii and Old Russia, Peg Weiss has highlighted the elements of Russian paganism and folklore in *Klänge,* based in part on Kandinskii's own ethnographic research in the Russian north. In "Videt'," for example, the seemingly enigmatic red cloth may be a reference to the practice of the Samoyed shaman who "shamanized with a cloth stiched with red thread over his eyes to indicate that he would see into the world of the spirits with his 'inner eye.'"[64] Kandinskii's interest in folklore and shamanism is akin to Remizov's artistic pursuits, and, within Russian futurism, to Khlebnikov's verbal incantations.

It becomes clear that by treating Kandinskii as a mere promoter of abstract art, we miss the essential thrust of his spiritual message. A modernist more by circumstance than by design, Kandinskii created a sort of "abstractionism with a human face" that opposed itself to the hard-edged, formalist approach of the cubists.[65] Interspersed with Kandinskii's "abstract" prose poems, one can also find texts of an entirely figurative nature, such as the following minimalist sketch, which only exists in the German version:

Vorfrühling

Ein Herr nahm in der Straße seinen Hut ab. Ich sah schwarz-weiße, fest mit Pomade rechts und links vom Scheitel klebende Haare.

Ein anderer Herr nahm seinen Hut ab. Ich sah eine große rosige, etwas fette Glatze mit bläulichem Glanzlicht.

Die beiden Herren sahen sich an, gegenseitig zeigten sie sich schiefe, gräulich gelbliche Zähne mit Plomben.[66]

Early Spring

A man on the street took off his hat. I saw black-and-white hair stuck down to the right and left of his part with hair cream.

Another man took off his hat. I saw a big pink, slightly greasy bald spot with a bluish highlight.

The two men looked at one another, each showing the other crooked, greyish yellowish teeth with fillings.[67]

This grotesque scene of urban life, which so radically deceives the expectations triggered by its title, seems to have more in common with the satirical drawings of George Grosz than with Kandinskii's own paintings. The use of colors, however, corresponds to the theory outlined in *Über das Geistige*. In spiritual terms, the picture represents a hateful "fallen" reality dominated by the lifeless color grey resulting from the mixing of black and white.[68] The inkling of pink and blue seems to announce the dawning of a new era which has not yet arrived—a *Vorfrühling* rather than a *Frühling*.

The fact that Kandinskii published his prose poems together with his woodcuts in a luxury album seems to lend support to Michel Beaujour's contention that there is an intimate connection between the genre of the prose poem and the "Préface d'exposition" or catalogue blurb. As Beaujour puts it: "The album, often issued by art galleries rather than regular publishers and intended for a wealthy public of connoisseurs and speculators, provided the French prose poem with the sort of *framing* necessary to support the claims that a prose text can indeed be poetic."[69] It would be too simplistic, however, to simply regard Kandinskii's prose poems as a comment on his woodcuts, or, vice versa, the woodcuts as an illustration of the prose poems. The relationship between text and image is in fact rather complex. The matter is complicated by the fact that the German edition of *Klänge* follows a different arrangement than the originally planned Russian edition. Like the prose poems, Kandinskii's woodcuts are quite heterogeneous in nature. Some are in color, some in black and white, and they range from a stylized representationalism reminiscent of *Jugendstil* and Russian folk art to total abstraction.[70] Richard Sheppard has argued that, rather than establishing a direct correspondence between individual texts and images, Kandinskii's woodcuts form a sequence that roughly parallels the development of the prose poems. As he puts it, "in visual terms, *Klänge* moves, gradually and haltingly, towards a sense that higher meaning, pattern, spirituality can emerge out of demonic conflict and the trials of pilgrimage."[71] Initially, images of violent conflict and centripetality prevail. As the work progresses, the style moves toward abstraction and a predominant circular pattern, Kandinskii's emblem of spirituality. Predominant imagery throughout the cycle includes a horse and horseman and allusions to crucifixion. The rider, a frequent figure in Kandinskii's oeuvre of the Munich period, could be read both as an apocalyptic allusion, a reference to St. George, or, as Peg Weiss has noted, as an image of the "World-Watching-Man and of the horse-riding shaman."[72]

The most thorough analysis of the relation between the prose poems and the woodcuts in *Klänge* can be found in Patrick McGrady's unpublished

Ph.D. thesis.[73] The author makes a convincing case that the correspondence between text and image is much closer than had previously been assumed. Although McGrady is quite compelling in showing the correlation between individual texts and images, even he has to admit that in some cases the specific placement of a poem or woodcut seems to defy explanation. In this sense, Kandinskii's *Klänge* preserves an element of mystery that seems to remain impenetrable to critical inquiry.

No discussion of the Russian futurist prose poem will be complete without mentioning the oeuvre of one more poet and artist who worked in this genre: Elena Guro (1887–1913). A painter by training, Guro was associated with the cubo-futurists and participated in their miscellanies (although not in *A Slap*). Her gentleness, delicacy, and spirituality form a sharp contrast to the boisterous machismo of her futurist colleagues. In fact, she has more in common with Kandinskii, of whom she was an early admirer. In a note that she wrote after visiting the twelfth exhibition of the Moscow Association of Artists in Petersburg in 1905, Guro praised the "fairy-tale like (*skazochnyi*) Kandinskii with his dense velvety fairy-tale tones of purple, emerald and azure."[74] Her evocation of a painting by Kandinskii featuring a couple on horseback, accompanied by "romantic swans," although in keeping with Kandinskii's neo-romantic work of that time, does not seem to correspond to any known picture by Kandinskii. Rather than assuming that "the work has probably been lost," as Nina Gourianova does,[75] one could also speculate that Guro's text is not the description of an actual painting, but a work of verbal art inspired by the example of Kandinskii's pictorial style.

Guro's literary tastes had much in common with those of Kandinskii. Among her favorite authors were Blok, Belyi, and Remizov, as well as the French and Belgian symbolists and decadents. It is certain that her sustained interest in the creative possibilities of the prose miniature was at least in part inspired by Baudelaire. Her undated sketch "Gavan'" ("Port") is a literal translation of Baudelaire's prose poem "Le Port."[76] Guro's use of the generic title *"stikhotvorenie v proze"* further indicates her indebtedness to her French models.[77] Lyric prose miniatures play an important role in all of Guro's poetic oeuvre. Vladimir Markov has argued that Guro's main historical importance may lie precisely in her "conscious effort to obliterate the difference between prose and verse."[78] In a diary entry of 1912, Guro specified her project of turning "prose into verse, verse into prose." She mentions "pieces of plot (*kuski fabul*) taken as colors and as leitmotivs," "concentration of the plot in two, three words," and "musical symphonism."[79] Her fusion of poetic, painterly, and musical elements is reminiscent of Kandinskii's *Klänge*, while the blurring of boundaries between verse and prose parallels Remizov's and Khlebnikov's early writings. Guro also shared with these writers an interest in Russian folklore and the worldview and artistic sensibility of children.

123

In her poetic practice, Guro was less radical than her fellow futurists. Overall, her style could be characterized as impressionistic. Many of her miniatures are lyric evocations of the Finnish landscape on the Karelian Isthmus north of St. Petersburg where she used to spend her summers, such as the following untitled fragment from the volume *Nebesnye verbli-uzhata* (*Baby Camels of the Sky*, 1913):

В лучезарной бледности небо. В раздавшихся в обе стороны светлых перьях облаков—знак ширины, знак полета, и во все это врезались мачтами кресты елок.

В ветвях сосен и всюду дремлют тысячи сонных ритмов.

Сосны испускают столько молчания, что оно поглощает звуки.

Золотые стволы, люди, дни, мысли—погружены, как рыбы, в светлый июнь.

Я молюсь покровителям тихим с крыльями широкими и нежными, как большое море и тихая дюна.[80]

The sky is radiantly pale. In the bright feathers of clouds as they spread—there's a sign of their span, a sign of soaring, and the fir's crosses cut like masts into all that.

In pine boughs—everywhere—thousands of sleepy rhythms drowse.

Pines give forth so much silence that it devours sound. Days, golden trunks, thoughts, people are immersed like fish, in bright June.

I pray to the quiet protectors, with their wings wide and tender, like a vast sea and a quiet dune.[81]

Guro's prose poem metaphorically combines clouds, pine trees, and the sea into a unified spiritual landscape. Like Kandinskii's *Klänge*, her miniatures include religious and musical overtones, as becomes evident in her use of crosses and praying and reference to rhythms, sounds, and silence. Curiously, it is precisely the absence of sound that creates an atmosphere of "abstract" musicality.

Two of Guro's prose poems seem inspired by "L'Etranger," the famous opening piece of Baudelaire's *Petits poèmes en prose* ending in a paean to clouds. Clouds, as we have seen from the previous quote, play a major role in Guro's poetics (one wonders whether her "Baby Camels of the Sky" did not originate in the whimsical interpretation of a cloud formation). A text with the generic title "*Stikhotvorenie v proze,*" first published only in 1919, evokes the spectacle of slowly moving clouds.[82] *Nebesnye verbli-uzhata* features a miniature dialog which imitates the form of "L'Etranger." As in Baudelaire's prose poem, the questioner in Guro's text addresses the poetic persona in the second-person singular, while the speaker answers back using the second-person plural. This distinction between informal and formal address marks the poetic speaker as a child or social inferior. Whereas Baudelaire's "L'Etranger" expresses a feeling of alienation, however, Guro focuses on a positive, childlike sense of connectedness with nature:

—Любишь ли ты песок?

—Люблю, он мягкий.

—Любишь ли ты сосну?

—Люблю, если к ней прижмешься щекой с солнечной стороны—она теплая . . .

—А ты любишь лошадь?

—Люблю. У нее милые ноздри.

—Ты любишь ли море?

—Да. Я заметил, в тихие дни оно любит меня.

—Ты любишь ли землю?

—Как вы можете это спрашивать, ведь она . . . —мне мать![83]

"Do you love sand?"

"I love it, it's soft."

"Do you love pines?"

"I love them—if you press a cheek against their sunny side, they're warm."

"And do you love that horse?"

"I love her. She has nice nostrils."

"Do you love the sea?"

"Yes. I've noticed that on quiet days it loves me."

"Do you love the earth?"

"How can you ask, after all, she's my mother!"[84]

The rather simple content of this dialogue is enhanced by its lilting sound effect, relying on the flow of the soft "l" generated by the repetion of "liubish' li" and "liubliu." The "Franciscan" communion with nature recalls Aleksandr Dobroliubov's collection *Iz knigi nevidimoi.* Guro's husband Mikhail Matiushin mentions Dobroliubov as one of her favorite writers.[85] Parallels exist not only on the level of content, but also in the similar form of both books, mixing prose miniatures with free verse poetry.[86]

Beside her prose poems, Guro practiced an even more laconic genre. Her "études," as she called them, are extremely condensed sketches of no more than a few words. A study of Guro's manuscripts reveals that she adopted this technique relatively late in her career.[87] Guro's impressionism achieves in these miniatures a *haiku*-like formal condensation. The minimalist style of these "études" parallels the simplified visual shapes in Guro's drawings. In the following example, the sparsity of form is motivated by the seasonal content of the piece. The text both evokes and embodies the concept of silence:

Осень

Сухой металлический шум деревьев.

———————

Черные металлические отражения уходят в свинцовую (молчаливую) глубь молчания.

———————

Молчанье над зимовкой барок. Скрипнуло и замолкло. Ставни домов закрыты. Все приготовилось к осаде.[88]

Fall

The dry metallic noise of trees.

————◆◆◆◆————

Black metallic reflections sink into the leaden (silent) depth of silence.

————◆◆◆◆————

Silence over the wintering of barges. It creaked and fell silent. The shutters of the houses are closed. Everything is prepared for the siege.

None of the texts discussed thus far lends much credence to Guro's classification as a futurist, and some futurists in fact questioned her belonging to this movement altogether. Livshits rather condescendingly called her work a "mixture of Maeterlinck and Jammes diluted with Russian kissel" (a kind of blancmange), and spoke about "the silent melopeia of lifeless words which Guro used to translate her astral luminescence into spoken language."[89] On the other hand, Guro was held in high esteem by Khlebnikov and, oddly enough, by Kruchenykh, perhaps the most radical of the cubo-futurists. The volume *Troe* (*The Three*), which came out a few months after Guro's premature death from leukemia in 1913, contained works by Guro, Khlebnikov, and Kruchenykh, with illustrations by Kazimir Malevich. Among Guro's contributions is the prose miniature "Skripka Pikasso" ("Picasso's Violin"), which provides an example of Guro's approach to the cubist avant-garde:

Скрипка Пикассо

В светлой тени на мраморе трепет люстры.

В имени счастливого полустрадальца, всю поднятость мучений на дощечке с золотым блеском черт выразило королевство тени нервными углами.

И длинный корпус музыканта, вырезанный вытянутым жилетом, был продолжением и выгибом истомленного грифа. Изворотиком гениальным скрипки очаровано скрытое духа и страна белых стен, и настал туман белой музыки и потонувшее в мир немоты, уводящее из вещей.

Избалованный страдалец с лицом иссиня бледным на диване, простерши измученные руки и протянув длинный подбородок к свету.

И как он, почти умирали цветы в хрустальном стакане с водой.[90]

Picasso's Violin

In the bright shadow on the marble the trembling of a chandelier.

In the name of the happy semi-sufferer, the whole liftedness of pains on the little plank with the golden brilliance of lines was expressed by the kingdom of the shadow in nervous angles.

And the long body of the musician, cut out with a drawn-in waistcoat, was the continuation and curve of the exhausted finger-board. A brilliant little twist of the violin enchants the secrets of the spirit and the country of white walls, and the fog of white music has begun, and what has sunk into the world of muteness, leading away from the things. The spoiled sufferer with a bluish-pale face on the couch, extending tired-out hands and stretching his long chin toward the light.

And like him, the flowers in the crystal glass with water almost died.

The title seems to be a reference to the violins and musicians appearing in many of Picasso's paintings of the cubist period, although no particular work comes to mind as a concrete model. As in her earlier sketch of Kandinskii, Guro uses the oeuvre of a visual artist as the springboard for the composition of an independent artistic text. "Skripka Pikasso" follows to some extent the poetics of cubism used by Livshits in "Liudi v peizazhe," featuring a complex, "angular" texture of imagery and a syntax characterized by a dearth of conjugated verbs. We can also find a (not particularly bold) neologism: "podniatost'" ("liftedness"). Nevertheless, the overall effect points in the direction of impressionism rather than cubism. As Nils Ake Nilsson has observed, the color of the face and the pathetic gesture of the spectator suggest Picasso's "blue period" rather than his cubist phase.[91] The elongated body of the violinist is also reminiscent of Marc Chagall. As far as literary models are concerned, the piece resembles most of all Innokentii Annenskii's dreamlike, synaesthetic evocations of musical sensations with their mixture of aesthetic bliss and existential pain.[92] A certain similarity also exists with one of Vsevolod Garshin's prose poems, where the sound of a cello evokes the pale face of his dying friend, the poet Semen Nadson.[93] Markov certainly has a point when he notes that in Guro's piece, Picasso receives a "turn-of-the-century, decadent treatment."[94]

In summary, we notice once again the wide spectrum of the futurist prose miniature. The attempt to translate the advances of modernist painting into prose stretched from fin de siècle impressionism to hard-edged cubist abstraction. Overall, the formalist approach of Livshits remained an exception, however. Khlebnikov's, Kandinskii's, and Guro's spiritualism and interest in the traditions of Russian folklore seem more representative for the culture of Russian modernism as a whole, which remained rooted to a large extent in the mystic quests of the symbolist generation and had little patience for the practice of "art for art's sake." In this sense, the fragmentation of the modernist prose text, the departure from traditional syntax and vocabulary, and the abolition of boundaries between poetry and prose served ultimately not a destructive, but a constructive purpose: the movement toward a syncretic, utopian "total art" of the future.

This optimistic, Promethean view of the role of art and literature was to become shattered in the work of a writer who began his career as a belated member of the futurist avant-garde. Daniil Kharms' minimalist "anti-stories" will be the subject of our next and final chapter.

127

Chapter Eight

Daniil Kharms' Minimalist Prose

DANIIL KHARMS' ultra-short prose works belong to the more baffling phenomena of twentieth-century Russian literature. A reader accustomed to traditional narratives will be quick to interpret these "mini-stories," with their utter lack of a conventional plot, as evidence for the typical avant-garde gesture of radical rupture from established norms. Nevertheless, it seems unsatisfactory to simply classify Kharms' oeuvre as a form of destructive "anti-literature" and leave it at that. It has long been recognized that even the most radical avant-garde aesthetic is in many ways indebted to a preexisting tradition. An example that readily comes to mind is Kazimir Malevich's suprematism, whose radical departure from realist figuration is rooted in the spiritualist geometry of Russian icon painting. Likewise, it can be argued that Kharms' (anti-) narrative prose did not emerge ex nihilo, but belongs to a specific generic tradition.

In his introduction to his landmark 1991 volume of Kharms criticism, Neil Cornwell made a remark that establishes a direct connection between Kharms' writings and the topic of this book. He notes that "the prose miniature—a form which Kharms may ultimately be judged to have made his own—has long been a genre more commonly found in Russian literature than elsewhere."[1] Casting a rather wide net, Cornwell mentions Dostoevskii's feuilletons, Turgenev's prose poems, the shortest stories of Garshin and Chekhov, and from the twentieth century, short pieces by Zamiatin, Olesha, and Zoshchenko, as well as the aphoristic writings of Siniavskii and the prose poems of Solzhenitsyn (the latter two, of course, postdating Kharms). This inventory is far from exhaustive, to be sure, and Cornwell did not follow up further on any of these connections.

The only attempt thus far to link Kharms' short prose with a concrete generic model from Russian literature is Ellen Chances' 1982 article on Kharms and Chekhov. Chances observed a row of parallels between Chekhov's short stories and Kharms' mini-stories, such as the incorporation of dramatic techniques into the narrative, the abundance of ostentatiously superfluous details, the use of zero endings, repetition as a structural device, children as narrators, a stark confrontation of beauty and ugliness, and so

on. However, Chances stresses as much the differences as the similarities between the two authors. Despite his modernist techniques, Chekhov, according to Chances, ultimately remains grounded in reality, whereas Kharms
engages in a sort of parodistic verbiage devoid of any referential meaning.
The Chekhovian story mutates into the Kharmsian anti-story, which Chances
finds lacking not only in referentiality, but also in relevance. As she notes
with some exasperation: "But so what? What has Xarms proved? What is he
saying? And who cares?"[2]

It seems clear that, whatever Kharms' attitude to Chekhov may have
been,[3] Chekhov's short stories do not constitute the only, or even the principal, generic model for Kharms' mini-stories. In this final chapter, I will
elaborate on Cornwell's insight by highlighting the similarities between
Kharms' mini-stories and the various Russian minimalist prose miniatures
that have been discussed earlier. As we have seen in the first chapter of this
book, laconicity and simplicity alone are not sufficient to qualify a text as
"minimalist." What is required is a conscious flaunting of established norms
of narrativity or literariness. Brevity, although not universally regarded as a
necessary ingredient of literary mimimalism, does play a crucial role in this
project. Kharms' minimalist stories test our threshold of generic acceptance
by consciously underbidding the minimal length that we consider necessary
for a text to qualify as a "story." This phenomenon is best illustrated with a
concrete example. The text I propose to look at is Kharms' "Vstrecha" ("A
Meeting"), the nineteenth piece in the cycle "Sluchai" ("Incidents"):

Встреча

Вот однажды один человек пошел на службу, да по дороге встретил
другого человека, который, купив польский батон, направлялся к себе
восвояси.
Вот, собственно, и все.[4]

A Meeting

The other day a man went to work, but on his way, he met another man, who
had bought a loaf of Polish bread and was on his way home, to his own place.
That's about all.[5]

The text contains several elements that we can associate with conventional
narrativity. It features a title and an opening formula which looks like the
traditional beginning of a story: a deictic marker (*vot*) points to a specific
temporal moment (*odnazhdy*) and individual (*odin chelovek*), whom we expect to be the principal character in the event that is going to unfold. The
rest of the opening sentence, introducing a second character, is hardly surprising, either. It confirms our expectations triggered by the title: since the
story is called "A Meeting," we expect the protagonist to encounter another
character. The fact that this person is carrying a *pol'skii baton*, a common

type of bread at that time, seems to add an element of daily-life realism. Several questions arise at this point: Does the narrator mention this detail simply for the sake of "atmosphere," or will the bread play a role in the story? At the same time, a potential tension, or conflict, arises: one character is going to work, while the other is going home. Why? Are they working on separate shifts? Does the first character perhaps resent the fact that he has to go to work, while the other one will be relaxing at home with his newly acquired loaf of bread? Have they met before, or are they complete strangers?

We will never know, of course. Just at the moment when our curiosity is triggered about the possible ramifications of this narrative opening gambit, the story is cut short. From his exposition, the narrator switches abruptly to a closing formula. This unexpected ending forces us to reconsider what we have just read. It turns out that what we have been considering was not the beginning of a story after all, it *was* the story. The encounter promised in the title did indeed happen, and, as it turns out, there is nothing else left to say. Although all the outward trappings of a conventional story, such as a title, an opening, and a conclusion, are present in the text, these elements seem to fulfill merely a structural, but not a functional role. As Jean-Philippe Jaccard has noted in his discussion of Kharms' ministories, "every element is in place (subject, title, plot, characters, etc.), but the participation of each of them in the narration frequently amounts to zero [. . .], similar to a car in which the steering wheel is in the correct place, but not connected to the wheels."[6]

The matter-of-fact tone of the narrator precludes speculations that the reported event is anything else than what it appears to be: two men crossing paths in the street, each going about his own business. To be sure, the fleeting anonymous encounter between strangers in the metropolis is a favorite topos of literary modernism, expressed perhaps most poignantly in Baudelaire's famous sonnet "A une passante." But there is no sense at all of portentous fatefulness and tragically missed opportunity in Kharms' deadpan narrative. What Kharms seems to be presenting is a simple, unadorned "slice of life" of utter banality, akin to the stack of bricks or plywood boxes of minimalist sculpture. The only shocking aspect of this story is the fact that it is told at all, since, after all, there seems to be nothing worth telling. The reader is left with the same frustration that might befall an art lover who visits a museum or gallery in search of aesthetic illumination and encounters only piles of bricks and stacks of plywood.

If "Vstrecha" leaves the reader's desire for narrative gratification unfulfilled, alternative approaches of reading prove equally unproductive. The text lacks the polished form or aesthetic appeal that we would associate with poetry, the pithily stated wisdom of a philosophical aphorism, or the witticism of an anecdote. Neither does it invite symbolic or allegoric interpretation. Even the notion of the fragment, so central to both romantic and modernist aesthetics, proves less than helpful in this case. "Vstrecha" is not presented as the broken splinter of a shattered whole, longing for a lost state of completeness. It seems in fact quite complete in itself. Just like a piece of minimalist sculpture, it is simply "there," a stubborn irritant to hermeneutic deciphering.

We can conclude then that the point of this story is hardly its "content," which is truly minimal. Rather, the focus of interest becomes the act of storytelling itself. Although there seems to be no content worth telling, the narrator nevertheless engages in an (aborted) act of narration. The reader's frustrated search for narrative gratification foregrounds the situation of literary consumption. The "encounter" thematized in the title of the story also relates to the relationship between reader and text.[7] In his study of French minimalist fiction, Warren Motte has pointed out that "minimalists invest very heavily indeed in the encounter, relying on the carefully constructed immediacy of their work and wagering boldly on the notion of *presence*."[8] As Jaccard has shown, Kharms' narrator focuses his lens on a specific "point zéro" in space and time. The characters of the story only exist for the brief moment in which they linger in the narrator's field of vision. Once they walk out of it, they disappear from the narration as well, and the story grinds to a halt.[9] This situation leads to a host of interrelated questions, which, mutatis mutandis, relate to any work of minimalist art: What do we expect from a story? What makes a story worth telling? Is a story in which nothing particular happens still a story?

Mary Louise Pratt has argued that the quality of "tellability" involves the narration of something "unusual, contrary to expectations, or otherwise problematic."[10] Kharms' mini-story seems to offer none of this. At best, the mere fact that the story is told could be called unusual, contrary to expectation and problematic. In this sense, Kharms' narrative strategy differs from the poetics of the "insignificant event" of such authors as Chekhov and Zoshchenko, where, as Cathy Popkin has shown, the violation of minimum standards of tellability is only apparent, since the seemingly trivial event emerges ultimately as "enormously significant."[11] Kharms' text remains stubbornly insignificant. According to the terminology established by the narratologist Gerald Prince, "Vstrecha" does not even qualify as a "minimal story," since the event reported by the narrator does not entail a qualitative change.[12]

The extreme brevity of "Vstrecha" constitutes one of the key elements of Kharms' poetics. As he noted in his diary, "Mnogoslovie mat' bezdarnosti" ("verbosity is the mother of mediocrity").[13] "Vstrecha" is by no means his shortest work. Many of Kharms' stories seem nothing more than "microtexts of concise inconsequentiality,"[14] as demonstrated by the following example: "An old man was scratching his head with both hands. In places where he couldn't reach with both hands, he scratched himself with one,

131

but very, very fast (*bystro-bystro*). And while he was doing it he blinked rapidly (*bystro*)."[15] Despite the furious activity described in this text, no narrative gain ensues. The word *bystro* (fast) which is repeated three times, functions as a metafictional comment: the story goes by so fast that it is over before it has really begun.[16]

The sudden death which befalls many of Kharms' characters could be read as another metanarrative allegory. Frequently, the story comes to a premature end through the passing away of the protagonist, such as in the following example: "A man with a stupid face ate an entre-côte, hiccuped and died. The waiters carried him into the corridor leading to the kitchen and put him on the floor along the wall, covering him with a dirty table-cloth."[17] Instead of a dramatic or tragic occurrence, death is presented as a banal nonevent. Ultimately, Kharms seems to mobilize his narratives liter-ally *for nothing.* Consider the following beginning of a story: "At 2 o'clock in the afternoon on Nevskii Prospekt, or rather, on the Prospekt of October 25, nothing particular happened."[18] Specific parameters of time and space are provided here only to serve as a framework for a zero-event.

It is important to note that such a reductionist approach was by no means Kharms' invention. The Russian avant-garde, of which Kharms was a belated member, had long experimented with minimal forms of writing. As the most extreme example and *non plus ultra* of a minimalist text in Rus-sian literature, mention should be made of "Poema kontsa" ("The Poem of the End"), the final piece in the collection *Smert' iskusstvu* (*Death to Art,* 1913) written by the futurist poet Vasilisk Gnedov (1890–1978). The poem consists of a page that, except for the title, number, and publisher's seal at the bottom, is left blank. Gnedov thus anticipated comparable phenomena in the realms of twentieth-century visual art and music, such as Yves Klein's notorious exhibition in the Iris Clert Gallery, Paris, in April 1958, which consisted of empty, white-washed walls, or John Cage's composition 4'33" (1952). In all these cases, a zero-degree work of literature, art, or music, like the zero value in mathematics, cannot be simply equated with noth-ing.[19] A frame provides temporal and spatial parameters which confine and define the reception of the piece as a specimen of music or art. In the case of Gnedov, the text has a title and appears as an item in a book of poems, where it occupies the last page. Cage's composition can be and is meant to be performed, with musicians gathering on stage in front of an audience, and emitting no sound for the prescribed time interval. The same per-formability applies to Gnedov's poem as well. Read by the author, the text was in fact a popular and much-demanded item in public lectures. Gnedov would raise his arm and then quickly let it fall in a dramatic gesture, elicit-ing stormy applause from the audience.[20] The fact that Gnedov labeled his text a *poema* rather than a *stikhotvorenie* underlines a potential narrative or epic content, which is presented, as it were, as a pure virtuality.

Many of Gnedov's other poems are only slightly less minimalist. Two of the fifteen poems in the collection *Smert' iskusstvu* consist of one letter each ("u," "iu"),[21] two others consist of one neologistic word. Nine texts are one-line poems. One of them simply repeats the word "Buba" three times.[22] The one-line poem in itself, of course, was not Gnedov's invention. The most notorious example of this genre in Russian literature is Valerii Briusov's "O, zakroi svoi blednye nogi" ("O, cover your pale legs"), which created a *succès de scandale* when it appeared in the 1895 collection *Russkie simvolisty*. The youthful bravado and desire to "épater les bourgeois" of the leading decadent of the 1890s had more than a passing resemblance to the iconoclasm and aggressive anti-philistinism of his futurist successors twenty years later (although both Briusov and the futurists were loath to acknowledge that parentage).[23] In this sense, Kharms' minimalism of the 1930s can also be read as a provocation against the officially enforced "middlebrow" taste of Stalinist culture. In their extreme laconicity, Kharms' mini-stories provide a counterpoint to the publicly encouraged monumentalism of Soviet literary production.[24]

One could argue that Gnedov's and Briusov's texts do not qualify as direct generic antecedents of Kharms' mini-stories, since they constitute examples of minimalist poetry rather than minimalist prose.[25] It is true, of course, that in extremely short texts the opposition between poetry and prose becomes neutralized. Given its title and the fact that it appears in a volume of poems, Gnedov's zero-text needs to be classified as poetry. But by attaching a "poetry" label to something that does not seem to warrant such a designation, it functions in a similar manner as a prose poem. We could call it a zero-degree prose poem that—to use a favorite expression of the formalists—lays bare the device of the genre.

In his "Sluchai" cycle, Kharms operates with similar techniques of (false) labeling. The most obvious example is the story "Sonet" ("A Sonnet"), which, at least on the surface, seems to have nothing to do with a sonnet.[26] The story relates how the narrator forgets which number comes first, seven or eight. It turns out that his neighbors suffer from the same predicament, and the explanation offered by the cashier in a food store ("seven comes after eight in those cases when eight comes after seven") does not provide much help. Attempts to settle the question by counting trees in a park end in failure and dispute. Finally, the characters are distracted by a child who, "fortunately," falls from a park bench and breaks both jaws, and they go home. Why is this text called a sonnet? Iampol'skii notes the connection between the topic of the arbitrariness of the numerical series, which was one of Kharms' general philosophical concerns, and the fact that the constituting elements of a sonnet enter in a structural relationship that makes them lose their autonomy.[27] In addition, Robin Milner-Gulland has observed that the text consists of exactly fourteen sentences divided in a proportion of 8:6.[28] Andrei Dobrytsin has gone even further in reading "Sonet" as a sonnet. He claims that the two "quatrains" and two "tercets" form a logical sequence that mimics the semantics of the classical sonnet form. He also notes that the number of words in the text is 196 (that is, 14 x 14), that seven and eight indeed change places when we count backward from fourteen, and he even discovers a system of anaphoric "rhymes."[29] In this sense, "Sonet" represents a "poem in prose" of a peculiar and unique kind. It translates, as it were, the constraints of the sonnet form into prosaic equivalents.

Should we consider then Kharms' mini-stories as prose poems? Although we find no reference in Kharms' writings to either Baudelaire's *Petits poèmes en prose* or Turgenev's *Stikhotvoreniia v proze*, there are some interesting biographical parallels that deserve to be mentioned. Just like Baudelaire and Turgenev, Kharms came to the form of the prose miniature late in his career. For all three authors, the new form was the product of a creative crisis that entailed the reevaluation and renunciation of previous literary practices. Baudelaire deconstructed his earlier verse poetry by rewriting it in prose. Turgenev explained the emergence of the prose poem with the death of the novel in his oeuvre. Kharms, like Baudelaire, arrived at the prose miniature through the renunciation of poetry. Up to the early 1930s, Kharms considered himself a poet first and foremost. Prose begins to play a predominant role in his work only after 1933 and 1934. Jaccard has interpreted this turn from poetry to prose as the result of a philosophical crisis. While the earlier poetry, with all its radical, avant-garde outlook and experimentation with "trans-sense" language, was driven by the utopian belief in the accessibility of an underlying total sense, this assumption became shattered in the 1930s. The kaleidoscopic "collision of meanings" advocated by OBERIU poetics, which was supposed to contain the wholeness of existence, turned instead into a chaotic fragmentation. Having become a true writer of the absurd, Kharms found in the prose miniature a more adequate form for his new "existentialist" worldview.[30]

It cannot be overlooked, of course, that the years 1933 and 1934 coincide with an important cultural divide, since it was during that time that the Soviet Writers' Union was established and Socialist Realism was enshrined as the sole acceptable form of Soviet art. The inception and gradual intensification of Stalinist terror, which would later claim Kharms' life, further contributed to an atmosphere of fear and despair. The backdrop of Stalinist Russia makes it tempting to explain the seemingly "absurd" nature of Kharms' fiction—the pervasive violence, the unmotivated disappearance of characters, the treatment of death as a banal occurrence, and so on—as a "realist" description of Russian society in the 1930s. Anthony Anemone went as far as to claim that Kharms' stories not only "add up to a stinging indictment of the ethical and moral climate of the Stalinist period," but also constitute a sort of mea culpa in acknowledging "the role of the avant-garde in preparing the way for the violence and immorality of Stalinism."[31]

134

Regardless of whether we consider Kharms' prose of the 1930s an expression of nihilist despair or a spirited attack against the dystopian Stalinist state, it remains beyond doubt that his mini-stories mark a departure from his previous literary production and express a disillusionment with his former utopian quests. In this sense, Kharms' career follows a similar trajectory to that of Baudelaire, who also became disenchanted with his revolutionary fervor of 1848. "Assomons les pauvres!" Baudelaire's ironic deconstruction of the egalitarian discourse, is an almost "Kharmsian" text in its dark humor and seemingly amoral depiction of violent behavior. Both authors go to grotesque lengths in their description of physical violence. Here is an excerpt from Baudelaire's text:

> Having next, with a kick directed to his back, forceful enough to break his shoulder blades, floored that weakened sexagenarian, I grabbed a big tree branch lying on the ground, and beat him with the obstinate energy of cooks trying to tenderize a beefsteak.[32]

In Kharms' "Istoriia Derushchikhsia" ("The Story of a Fight"), one of many examples of gratuitous violence in the "Sluchai" cycle, the tree branch has been replaced by a more bizarre instrument:

> Aleksei Alekseevich, who did not expect such a fast attack, fell on the floor, and Andrei Karlovich sat down on top of him, pulled a prosthetic jaw out of his mouth and gave Aleksei Alekseevich such a work-over, that Aleksei Alekseevich got up from the floor with a completely maimed face and torn nostrils.[33]

Many of Baudelaire's prose poems, just like Kharms' mini-stories, are devoted to the narration of "strange" events, while frustrating at the same time the reader's quest for a moral message. Kharms uses this technique in an even more overt manner. Frequently, his texts end with a pithily stated aphoristic line that seems to sum up the "lesson" of the story, but does really nothing of the sort. "Sluchai" ("Incidents"), the title story of the cycle, after enumerating a series of absurd deaths and misfortunes, ends with the remark, "Good people, but they don't know how to take themselves in hand."[34] This technique of a false moral ending becomes most explicit in a story with the generic title "Basnia" ("A Fable").[35] A man who is frustrated by his small height declares that he would be ready for anything if only he were a bit taller. At this moment, a fairy appears and asks him to make a wish. The man is so frightened that he is unable to say a word. The fairy disappears, and the man begins to cry and bite his nails. In the manner of the classic fable tradition, the story closes with a sententious address to the reader: "Reader, think hard about this fable, and you will feel strange." Similar to Baudelaire's "Les dons des fées," Kharms' fable mocks the folktale plot of good fairies as providers of help to humans. While Baudelaire's fairies bestow their gifts in a capricious and arbitrary manner, in Kharms' version no transaction at all occurs due to the character's incapability to express his wish. The story can be read as an allegory of its own minimalism: like its protagonist, it is too short, and the hopes of lengthening it through supernatural intervention are thwarted by the author's refusal to come to the rescue of either his character or the hapless reader, both of whom are left to bite their nails in frustration.

While the subversive use of narrative creates a typological parallel between Kharms and Baudelaire, the relationship to Turgenev's prose poems seems less obvious. A resemblance exists on the purely formal level, to be sure: both authors created a cycle of miniature prose pieces interspersed with occasional short dialogues. But with all his bouts of pessimistic nihilism, Turgenev, as we have seen, nevertheless tried to place Baudelaire's subversive genre on a more firm moral grounding. Interestingly enough, a text more akin to Kharms' mini-stories can be found not in Turgenev's *Stikhotvoreniia v proze* per se, but in a parody of Turgenev's prose poems published in the satirical journal *Strekoza:*

Рассказ без названия

Нас было в комнате человек одиннадцать и все мы ужасно много говорили.
  Был теплый майский вечер . . .
  Вдруг мы все замолчали.
  —«Господа, пора расходиться!» сказал один из нас.
  Мы встали и разошлися . . .[36]

A Tale without a Title

There were about eleven of us in the room and we all talked an awful lot.
  It was a warm May evening . . .
  Suddenly we all grew silent.
  —"Gentlemen, it is time to go!" said one of us.
  We all stood up and left . . .

The anonymous author of this parody lampoons the plotlessness of the prose poem. A motivation for the lack of narrative is provided by the lyrical nature of Turgenev's prose poetry (a mood parodistically alluded to with the reference to a "warm May evening"), but it clashes with the expectation of a plot generated by the prosaic form and the generic title "rasskaz" (story). Just like Kharms' "Vstrecha," the entire story is concerned with the narration of a banal nonevent. The number eleven seems to have been deliberately chosen to preclude from the outset any kind of allegoric interpretation, since eleven is devoid of any obvious symbolic connotations. Although we are told that the characters do a lot of talking, they do not appear to be saying anything worthwhile. Lacking a memorable event, the narrator can't even think of a title for the story. He resorts to a purely generic label, which leaves the reader frustrated, since the promised story fails to materialize. Like its characters, the story suddenly falls silent.

A parody usually has the benefit of foregrounding (and exaggerating) the dominant features of the text or genre it refers to. In the present case, the parody makes visible a latent trait not fully realized in Turgenev's texts. It points to the "destructive" potential inherent in the genre of the prose poem, whose paradoxical ontological status between poetry and prose has led many twentieth-century authors from anti-poetry to a form of anti-narrative prose. In the history of modernist poetics, the boundaries between a parody and a "serious" text can become quite permeable, as one author's parody is appropriated by others as a fruitful innovation. Vladimir Solov'ev's spoofs at Briusov's decadent lyrics of the 1890s, for example, anticipate the later "trans-sense" experiments of the futurists and *oberiuty*.[37] Similarly, the plot-lessness of the decadent prose poem can become in the oeuvre of avant-garde writers a consciously applied technique of narrative estrangement.

It will have become obvious that many of the prose miniatures discussed earlier in this book bear a resemblance to Kharms' mini-stories. The similarity is particularly striking in the case of Sologub's fairy tales, many of which, as we have seen, operate with minimalist (non-) narratives and *faux* closures.[38] Both writers evoke a "fallen" world of depressing banality, shot through with acts of random violence and occurrences of unmotivated, sudden death. Sologub's dream about people being burned in a stove as fire logs anticipates the dehumanized universe of Kharms' "Son" ("A Dream"), which ends with the protagonist being folded in two and thrown out with the trash.[39] With both writers, possible escapes into a transcendent counterreality are hinted at, but remain vague.[40]

Most important, both Kharms and Sologub rely on fairy tale patterns to create a minimalist genre of *Anti-Märchen*.[41] The role of the Russian folktale in Kharms' "Sluchai" cycle has been studied by Frank Göbler.[42] Many of his findings apply as well to Sologub's fairy tales. Göbler mentions the lack of a text-internal narrator, an alogical narrative style, iterative and durative structures of chronology typical for both absurd drama and fairy tales, plots marked by cruelty, and de-individualized, de-emotionalized characters. In a strange twist, Kharms inverses the practice of the folktale which endows animals with human attributes by populating his seemingly realistic world with dehumanized figures. Whereas the literary *Kunstmärchen* usually psychologizes the folktale, Kharms' (and Sologub's) tales represent the opposite: they constitute examples of de-psychologized *Kunstmärchen*, signaling, in some respects, a return to a more primitivist folk mythology.

Kharms himself marked the adherence to and deviation from the folktale model (*skazka*) with two titles that allude to the folktale and deform it at the same time: *Skasska* and *Skavka*.[43] The former is the story of a character named Semenov who keeps losing one thing after the other. First he loses his handkerchief, then his hat, then his jacket, and then his boots. At this point, he decides to go home, but gets lost. He sits down and falls asleep, which brings the story to a close. The formulaic repetition of misfortunes, a frequently encountered element in Kharms' narrative prose, points to the folktale tradition, which is also evoked with the opening "Zhil-byl odin chelovek" ("Once upon a time there lived a man"). But nothing miraculous or even particularly interesting happens in this story. At best, we must conclude that Semenov is a complete idiot. His misfortunes are reported in an unemphatic, matter-of-fact style. He is such an insignificant character that, after he falls asleep, the narrator seems to lose interest in him. As Thomas Grob has noted, compared to the violence in other texts, Semenov's fate is relatively benign; however, the story ends untragically, even peacefully.[44]

The second text with a misspelled fairy tale title, "Skavka," takes the form of a minimalist poem:

восемь человек сидят на лавке
вот и конец моей скавке

eight people sit on a bench
here my story comes to an ench

The distortion of the generic title word (making it rhyme, incidentally, with Kafka!) is motivated by a rhyme constraint. Unlike the word "Skasska," which, although misspelled, is at least phonetically correct, "Skavka" constitutes a genuine neologism. Jaccard has pointed to the important transitional nature of this poem in Kharms' oeuvre. Written in 1930, it combines the deformative avant-garde poetics of his earlier style with the laconic minimalism of the later prose narratives.[45] Significantly, Kharms uses the material of the folktale to demonstrate the impossibility of traditional narration. As we remember, ultra-short "anti-narratives" of this kind can also be found in Afanas'ev's collection of *Dokuchnye skazki.*[46]

While "Skavka" still presents itself as a "complete" literary text, other examples document the breakdown of an attempted act of storytelling. Afanas'ev's tale of the white bull, which was also used by Sologub, finds its equivalent in an untitled text of 1934–35.[47] The story begins with the announcement, "Khotite, ia rasskazhu vam rasskaz pro etu kriukitsu?" ("Shall I tell you the story of this kriukitsa?"). The story never gets off the ground, however, because the narrator can't remember what to call his fairy tale creature—kriukitsa? kiriukitsa? kuriakitsa? kirikriukitsa? kurikriakitsa? kirikuriukitsa? kirikukukrekitsa? and so on. Unlike "Skasska," where it is the character of the story who seems mentally challenged, here we have to doubt the intellectual capacities of the narrator himself. The same could be said about the implied author of "Skavka," who takes delight in forging idiotic rhymes. Kharms' linguistic play with letters and syllables, which he inherited from the trans-sense language of the futurists, leads here to the breakdown of communication and makes any storytelling impossible.

In at least one instance, Kharms borrows a technique of communicative disturbance directly from Sologub's fairy tales. Sologub's story "Tik" features a boy who has the annoying habit of interrupting all his sentences with the word "tik!"[48] In Kharms' "Sluchai" cycle, the same motif appears in a vaguely Chekhovian dramatic scene with the title "Tiuk!"[49] The little boy has turned into an elderly man who drives his female companion crazy by constantly uttering the word "tiuk!" when she hits a log of firewood with her axe. The shift from child to adult is significant. While the young age of the character in Sologub's text provides a natural explanation for a behavior which, although annoying, constitutes a form of essentially harmless play, the adult character in Kharms' scene seems positively deranged.

The self-stylization of the author as an infantile character, as evidenced in the matter-of-fact-like and disturbingly unemotional reporting of absurd, cruel, and shocking events, is a technique that can also be observed in Remizov's work.[50] In their absurdist laconicity, as well as in their at times violent content, many of Remizov's dreams anticipate Kharms' mini-stories. In some instances, Remizov, just like Kharms, engages in metafictional comments on his own narrative minimalism. In one of Remizov's dreams, the narrator is confronted with "paper from the fourth dimension" on which it is impossible to write with either pencil or pen. The whole secret, he is told by someone, consists in "making something from nothing."[51] In another dream, the narrator is hauling a cart loaded with sand to a mountain village. When he arrives, the women of the village inform him that the sand will be used to weave cloth.[52] The paradox of a woven structure—a text!—made of sand points to the problem of creating a coherent, overarching narrative out of autonomous minimal units. Dreams play a major role in Kharms' fiction as well. Two of the texts in the "Sluchai" cycle carry the word "dream" in their title, and several more stories are concerned with the topic of sleep and dreaming.[53] As Mikhail Iampol'skii has shown, the dream had a special significance in Kharms' philosophy as a means of stopping, or even reversing, the flow of time.[54]

A further parallel between Kharms' prose and the "dream-text" of a symbolist predecessor has been highlighted by A. A. Aleksandrov in his foreword to the first Soviet edition of Kharms' works.[55] Aleksandrov quotes the following excerpt from Aleksandr Blok's "Ni sny, ni iav":

> . . . все и пошло прахом. Мужики, которые пели, принесли из Москвы сифилис и разнесли по всем деревням. Купец, чей луг косили, вовсе спился и с пьяных глаз сам поджег сенные сараи в своей усадьбе.
>
> Дьякон нарожал незаконных детей. У Федота в избе потолок совсем провалился, а Федот его не чинит. У нас старые стали умирать, а молодые стариться. Дядюшка мой стал говорить глупости, каких никогда еще не говорил. Я тоже на следующее утро пошел рубить сирень.[56]

. . . everything went to ashes. The singing peasants brought syphilis from Moscow and spread it through all the villages. The merchant, whose meadow they had been mowing, became a complete alcoholic and in his drunken state himself set fire to his hey-lofts and estate. The deacon fathered illegal children. In Fedot's hut the ceiling caved in, and Fedot didn't fix it. Our old people began to die, and the young ones got old. My uncle began to talk such nonsense as he never had before. I, too, the following morning went to cut down the lilac.

Blok's tale of the destruction of his grandfather's estate during the revolution becomes a vision of universal degradation and disintegration. His technique of laconically enumerating a series of calamities without indicating any causal linkage anticipates Kharms' story "Sluchai" ("Incidents"), which begins: "Once Orlov ate too many ground peas and died. Krylov found out about it and died too. Spiridonov up and died all by himself. Spiridonov's wife fell off the cupboard and also died. Spiridonov's children drowned in the pond. Grandma Spiridonov took to drink and hit the road. . ."[57] Blok's account of destructive violence, prompted by his disillusionment with the revolution, sounds only slightly less absurd than Kharms' deadpan enumeration of deaths and misfortunes.

A certain similarity also exists between Kharms' mini-stories and Kandinskii's prose poems, although of course there can hardly be a question of direct influence (the only prose poems by Kandinskii that could have been known to Kharms are the four pieces published in *A Slap in the Face of Public Taste*).[58] The "Kharmsian" ending of Kandinskii's "Kletka" has already been noted.[59] The Kandinskii scholar Boris Sokolov pointed to several parallels between *Klänge* and the poetics of the *oberiuty*. He mentions objects and people appearing and disappearing from a "different reality," absurd plots, neologisms, psychologization of animals and objects, and openings into a spiritual world amidst the ugliness of humdrum reality.[60] Kandinskii's grotesque "Vorfrühling" quoted earlier would easily fit into Kharms' "Sluchai" cycle. However, Kandinskii's spiritual messianism would have been alien to Kharms, who, rather than witnessing the purported dawn of a new spiritual age, experienced the exact opposite phenomenon.

Perhaps even more surprisingly, similarities can also be found with Bunin's *Kratkie rasskazy*, which, like Kharms' mini-stories, were written in the 1930s. This parallel may appear unlikely in light of Bunin's proclaimed traditionalism and hostility to the modernist avant-garde. Yet we find in Bunin stories such as the following:

Летний день

Слобода, бесконечный летний день.

И весь день сидит босой, распоясанный сапожник возле своей ветхой мазанки, на гнилой лавочке, подставив под солнце свою раскрытую лохматую голову. Сидит и занимается с рыжим кобельком:

—Дай лапку!

Кобелек не понимает, не дает.

—Говорят тебе, дай лапку! Ну?

Кобелек не дает. И он бьет его по морде. Кобелек с отвращением моргает, отворачивается, кисло-сладко оскаляется, неуверенно поднимает лапу и тотчас опять опускает ее. И опять пощечина, и опять:

—Дай, сукин сын, лапку![61]

A Summer Day

A village, an endless summer day.

And the whole day, a shoemaker, barefoot, with unfastened belt, is sitting by his ramshackle cottage, on a rotten bench, placing his bare disheveled head in the sun. He is sitting and busying himself with a red-haired puppy dog:

"Give your paw!"

The dog doesn't understand. He doesn't do it.

"You're told to give your paw. So?"

The dog doesn't do it. And he hits him in the snout. The dog blinks with disgust, turns away, shows his teeth in a sour-sweet manner, lifts hesitantly his paw and lets it sink right away. And again a slap, and again:

"Give your paw, you son of a bitch!"

While the innocuous title of Bunin's story seems to promise some idyllic nature scene, the actual content deceives this expectation. Kharms used the same technique in his "Nachalo ochen' khoroshego letnego dnia. Simfoniia" ("The Beginning of a Very Beautiful Summer Day. A Symphony").[62] The content of this "symphony" also contradicts the promise of its title. Despite its bucolic opening, evoking the crowing of a rooster, and the idyllic closing phrase ("Thus begun a beautiful summer day"), the main body of Kharms' text consists of a sort of tableau vivant depicting random acts of vulgar and violent behavior, with various people shouting insults and beating each other up. In both Bunin's and Kharms' texts, the linear flow of time is abolished. Bunin uses the device of cyclic repetition to create the effect of "endlessness" announced in the opening sentence, while Kharms presents a picture of synchronous simultaneity. As Jaccard has observed, Kharms' narrator switches midway in the text from the perfective to the imperfective verbal aspect. The resulting passage from narration to description creates an effect of "frozen reality."[63] Among the victims in Kharms' "symphony" is a little dog who rolls around on the pavement with a broken leg. The abolition of the boundaries between animals and humans, exemplified by the "bestial" behavior of Kharms' protagonists, is foreshadowed in the punchline of Bunin's story with its strange conflation of the figurative and literal meaning of the expression "son of a bitch."

141

Despite the fact that Bunin and Kharms could hardly have been aware of each other's work, the similarity between the two texts is striking. Both writers make maximum use of the ambiguity and inherent tension between the "poetic" and the "prosaic," as evidenced by the clash between the idyllic scene promised in the title and the gratuitous violence depicted in the story. Although seemingly very different from each other, Bunin and Kharms are both located at the intersection of realism and modernism. As a self-proclaimed traditionalist, Bunin was nevertheless affected by the modernist age, while Kharms, a belated member of the Russian avant-garde, created with his absurdist tales a grim comment on Stalinist reality. In addition, both writers arrived at their laconic prose style by rejecting their earlier, more "poetic" mode of writing. In this sense, the common essence between Bunin and Kharms could be found in a shared neo-classicist approach to form. In a speech at the Leningrad Writers' Union in 1936, Kharms expressed his distaste for "impressionism, decadence and symbolism" and declared Mozart and Pushkin to be his artistic models.[64] As a matter of fact, Kharms' prose works from the 1930s feature none of the neologisms and syntactical ungrammaticalities that had been the hallmark of futurist and OBERIU poetics. Their "strangeness," rather than being created by a deformed linguistic medium, is now located at the level of content and plot. As in the fiction of Franz Kafka, even the most absurd events are rendered in a "neutral" style of classic economy and simplicity.

In conclusion, we note that the theory of the prose poem provides an overarching generic locus for the various examples of minimalist prose that we have identified as possible antecedents of Kharms' mini-stories. The extreme brevity of Kharms' prose miniatures can be interpreted as an outgrowth of the negativity inherent in the form of the prose poem. As we have seen, brevity is a defining feature of this genre. With its reduced dimensions, the prose poem imitates the compactness of the lyric, and draws a distinction with narrative prose. Given its prosaic form and miniature size, the prose poem is *neither a poem nor a story,* although it seems to allude to both of these genres. As we have seen before, not every prose poem follows a minimalist aesthetic, but it is noteworthy that several authors who began their career with "lyric prose"—Ivan Bunin, Aleksei Remizov, Velimir Khlebnikov, Elena Guro—later developed an extremely laconic, minimalist style. This development from poetic prose to prosaic minimalism finds its logical conclusion in the absurdist anti-stories of Daniil Kharms.

By associating Kharms' miniatures with the theory of the prose poem, I do not mean to imply that Kharms should be considered a conscious follower of Turgenev or Baudelaire. The similarity is typological rather than genealogical. In their minimalist subversion of traditional narrative, Kharms' anti-stories question literariness in the same way as the prose poem's impossible binarism between poetry and prose questions the notion of poetic-

ity. Just like minimalist sculpture that hovers uneasily on the margins between art and nonart, the prose poem can be defined as "any short text
which, by dint of transgressing the canons of accepted literary discourses,
borders on a nonliterary or 'para-literary' discourse."[65] Anna Gerasimova
stated something very similar when she characterized the literary production of Kharms and the *oberiuty* as "a phenomenon, as it were, on the limit
of literature (*na grani literatury*), bordering on play, science, philosophy,
contemporary mythology, a new syncretism; on the limit between the comical and the serious; on the limit between art and life, bordering on spontaneous life-building (*zhiznetvorchestvo*)."[66]

Many of Kharms' texts are difficult to classify if we adhere to a strict
binary system of "literature" vs. "non-literature." This becomes evident in
the curious publication history of his work. The fact that his oeuvre appeared posthumously has meant that editors and publishers had to decide
which of his prose texts fall into the category of fiction (*khudozhestvennaia
literatura*) and which ones remain outside this category. Kharms' notebooks
seem to freely mix fictional and nonfictional texts, and the persona in his diaries is a literary construct rather than an autobiographical self. In comparing the various editions of Kharms' works that have appeared over the past
few years, we note that a growing number of texts are placed into the category of *khudozhestvennaia literatura*. The quite arbitrary decision of lifting
a text or text fragment from a diary or notebook and declaring it to be a
piece of "literature" has far-reaching consequences for its reception. As in
the case of the prose poem, it is the "frame" rather than any intrinsic quality that places the text into a different aesthetic category.[67]

It is interesting to note that Kharms himself engaged in a similar
process of framing and (re)contextualizing. The title of the opening piece of
the "Sluchai" cycle, "Golubaia tetrad' No. 10," is revealing of this proce-
dure. In attaching the number ten, rather than one, to his first story, Kharms
marks the text as appropriated from a different environment, the "Blue Notebook."[68] By openly proclaiming the text as a transplant from this heterogeneous collage of sketches, diary entries, aphorisms, and poems, Kharms is
"laying bare the device" of citing and reinserting a text as a sort of "ready
made" into his cycle of mini-stories. As we have seen, minimalist art similarly relies on techniques of framing and recontextualization in order to establish itself as art. "Golubaia tetrad' No. 10," perhaps Kharms' best-known
story, embodies this problem in exemplary fashion:

Голубая тетрадь No. 10

Был один рыжий человек, у которого не было глаз и ушей. У него не было
и волос, так что рыжим его называли условно.

Говорить он не мог, так как у него не было рта. Носа тоже у него не
было.

143

У него не было даже рук и ног. И живота у него не было, и спины у него не было, и хребта у него не было, и никаких внутренностей у него не было. Ничего не было! Так что непонятно, о ком идет речь.

Уж лучше мы о нем не будем больше говорить.[69]

Blue Notebook No. 10

There was once a red-haired man who had no eyes and no ears. He also had no hair, so he was called red-haired only in a manner of speaking.

He wasn't able to talk, because he didn't have a mouth. He had no nose, either.

He didn't even have any arms or legs. He also didn't have a stomach, and he didn't have a back, and he didn't have a spine, and he also didn't have any other insides. He didn't have anything [Or: There was nothing]. So it's hard to understand whom we're talking about.

So we'd better not talk about him anymore.[70]

As a sort of programmatic opening manifesto of the "Sluchai" cycle, "Golubaia tetrad' No. 10" points to the narrative dilemma of "creating something out of nothing" (as Remizov put it in his dream).[71] How can we refer to a character with no hair as a "red-haired man"? In the same manner, one could argue, as we refer to a text with no obvious poetic qualities as a prose poem, or an object with no obvious aesthetic attributes as a work of minimalist art—it all happens "as a manner of speaking" (*uslovno*).[72] This insight leads to a more wide-ranging ontological dilemma: How can we talk about someone or something at all in the absence of any perceptible attributes? The resulting disintegration of the narrative ends in the ultimate vanishing point of all minimalist art: the empty canvas, the white page, the protracted silence. Confronted with an artifact that appears to be lacking in aesthetic complexity, poeticity, or narrativity, the reader or beholder is left alone to ponder his or her own operative assumptions about the meaning of art and life.

That's about all.

Epilogue

> This would seem to be the end. But perhaps
> some of our readers would care to know what
> each of the characters we have introduced is
> doing in the present, the actual present. We are
> ready to satisfy him.
>
> —Turgenev, *Fathers and Sons*

THE NEGATIVITY ALREADY INHERENT in Turgenev's prose poems attained its outer limit with Kharms' minimalist prose miniatures. We seem to have reached "the end" in some absolute sense. "Blue Notebook No. 10" exhorts us, in the manner of Wittgenstein, to be silent about what cannot be fathomed in language. The modernist breakdown of traditional narrative prose foreshadowed in Turgenev's "Senilia" seems to have run its course with Kharms' anti-stories.

To be sure, this does not necessarily mean that we have reached the end of literature. As Samuel Beckett's narrator in *L'innomable* puts it, even when there is nothing to say, "the discourse must go on."[1] Such an attitude typifies a postmodern aesthetic, which, according to some critics, Kharms' miniatures anticipate.[2] In a 1997 issue of the journal *Novoe literaturnoe obozrenie* devoted to "minimalism and mini-forms in contemporary literature," Sergei Biriukov lists Kharms among the "proto-minimalist" forerunners of postmodern minimalism.[3] Some of the examples of contemporary minimalist writing collected here address the idea of the "end of the story" in a manner reminiscent of Kharms. This becomes particularly evident in Stella Morotskaia's two contributions:

Сказке конец

Он жил долго и умер в один день

The End of the Fairy Tale

He lived a long time and died in one day

Стихотворение о совершенности прекращения как логическом конце
несовершенности продолжения

жил и умер

A Poem about the Perfection of Cessation as the Logical End
to the Imperfection of Continuation

he lived and died[4]

While a comprehensive discussion of postmodern minimalism in Russian literature remains beyond the scope of this brief epilogue, I will demonstrate its salient features by focusing on one prominent author. Perhaps the best-known representative of minimalism in contemporary Russian literature is Lev Rubinshtein (born 1947). Together with Dmitrii Prigov and Vladimir Sorokin, he is a leading member of the so-called Moscow conceptualist school, which began as an underground movement in the late 1960s. Rubinshtein is the inventor and sole practitioner of a unique genre, the card catalogue. Partially inspired by his former work as a librarian and bibliographer, Rubinshtein writes his texts on loose sheets and index cards that he arranges in numbered sequences. Rather than forming a coherent whole, they remain a compilation of fragments, and in this sense constitute a sort of "rebellion against the book," as Rubinshtein explained in a 1999 interview.[5] In accordance with the parameters of conceptualism, Rubinshtein's texts do not express an autonomous authorial voice, but reflect a montage of discourses, including pastiches of various literary styles. The spectrum of cited texts ranges from vulgar street jargon through banal conversations to examples of Soviet ideological and literary prose and quotations from classical Russian literature. The author has deliberately withdrawn from his text, leaving the reader with a bewildering array of citations and instructions, such as the injunction to "stop and think," followed on the next card by a request to "stop and think of something else."[6]

It is obvious that Rubinshtein's texts fail to fulfill any kind of traditional expectation in terms of narrative prose or poetry. They contain no "story" and are written in a deliberately banal manner devoid of metaphors or formal ornamentation. Frequently, they develop a series that repeats the same formula with minimal variations. Many of his catalogues are based on the anaphoric repetition of an opening formula that reproduces itself on every index card. For example, his "Katalog komediinykh novshestv" ("A Catalogue of Comical Novelties," 1976) consists of one hundred and ten cards that all begin with the word "mozhno" ("one can").[7] This serial quality makes Rubinshtein's texts akin to minimalist music, which he has named among the main inspirations for his literary oeuvre.[8] Gerald Janacek has pointed to the importance of John Cage in particular as a model for Rubinshtein's aleatory poetics.[9] A moment of chance is introduced by making the reader an active agent in the text production. The performative aspect becomes a key ingredient in Rubinshtein's project, as the rhythm of leafing through the card catalogue serves as a structuring element in the reception of the text.

146

An important component of Rubinshtein's work is the use of blank space. Some of his catalogues contain empty cards, which translate into pauses in public readings of his work. This zero form culminates in the series "Tridtsat' piat' novykh listov" ("Thirty-Five New Sheets," 1981).[10] Each sheet is completely blank except for a title and a footnote with instructions about what should be written in the empty space or done with the sheet. We learn, for example, that sheet 23 "has to express a completely clear authorial position," although what this position consists of remains unstated. The capitalized "Author" appears again on sheets 27 through 32, which contain the following instructions:

> Sheet 27 must remind us in a completely clear manner of the Author
> Sheet 28 must lie permanently on the table, reminding us of the Author
> Sheet 29 must hang permanently on the wall, reminding us of the Author
> Sheet 30, folded up, must be used as a jacket for the book being read at this moment, serving as a permanent reminder of the Author
> Sheet 31 must be permanently kept somewhere near and be produced to acquaintances as a reminder of the Author
> Sheet 32 must get lost among other papers, but when found by chance must without fail remind us of the Author

The beginning and ending sheets of the series are to remain blank. In its ironic deconstruction of the author-function, Rubinshtein's text resembles "computer software templates whereby a structure is provided for a composition to be filled in by an Author," as Gerald Janacek has observed.[11] The German critic Stephan Küpper has placed Rubinshtein's use of blank cards in the tradition of Zen Buddhism, apophatic theology, romantic irony, Wittgenstein's philosophy of the *Tractatus logico-philosophicus,* and Jacques Derrida's concept of *différance.*[12] One could add to this list the "homegrown" tradition of Russian minimalism, in particular Vasilisk Gnedov's "Poema kontsa."

While it may seem counterintuitive as first sight, there are also certain similarities between Rubinshtein's card indexes and Turgenev's prose poems. Turgenev too wrote his texts on loose sheets and cited them as evidence for the death of the novel in his oeuvre. In his conversation with Stasiulevich, he indicated that his texts did not add up to a coherent whole, but constituted merely a sort of raw "material" not unlike Rubinshtein's conceptualist corpus of discourses. In his preface to the published version, Turgenev recommended an aleatory mode of reading for his prose poems. Similarities also exist on the level of genre. Rubinshtein, in the foreword to a collection of his texts published in 1996, characterized his mode of writing as an "intergenre, combining features of poetry, prose, drama, the visual arts, and performance."[13] The same could be said about Turgenev's prose poems. Like Rubinshtein's, Turgenev's texts occupy an uncertain generic locus between poetry, prose, and drama (some of them assume the form of mini-playlets). They overlap with the visual arts both in their designation as an "artist's sketches" and in their frequent preoccupation with ekphrasis. An ekphrastic element also informs Rubinshtein's poetics. The catalogue "Eto ia" ("That's Me," 1995), for example, consists mostly of legends to imaginary photographs.[14] Both Turgenev and Rubinshtein make use of dream narratives.[15] Finally, we should not forget that it was Turgenev's own performance of his texts that swayed Stasiulevich to initiate their publication.

To be sure, for reasons that we have discussed before, it would never occur to anyone to refer to Rubinshtein's texts as "stikhotvoreniia v proze." As we have seen, Turgenev's conservative appropriation made this term ill-suited as a label for any kind of avant-garde experimentation. At the same time, the designation "prose poem" continues to appeal to writers of a more traditionalist bent. The conservative legacy of Turgenev's prose poetry has survived to this day in a form of writing that situates itself at the opposite end of Rubinshtein's postmodernist minimalism.

Among the practitioners of this conservative prose poem in contemporary Russia is Aleksandr Solzhenitsyn (born 1918). He began working in the genre of the prose miniature in the 1950s and early 1960s. His cycle of *Krokhotki* ("Crumbs") or *Krokhotnye rasskazy* was first published in the émigré journal *Grani* in 1964 after circulating in samizdat form. Solzhenitsyn himself referred to these texts in 1967 as *stikhotvoreniia v proze,*[16] thereby placing them explicitly in the Turgenevan generic tradition. If Solzhenitsyn was inspired by Turgenev's prose poems, it was mostly by their didactic nature. However, while Turgenev appropriated the model of the moral tale for the propagation of an essentially secular system of ethics, Solzhenitsyn reinstated the model's original religious significance. As John Dunlop has observed, Solzhenitsyn's collection of sixteen miniature sketches was motivated by the desire to indict "the spiritual inadequacy of modern life" in general, and the "seedy, secular and arrogantly Promethean present of the USSR" in particular.[17] Faithful to the outlook of a *derevenshchik,* or rural prose writer, Solzhenitsyn presents the unspoiled nature of the Russian countryside and the spirituality of the Orthodox Church as alternatives to the modern malaise of Soviet and post-Soviet society.

The title "Crumbs" has both formal and spiritual implications. The metaphor of the crumb denotes the smallness and fragmentary form of these texts, but it also reveals them as pieces of a potential whole—the original "loaf of bread"—providing a source of nourishment and sustenance. In the theological sense, the image of the crumb takes on both eucharistic and eschatological overtones. Solzhenitsyn's prose poems are an attempt to re-spiritualize contemporary secularized reality. As he explains in the prose poem "Puteshestvuia vdol' Oki" ("Traveling along the Oka"), without an awareness of divine transcendence, we are left to "walk on all fours."

Rhetorically, Solzhenitsyn's prose poems are built on a structure of binaries such as new and old, body and soul, materialism and idealism. One side is represented, for example, by "back-firing motorcycles, howling radios and crackling loudspeakers" (in the prose poem "Dykhanie" ["Breathing"]), barbed wire, and a garish propaganda poster of a Soviet worker holding an African baby in his arms ("Prakh poeta" ["The Ashes of a Poet"]), or the ritual of morning gymnastics ("Pristupaia ko dniu" ["Starting the Day"]). These realities of modern life are contrasted, respectively, with the smell of a blooming apple tree after a rain shower, the remains of an old monastery, and the ritual of prayer that the morning gymnastics falsely evoke. Solzhenitsyn uses the bipolar structure, a constitutive feature of the prose poem, to validate one pole and denigrate the other. Essentially, his "Krokhotki" constitute an attempt to reinstate the claims of "poetry" in a world that has grown "prosaic."

In their anti-Soviet stance and nostalgia for a "lost" Russia, Solzhenitsyn's prose poems bear a certain resemblance to Bunin's miniatures, which we have identified earlier as prime examples of twentieth-century realist prose poems. However, their straightforward orientation toward delivering a moral message eschews the ambivalence of Bunin's texts. They are informed by a Manichean struggle between "good" and "evil." Polar opposites also surface in Bunin and Turgenev, as we have seen, but in Solzhenitsyn's case, the author remains squarely on one side of the divide, and the opposite side is only evoked in order to be polemically dismissed. With this didactic thrust, Solzhenitsyn turns the prose poem into a completely "monological" genre, situating it at the opposite extreme of Baudelaire's subversive approach. His prose poems are not meant to question or challenge the notions of poetry and narrative prose, but to mobilize their resources for his moral message.

Solzhenitsyn's hostility toward the realities of post-Soviet Russia is no less fervent than his critique of Soviet Communism. After a long hiatus that was mainly spent working on the monumental *Red Wheel* cycle, he has recently returned to the genre of the prose miniature. In 1997, he published a series of nine new "Krokhotki" in the journal *Novyi mir*.[18] Thematically, Solzhenitsyn's latest prose poems can be divided into three categories: comments on the author's old age and failing health, allegoric nature images used to elucidate human psychology, and allegoric references to Russian history and the current political situation in Russia. The first category creates an obvious connection with the model of the genre, Turgenev's "Senilia." However, while both authors dwell on the topic of old age and impending death, Solzhenitsyn explicitly refutes Turgenev's views on those matters. Unlike Turgenev, he does not highlight the pains of senile decrepitude and the horror of death. His text "Starenie" ("Old Age") begins with the words: "How much has there been written about the horror of death, but also: what a natural link (*zveno*) is it, if it is not brought about violently." As a natural occurrence, death is to be welcomed, and old age is a blessing rather than a burden. Diminished enjoyment of bodily pleasures only serves to reassert the triumph of man's spiritual nature over matter. The shortened lease on life leads not to depression, but to a heightened enjoyment of every new day as an additional gift from God.

The didactic model becomes most obvious in the texts where Solzhenitsyn uses imagery of nature as a comment on human psychology. In each case, a description of a plant is followed by an explicit exegesis, revealing the allegoric nature of the preceding image. A larch ("Listvennitsa"), with its annual shedding of needles and the sturdiness of its wood, represents both compassion and firmness; a pine-tree split by a lightning ("Molniia") is an emblem of a mind wracked by the punishment of conscience, and a proliferating weed ("Likhoe zel'e") indicates the power of evil in the world.[19] When addressing the plight of his homeland, Solzhenitsyn's language becomes most explicit and vigorous. Just like the earlier series of "Krokhotki," this latest installment also constitutes an indictment of the Russian rulers and a lament over the calamitous course of Russian history. In "Kolokol Uglicha" ("The Bell of Uglich"), the narrator draws an explicit parallel between the original *Smuta* ("Time of Troubles") four hundred years ago and the present "Third *Smuta*" (the second *Smuta*, presumably, is represented by the Bolshevik Revolution). "Kolokol'nia" ("The Bell-Tower") relies on an analogy familiar from Valentin Rasputin's "Farewell to Matyora." A village submerged in the floods created by a hydroelectric dam becomes emblematic of the fate of Russian culture under the Soviet and post-Soviet regimes. Of all the buildings, only the church bell-tower still rises above the water. Miraculously, even the cross on the roof has been preserved. As if this symbolism were not explicit enough, the narrator ends by equating the tower with "our hope" and "our prayer." As he states, "no, *all* of Russia to the end will the Lord not allow to be drowned. . . ."

The most categorical critique of contemporary Russia occurs in the prose poem "Pozor" ("Shame"). The narrator feels indelible shame for his homeland (referred to as "Rodina" and with capitalized pronouns), for the thoughtlessness and greed of Her rulers, for the arrogant face She shows to the world, for the "decaying swill" (*tlennoe poilo*) that She is given instead of healthy spiritual food, and for the ruin and poverty of popular life. A glance into history books reveals that entire peoples have perished in the past. Will Russia meet the same fate? Solzhenitsyn is optimistic, but only because he has found hope in the Russian provinces, where he still encountered "living, familiar people with generous souls." However, the text concludes on a bitter note: "But Shame keeps hanging over us, like a yellow-pink cloud of poisoned gas, and it is eating our lungs. And even if we blow it away—we will never remove it from our history."

Of course, Solzhenitsyn was not the only Russian writer to deplore the soullessness of modern civilization and to extol the virtues of rural life. In a more cautious form, this attitude became the hallmark of the so-called village prose writers, who were able to publish their works legally in the Soviet Union in the 1960s and 1970s. Some of them also wrote prose miniatures that are comparable to Solzhenitsyn's "Krokhotki," although they refrain from expressing any overtly anti-Soviet positions.[20] Perhaps most comparable to Solzhenitsyn's are Iurii Bondarev's prose miniatures, despite the fact that this writer's pro-Soviet attitude made him, to some degree, Solzhenitsyn's opposite. The collapse of the Soviet Union encouraged a rapprochement between the two as both of them now represent the conservative Russian nationalist position. Bondarev's *Mgnoveniia* (*Moments,* first published in 1977), a collection of about two hundred prose miniatures varying in length from two lines to several pages, shares many features with Solzhenitsyn's prose poems. Without espousing a religious viewpoint, Bondarev also deplores modern body-centered decadence, which he locates mainly in Western capitalist society. For example, he juxtaposes the garish sex-appeal of a *Playboy* centerfold with the "pure beauty" of the peasant women in the paintings of Ivan Kramskoi and Zinaida Serebriakova.[21] Both Bondarev and Solzhenitsyn cherish the memories of World War II as a heroic age of selfless struggle, in comparison with which the present self-centered age seems wanting. They both condemn postmodernism and stress the writer's moral mission. Bondarev ends his collection with a homage to Lev Tolstoi, quoting excerpts from his diaries and presenting him as his role model in the struggle for the betterment of humanity. As he claims: "The meaning of [Tolstoi's] whole life was to increase the love of man for man."[22]

More than anything else, Bondarev's deference to Tolstoi demonstrates how far the conservative Russian prose poem has evolved from its Baudelairean origins. Ironically, in his attack on French decadence, Tolstoi had singled out Baudelaire's *Petits poèmes en prose* for special scorn. In the tenth chapter of *What Is Art?* (1898), he quoted three of Baudelaire's prose poems in extenso to demonstrate their absurdity. Tolstoi was particularly vexed by the fact that in a prose text, "the author could have talked simply, if he wanted to."[23] It looks as if Bondarev took Tolstoi's criticism to heart when he turned the genre of the prose poem into a vehicle for straightforward moral preaching.[24]

Within the context of the "subversive" modern European prose poem, the Russian conservative *stikhotvorenie v proze* presents a distinct anomaly. Nothing illustrates this better perhaps than the titles given to the translation of Solzhenitsyn's *Krokhotki*. English seems to be the only language in which these texts received the title "Prose Poems."[25] In France, the country of the poème en prose par excellence, they were published first as "Esquisses et petits récits" and later as "Etudes et miniatures." The French, so accustomed to their experimental avant-garde prose poem, no longer recognized their own genre of the *poème en prose* in Solzhenitsyn's resolutely anti-modernist and anti-postmodernist texts.

There is no greater contrast in contemporary Russian literature than Solzhenitsyn and Rubinshtein. Perhaps the only point they would agree on is an acknowledgment of a sense of crisis in post-Soviet Russian literature. But while Solzhenitsyn is desperately trying to salvage the traditional Russian role of the author as a beacon of morality in a corrupt world, Rubinshtein questions the legitimacy of any moralizing literary discourse in a post-Auschwitz and post-Gulag universe. Solzhenitsyn has made no secret of his contempt for postmodernism, and there can be little doubt that he would dismiss Rubinshtein's writings as an example of the "decaying swill" that is nowadays fed to the Russian people in lieu of spiritual sustenance. Rubinshtein, for his part, would no doubt see in Solzhenitsyn's writings precisely the kind of naively logocentric ideological discourse (be it Soviet or anti-Soviet) that he is trying to deconstruct in his card catalogues.

Unlike in France, where Baudelaire's prose poems provided both the generic term and the "subversive" model for such works, the two criteria do not overlap in Russia. As we have seen in our discussion of the realist Russian prose poem, texts with the generic title *stikhotvorenie v proze* tend to follow a conservative rather than an innovative poetics, while the authors of avant-garde experimental prose miniatures, unlike their colleagues in the West, usually shun the "prose poem" label.[26] Nevertheless, although they seem to have nothing in common and their authors openly despise each other's concept of literature, Rubinshtein's card catalogues and Solzhenitsyn's prose miniatures are both distant descendants of Turgenev's *Stikhotvoreniia v proze*. While Solzhenitsyn's "Krokhotki" develop Turgenev's didactic side and limit their minimalism to the miniature form of the "crumb," the more radical minimalism inherent in the genre of the prose poem has come to full fruition in Rubinshtein's postmodernist anti-literature. The bifurcated legacy of Turgenev's protean form—both conservative and subversive—is thus still alive and well.

Notes

PREFACE

1. For a useful bibliography, see Anne Craver, "Critical Studies of the Prose Poem," *L'esprit créateur* 39, no. 1 (Spring 1999), 84–92.

2. The expression is Robin Milner-Gulland's. See "Beyond the Turning-Point: An Afterword," in *Daniil Kharms and the Poetics of the Absurd: Essays and Materials,* ed. Neil Cornwell (Houndmills: Macmillan, 1991), 265.

3. The Russian prose poem has been addressed mostly in peripheral provincial publications in the Soviet Union and in the former Eastern and Central European satellite nations. The only Ph.D. thesis devoted to this topic was defended in 1969 at the University of Voronezh (see L. N. Issova, *Zhanr stikhotvoreniia v proze v russkoi literature [I. S. Turgenev, V. M. Garshin, V. G. Korolenko, I. A. Bunin]. Avtoreferat dissertatsii.* Voronezh, 1969). Articles on the *stikhotvorenie v proze* have appeared in East Germany, Hungary, Bulgaria, Romania, and Yugoslavia. The most comprehensive bibliography can be found in Zsuzsa D. Zöldhelyi, *Turgenyev prózai költeményei* (Budapest: Tankönyvkiadó, 1991), 341–72. In the West, the Russian prose poem has been addressed in articles by Walter Koschmal and Elizabeth Allen. See Walter Koschmal, "Das Prosagedicht als Gattung des evolutionären Wechsels: Ein Beitrag zur slavischen Komparatistik," in *Russische Literatur an der Wende vom 19. zum 20. Jahrhundert. Oldenburger Symposium,* ed. Rainer Grübel (Amsterdam: Rodopi, 1993), 143–61; and Elizabeth Cheresh Allen, "Turgenev's Last Will and Testament: Poems in Prose," in *Freedom and Responsibility in Russian Literature. Essays in Honor of Robert Louis Jackson,* ed. Elizabeth Cheresh Allen and Gary Saul Morson (Evanston: Northwestern University Press and The Yale Center for International and Area Studies, 1995), 53–68.

4. As Neil Cornwell puts it: "Kharms, the black miniaturist, is an exponent not so much of the modernist 'end of the Word' (in a Joycean sense) as of a post modernist, minimalist and infantilist 'end of the Story' (in a

sense perhaps most analogous to Beckett)." "Introduction: Daniil Kharms, Black Miniaturist," in *Daniil Kharms and the Poetics of the Absurd,* 18–19.

5. "Minimalizm: Strategiia i taktika," *Novoe literaturnoe obozrenie* 23 (1997), 261.

6. See on this Sergei Biriukov, "O maksimal'no minimal'nom v avan-gardnoi i postavangardnoi poezii," ibid., 290.

7. See "Minimalizm: Strategiia i taktika," 261.

8. Iu. Orlitskii, "Miniume," ibid., 342.

9. "Cutting Baudelaire's Rope: Ivan Turgenev's Re-Writing of 'La Corde,'" *Comparative Literature Studies* 34, no. 1 (1997), 31–40; "From Subversion to Affirmation: The Prose Poem as a Russian Genre," *Slavic Review* 56, no. 3 (1997), 519–41; "Aleksei Remizov's Dreams: Surrealism *Avant la Lettre?" The Russian Review* 58, no. 4 (1999), 599–614; "Russian Minimalist Prose: Generic Antecedents to Daniil Kharms' 'Sluchai,'" *Slavic and East European Journal* 45, no. 3 (2001), 451–72.

CHAPTER ONE

1. For a discussion of American minimalist fiction of the 1980s, see the special issue of *Mississippi Review* (vols. 40–41, 1985), with an intro-duction by Kim Herzinger.

2. Warren Motte, *Small Worlds: Minimalism in Contemporary French Literature* (Lincoln: University of Nebraska Press, 1999), 24.

3. See Frances Colpitt, *Minimal Art: The Critical Perspective* (Ann Arbor: UMI Research Press, 1990), 3, and Kenneth Baker, *Minimalism: Art of Circumstance* (New York: Abbeville Press, 1988), 17–18. In his 1937 tract "System and Dialectics of Art," published in Paris, Graham offered the following definition of minimalism: "*Minimalism* is the reducing of painting to the minimum ingredients for the sake of discovering the ultimate, logi-cal destination of painting in the process of abstracting. Painting starts with a virgin, uniform canvas and if one works ad infinitum it reverts again to a plain uniform surface (dark in color), but enriched by process and experi-ences lived through. Founder: Graham." *John Graham's System and Dia-lectics of Art,* ed. Marcia Epstein Allentuck (Baltimore: Johns Hopkins University Press, 1971), 115–16. The term "minimalism" had been used a few years before by David Burliuk in a 1929 catalogue essay on Graham. See Eleanor Green, *John Graham, Artist and Avatar* (Washington, D.C.: The Phillips Collection, 1987), 38, n. 13. According to Kenneth Baker, "it is un-clear whether he borrowed the term from Graham or vice versa" (134, n. 6).

4. See Barbara Rose, "ABC Art," in Gregory Battcock, ed., *Minimal Art: A Critical Anthology* (New York: Dutton, 1968), 275.

5. See Gerald J. Janecek, "Minimalism in Contemporary Russian Poetry: Vsevolod Nekrasov and Others," *The Slavonic and East European*

Review 70, no. 3 (July 1992), 401–19. This article has been republished in Russian, together with several other contributions, in "Minimum=Maximum: Minimalizm i mini-formy v sovremennoi literature," *Novoe literaturnoe obozrenie* 23 (1997), 245–342. For a recent interdisciplinary collection of essays devoted to minimalism in Russian literature, art, philosophy, film, music, and architecture, see Mirjam Goller and Georg Witte, eds., *Minimalismus: Zwischen Leere und Exzeß* (Vienna: Wiener Slawistischer Almanach, Sonderband 51, 2001). Caroline Schramm's Ph.D. thesis, *Minimalismus: Leonid Dobyčins Prosa im Kontext der totalitären Ästhetik* (Frankfurt a.M.: Peter Lang, 1999) raises the issue of minimalism in the narrative prose of the novelist Leonid Dobychin. Schramm's concept of a "minimalism of signifiers" leading to an aesthetic condensation of the signified has been criticized for misrepresenting the nature of minimalism, in particular for ignoring the minimalist aesthetics of non-art and lack of "depth." See Holt Meyer, "Humilitas, minima modernitas: Für eine historische Pragmatik der 'Untiefen' des Minimalismus (nicht nur) in Rußland (am Beispiel der Karthotek[en] Lev Rubinštejns)," in Goller, *Minimalismus*, 447–75. Meyer sees the quintessential minimalist work of Russian literature in Lev Rubinshtein's card catalogues. Among the writers of the late Soviet era, Vasilii Shukshin and Evgenii Popov have been characterized as minimalists for opposing the "false culture of maximalism" in their short stories. See Raul' Eshel'man, "Kakaia, brat, pustota': Minimalizm v sovetskoi novelle," in *Russkaia novella: Problemy teorii i istorii. Sbornik statei*, eds. V. M. Markovich and V. Schmid (St. Petersburg: Izdatel'stvo S.-Peterburgskogo Universiteta, 1993), 249–73.

6. An anthology of contemporary Russian monostichs has recently been published in Switzerland. See *Geballtes Schweigen: Zeitgenössische russische Einzeiler*, ed. Felix Philipp Ingold (St. Gallen: Erker-Verlag, 1999).

7. *Novoe literaturnoe obozrenie* 23 (1997), 266 (in order to save paper, the printed version omits lines 23 through 999,986).

8. See the essay "The Work of Art in the Age of Mechanical Reproduction" in Walter Benjamin, *Illuminations. Essays and Reflections*, ed. Hannah Arendt, trans. Harry Zohn (New York: Schocken Books, 1968), 217–51.

9. John Perreault, "Minimal Abstracts," in Battcock, *Minimal Art*, 262.

10. Michael Riffaterre, "On the Prose Poem's Formal Features," in *The Prose Poem in France: Theory and Practice*, eds. Mary Ann Caws and Hermine Riffaterre (New York: Columbia University Press, 1983), 117.

11. See Ulrich Fülleborn, *Das deutsche Prosagedicht: Zu Theorie und Geschichte einer Gattung* (Munich: Wilhelm Fink Verlag, 1970), and Riffaterre's article cited above.

155

12. John Simon, *The Prose Poem as a Genre in Nineteenth-Century European Literature* (New York: Garland, 1987), 698.

13. See Fülleborn, *Das deutsche Prosagedicht,* 29–30.

14. Suzanne Bernard, *Le poème en prose de Baudelaire jusqu'à nos jours* (Paris: Nizet, 1959). On Baudelaire in particular, see 103–50.

15. John Simon, "Prose Poem," in *Princeton Encyclopedia of Poetry and Poetics* (2nd ed.), eds. Alex Preminger, Frank J. Warnke, and O. B. Hardison (Princeton: Princeton University Press, 1965), 665.

16. F.-J. Schaarschuh, "Das Problem der Gattung 'Prosagedicht' in Turgenevs 'Stichotvorenija v proze'," *Zeitschrift für Slawistik* 10, no. 4 (1965), 511, 518.

17. See the section "Metri i ritmy" in Grossman's essay "Posledniaia poema Turgeneva" (1918), reprinted in Leonid Grossman, *Sobranie sochinenii v piati tomakh* (Moscow: Sovremennye problemy, 1928), 3:75–94.

18. V. Zhirmunskii, "O ritmicheskoi proze," *Teoriia stikha* (Leningrad: Sovetskii pisatel', 1975), 579.

19. Fritz Nies, *Poesie in prosaischer Welt: Untersuchungen zum Prosagedicht bei Aloysius Bertrand and Baudelaire* (Heidelberg: Carl Winter, 1964).

20. Richard Terdiman, *Discourse/Counter-Discourse: The Theory and Practice of Symbolic Resistance in Nineteenth-Century France* (Ithaca, N.Y.: Cornell University Press, 1985); Jonathan Monroe, *A Poverty of Objects: The Prose Poem and the Politics of Genre* (Ithaca, N.Y.: Cornell University Press, 1987); Margueritte S. Murphy, *A Tradition of Subversion: The Prose Poem in English from Wilde to Ashbery* (Amherst: The University of Massachusetts Press, 1992).

21. Steven Monte, *Invisible Fences: Prose Poetry as a Genre in French and American Literature* (Lincoln: University of Nebraska Press, 2000), 86.

22. "I do not deny prose poetry revolutionary potential, but I am anti-essentialist when it comes to questions of form or genre: the fact that a poem is written in prose does not necessarily mean it is subversive." Ibid., 8.

23. Michel Beaujour, "Short Epiphanies: Two Contextual Approaches to the French Prose Poem," in *The Prose Poem in France,* 40.

24. Several scholars have pointed to Gor'kii's "Burevestnik" as a prime example of a Russian *stikhotvorenie v proze.* See, for example, F.-J. Schaarschuh, "Das Problem der Gattung 'Prosagedicht'," 506, and Albert Kovács, "Zhanr stikhotvoreniia v proze v russkoi literature kontsa XIX – nachala XX veka," *Romanoslavica* 19 (1979), 275.

25. The only exceptions seem to be Margueritte Murphy and Steven Monte, who both include John Ashbery's lengthy *Three Poems* in their discussion of the prose poem. Murphy claims that "[t]here is no essential constraint that would prohibit the prose poem from indefinite expansion" (*A Tradition of Subversion,* 213). However, she admits herself that Ashbery

"unambiguously rejected the rubric of 'prose poem' in the French sense for [his] works" (5).

26. See "Short Epiphanies," 40–42.

27. David Young, "Introduction," *Models of the Universe: An Anthology of the Prose Poem,* ed. Stuart Friebert and David Young (Oberlin: Oberlin College Press, 1995), 18.

28. A *poema v proze* is obviously something quite different. As possible examples of this genre, one could mention Gogol's *Mertvye dushi* (*Dead Souls*), subtitled "Poema," or Dostoevskii's *Dvoinik* (*The Double*), subtitled "Peterburgskaia poema." Ivan Karamazov calls his legend of the Grand Inquisitor a "poema v proze." The fact that some of Baudelaire's prose poems were given the title *poemy v proze* in Russian translation is probably best explained as a simple calque from the French (*poème=poema*).

29. For examples of such attributions, see Zh. Zel'dkheii-Deak [Zsuzsa Zöldhelyi], "'Stikhotvoreniia v proze' I. S. Turgeneva: K probleme zhanra." *Russkaia literatura,* vol. 2 (1990), 191. Ulrich Fülleborn does not hesitate to isolate "latent" prose poems from novels (*Das deutsche Prosagedicht,* 31–32). Of course, de facto prose poems can be created by editors when they isolate a segment from a larger context and print it in an anthology of prose poetry (as did Fülleborn in his two anthologies of German prose poems).

30. Walter Koschmal has suggested that it is this cyclization, with its establishment of a network of symbolic correspondences, that makes the prose poem a symbolist or modernist genre, whereas the individual prose poem, taken by itself, still belongs to the realist school. See "Das Prosagedicht als Gattung des evolutionären Wechsels," 155–56.

31. See "A Arsène Houssaye" in Charles Baudelaire, *Oeuvres complètes,* ed. Claude Pichois (Paris: Gallimard, 1975), 1:275, and "K chitateliu" in I. S. Turgenev, *Polnoe sobranie sochinenii i pisem,* 2d ed., *Sochineniia,* 12 vols. (Moscow: Nauka, 1978–86), 10:125.

32. Marie Maclean, *Narrative as Performance: The Baudelairean Experiment* (London: Routledge, 1988), 45.

33. *The American Prose Poem,* 13.

34. *Daniil Kharms and the Poetics of the Absurd,* 15.

35. See Gérard Genette, *Palimpsestes* (Paris: Seuil, 1982), 9.

36. *A Tradition of Subversion,* 64.

37. Thomas O. Beebee, *The Ideology of Genre: A Comparative Study of Generic Instability* (University Park: Penn State University Press, 1994), 128.

38. Gary Saul Morson, *The Boundaries of Genre: Dostoevsky's Diary of a Writer and the Traditions of Literary Utopia* (Austin: University of Texas Press, 1981), 48–49.

39. Barbara Johnson, *Défigurations du langage poétique: La Seconde Révolution Baudelairienne* (Paris: Flammarion, 1979), 37.

40. "The Prose Poem's Deconstruction of Literariness," in *Difference Unbound: The Rise of Pluralism in Literature and Criticism* (Amsterdam: Rodopi, 1995), 94–95.

41. Peter Johnson, "An Interview with Russell Edson," *The Writer's Chronicle* 31, no. 6 (May/Summer 1999), 30. Although Edson never mentions Kharms, some of his absurdist fables bear a striking resemblance to Kharms' mini-stories.

42. The latest edition of the standard *Princeton Encyclopedia* reports a "rapidly increasing interest" in the prose poem. See Mary Ann Caws, "Prose Poem," in *The New Princeton Encyclopedia of Poetry and Poetics,* eds. Alex Preminger and T. V. F. Brogan (Princeton: Princeton University Press, 1993), 977. The 1990s witnessed the birth of two specialized journals and the appearance of several anthologies devoted to the prose poem. For a good survey, see Michel Delville, *The American Prose Poem: Poetic Form and the Boundaries of Genre* (Gainesville: University Press of Florida, 1998).

CHAPTER TWO

1. M. M. Stasiulevich, "Iz vospominanii o poslednikh dniakh I. S. Turgeneva" (1883), quoted in I. S. Turgenev, *Polnoe sobranie sochinenii i pisem,* 2d ed., *Sochineniia,* 12 vols. (Moscow: Nauka, 1978–86), 10:452. This edition will be referred to as "PSS" in the text. Unless otherwise noted, all English translations are my own.

2. Thirty-two more texts were later discovered among Turgenev's papers by the French Slavist André Mazon, who published them in 1930. Together with a previously published posthumous piece, this brings the total number of Turgenev's prose poems to eighty-three.

3. Despite Stasiulevich's opposition, the title "Senilia" was used in later editions of Turgenev's prose poems.

4. Quoted in PSS 10:454.

5. N. G. Chernyshevskii to A. N. Chernyshevskii, Astrakhan, March 5, 1885, *Polnoe sobranie sochinenii,* 15 vols. (Moscow: GIKhL, 1950), 15:518.

6. February 18, 1885. Ibid., 513.

7. See Peter Brang, *I. S. Turgenev: Sein Leben und sein Werk* (Wiesbaden: Otto Harrassowitz, 1976), 204.

8. For a discussion of the concept of "family resemblance" in relation to genre theory, see Alastair Fowler, *Kinds of Literature: An Introduction to the Theory of Genres and Modes* (Cambridge, Mass.: Harvard University Press, 1982), 40–44.

9. Sonya Stephens, *Baudelaire's Prose Poems: The Practice and Politics of Irony* (Oxford: Oxford University Press, 1999), 1.

10. Since the late 1980s, no fewer than five monographs have appeared on Baudelaire's prose poems—incidentally, all of them in English. See the books by Maclean, Hiddleston, Kaplan, Evans, and Stephens.

11. Barbara Johnson, *Défigurations du langage poétique: La seconde révolution baudelarienne* (Paris: Flammarion, 1979).

12. Baudelaire, *Oeuvres Complètes,* 2 vols. (Paris: Gallimard, 1975), 1:275–76.

13. Rosemary Lloyd, "Horrifying the Homais: The Challenge of the Prose Poem," *L'esprit créateur* 39, no. 1 (Spring 1999), 41.

14. Quoted in Baudelaire, 1:1298.

15. Ibid.

16. For a discussion of this question, see Zel'dkheii (Zöldhelyi), "'Stikhotvoreniia v proze' I. S. Turgeneva," 188–89. Readers fluent in Hungarian will find a more substantial treatment in Zöldhelyi's *Turgenyev prózai költeményei.*

17. See PSS 10:447–48.

18. See "Liste de projets" in Baudelaire, 1:366.

19. Baudelaire, 1:275.

20. In addition to Zsuzsa Zöldhelyi's and Elizabeth Allen's articles, see Nana Bogdanovich, "Pokushai jedne knizhevne paralele: Pesme u prozi I. Turgeneva i Sh. Bodlera," *Letopis Matice srpske* 375, vol. 6 (June 1955), 562–74; Boris Pavlov, "Turgenevite 'Stikhotvoreniia v proza' i 'Malki Poemi v proza' na Sharl Bodler," *Literaturna Misul* 27, vol. 9 (1983), 25–31; and V. A. Pesterev, "Zhanr stikhotvoreniia v proze v tvorchestve I. S. Turgeneva i Sh. Bodlera," in *Rol' russkoi klassiki v razvitii i vzaimoobogashchenii literaturnykh zhanrov* (Ordzhonikidze: Severo-Osetinskii gos. universitet im. K. S. Khetagurova, 1986), 119–29.

21. "Turgenev's Last Will and Testament," 60.

22. Zöldhelyi, "'Stikhotvoreniia v proze' I. S. Turgeneva," 189.

23. Walter Koschmal considers allegory the defining generic feature of the prose poem for both Baudelaire and Turgenev (see "Das Prosagedicht als Gattung des evolutionären Wechsels," passim).

24. Pesterev, "Zhanr stikhotvoreniia v proze," 121.

25. See PSS 10:474.

26. See *Trésor de la langue française* (Paris: Edition du Centre National de la Recherche Scientifique, 1978), 6:175, for examples in French literary texts.

27. Baudelaire's use of popular sayings in his *Petits poèmes en prose* is discussed in J. A. Hiddleston, *Baudelaire and Le Spleen de Paris* (Oxford: Clarendon Press, 1987), 40–41.

28. Marie Maclean, *Narrative as Performance: The Baudelairean Experiment* (London: Routledge, 1988), 59.

29. This is a topic which surfaces elsewhere in Turgenev's cycle of prose poems. "White-hand" has to be seen in conjunction with the nameless heroine of the prose poem "Porog" ("The Threshold"), which was written one month later. This young woman, who is about to enter a life of terrorism, like the intellectual who sacrifices his life for the cause of revolution, is presented as both a "fool" and a "saint" (see Turgenev 10:147–48).

30. Perhaps Turgenev was simply following Baudelaire's own advice to the reader. In his preface to *Petits poèmes en prose*, Baudelaire recommends to "hack [the cycle of prose poems] into numerous fragments, and you will see that each can exist by itself" (Baudelaire 1:275).

31. In a variant of the text, the version published in *L'Artiste* on 1 November 1864, Baudelaire added a more explicit comment at the end: "'Parbleu!'—I answered my friend, '—a meter of a hanged person's rope, at a hundred francs the decimeter, all in all, each paying according to his means, that makes a thousand francs, a real, an effective relief for that poor mother'" (Baudelaire 1:1339). The seeming approval of the first-person narrator adds another layer of irony to Baudelaire's text.

32. Baudelaire, 1:328.

33. The theme surfaces not only in Turgenev's prose poems, but is also evident in his previous work. See, for example, the following scene from *Fathers and Sons*: "The door opened, and Fenichka came in with Mitya in her arms. She had put on him a little red smock with an embroidered collar, had combed his hair and washed his face [. . .] Fenichka had put her own hair in order, too, and had arranged her kerchief better; but she might well have remained as she was. And really is there anything in the world more captivating than a beautiful young mother with a healthy baby in her arms?" *Fathers and Sons*, trans. Constance Garnett, ed. Ralph E. Matlaw (New York: Norton, 1989), 28.

34. Charles Baudelaire, *Petits Poëmes en prose*, ed. Robert Kopp (Paris: José Corti, 1969), 305.

35. René Galand, *Baudelaire: poétique et poésie* (Paris: Nizet, 1969), 502.

36. Edward K. Kaplan, *Baudelaire's Prose Poems: The Esthetic, the Ethical and the Religious in* The Parisian Prowler (Athens: The University of Georgia Press, 1990), 107.

37. "Baudelaire, Manet et 'La Corde'," *Bulletin Baudelairien* 19, vol. 1 (April 1984), 7–11. See also Hiddleston, *Baudelaire and Le Spleen de Paris*, 9–11.

38. Steve Murphy, "Haunting Memories: Inquest and Exorcism in Baudelaire's 'La Corde'," *Dalhousie French Studies* 30 (1995), 65–91.

39. Ibid., 91.

40. *Baudelaire and Le Spleen de Paris*, 10.

41. I have discussed this topic in detail in my book *Baudelaire in Russia* (Gainesville: University Press of Florida, 1996).

42. Edward K. Kaplan, *Baudelaire's Prose Poems*, 156.

43. An interesting variant of this motif is the refused handshake, which we find in "Ch'ia vina?" ("Whose fault is it?" January 1878, PSS 10:179). The narrator refuses to seize the outstretched hand of a young woman because she is "youth" and he is "old age." With this allegorizing explanation, he postulates an unbridgeable gap between these two opposed stages of life.

44. A useful survey of the critical response to "Assomons les pauvres!" can be found in Richard D. E. Burton, *Baudelaire and the Second Republic: Writing and Revolution* (Oxford: Clarendon Press, 1991), 326–28. In addition to the books by Monroe and Kaplan mentioned above, see also Marie Maclean, *Narrative as Performance,* which interprets the text as an allegory of reading (162–76). Dolf Oehler, rather unconvincingly, has read "Assomons les pauvres!" as Baudelaire's call for revolutionary violence and class struggle. See "Assomons les pauvres! Dialektik der Befreiung bei Baudelaire," *Germanisch-Romanische Monatschrift* 56 (1975), 454–62.

45. Richard Terdiman, *Discourse/Counter-Discourse*, 316.

46. On "Assomons les pauvres!" see *Baudelaire and Le Spleen de Paris,* 39–40.

47. Nana Bogdanovich, the first scholar to notice the parallels between "Nishchii" and "Assomons les pauvres!" raises the question of whether, despite appearances, Baudelaire should not be considered more humane than Turgenev, "to the extent that he does not allow the possibility of hypocrisy" (Bogdanovich, "Pokushai jedne knizhne paralele," 573).

48. Koschmal even suggests a concrete link between "Nishchii" and chapter 35 of *Magnum speculum,* translated into Russian in the seventeenth century as *Velikoe zertsalo* (see "Das Prosagedicht," 144).

49. See the prose poem "Khristos" (PSS 10:161–62).

50. Not surprisingly, such a conciliatory attitude provoked the scorn of Soviet critics. S. E. Shatalov, the author of the only Soviet monograph on Turgenev's *Stikhotvoreniia v proze,* denounced the ending of "Milostynia" as "false" and "forced." See *"Stikhotvoreniia v proze" I. S. Turgeneva* (Arzamas: Arzamasskii gos. ped. institut, 1961), 58.

51. Baudelaire, *Oeuvres,* 1:323–24.

52. Charles Baudelaire, *The Parisian Prowler,* trans. Edward K. Kaplan (Athens: The University of Georgia Press, 1989), 70.

53. Ibid., 33.

54. Baudelaire, *Oeuvres,* 1:344.

55. *The Parisian Prowler,* 101.

56. See Hiddleston, *Baudelaire and Le Spleen de Paris,* 78–80.

57. Lloyd, "Horrifying the Homais," 40.

58. Kaplan, *Baudelaire's Prose Poems,* 132.

59. See, for example, "Razgovor" ("A Conversation," PSS 10:127–28, or "Priroda" ["Nature"]), PSS 10:164–65.

60. "Turgenev's Last Will and Testament," 67–68.

61. See her analysis of "La Chevelure" vs. "Un Hémisphère dans une chevelure" and the two versions of "L'Invitation au voyage" in *Défigurations du langage poétique,* 31–55, 103–60.

62. See "Turgenev's Last Will and Testament," 54. For a comparison of Turgenev's prose poems with his verse lyric, see Walter Koschmal, "Zur Evolution des binären Weltmodells in I. S. Turgenevs Lyrik," *Slavistische Studien zum IX. Internationalen Slavistenkongress in Kiev 1983* (Cologne: Böhlau Verlag, 1983), 235–66.

63. "'Stikhotvoreniia v proze' I. S. Turgeneva. K probleme zhanra," 191–93.

64. Elizabeth Allen fails to take this context into account when she claims that Baudelaire's prose poems are more "poetic" and Turgenev's more "prosy," simply because Baudelaire was a poet and Turgenev a prose writer (see "Turgenev's Last Will and Testament," 60–61). The greater formal complexity of Baudelaire's prose poems noted by Allen does not in itself justify the claim that these texts are more "poetic."

65. See Christa Gasde, "Das Prosagedicht—ein Traum: Zu Turgenevs 'Starucha' und einem Feuilleton von Ludwig Pietsch," in J. Holthusen, ed., *Beiträge und Skizzen zum Werk Ivan Turgenevs* (Munich: Otto Sagner, 1977), 126.

66. For a brief but useful survey of the critical response, see Allen, "Turgenev's Last Will and Testament," 55–56.

67. See Ia. P. Polonskii, "Dve fialki" (1870–75), *Polnoe sobranie stikhotvorenii* (St. Petersburg: A. F. Marks, 1896), 2:125–27; and "Stikhotvoreniia v proze," in *Povesti i rasskazy (Pribavlenie k polnomu sobraniu sochinenii),* ch. 1–2 (St. Petersburg: Tip. V. V. Komarova, 1895), 279–80.

CHAPTER THREE

1. B. M. Eikhenbaum, *L. N. Tolstoi. Semidesiatye gody* (Leningrad: Sovetskii pisatel', 1960), 185.

2. See V. M. Garshin, "Stikhotvoreniia v proze" (1875, 1884), in *Sochineniia* (Moscow-Leningrad: GIKhL, 1951), 386–88.

3. See L. N. Issova, "Zhanr stikhotvoreniia v proze v tvorchestve V. M. Garshina," *Uchenye zapiski kaliningradskogo universiteta,* vol. 5 (1970), 133–44; and Iu. B. Orlitskii, "Stikhotvoreniia v proze v tvorchestve V. M. Garshina," in Peter Henry et al., eds., *Vsevolod Garshin on the Eve of the Millennium: An International Symposium in Three Volumes* (Nottingham: Astra Press, 1999), 2:579–80.

4. See, for example, Turgenev's "Zhiteiskoe pravilo" ("A Rule of Life"), PSS 10:179, or "Vostochnaia legenda" ("An Eastern Legend"), PSS

10:138–39. The main character in this story, Dzhiaffar, has the same name as the protagonist of Garshin's text.

5. A substantial number of the prose poems published in turn-of-the century Russian journals were translated from Polish. See, for example, A. Nemoevskii (Andrzei Niemojewski), "Eskizy i stikhotvoreniia v proze," *Novoe Slovo*, 1897, October, kn. 1 (104–12), kn. 2 (164–70), and by the same author, "Stikhotvoreniia v proze," *Zhizn'*, 1899, no. 6, 97–102. Niemojewski's prose poems fall into the category of socially engaged literature, dealing mainly with topics like coal mines, machines, and workers.

6. "Skitalets" ("The Wanderer") was the pseudonym of S. G. Petrov (1869–1941). A. Kornev's real name was A. V. Iarovitskii (1876–1903). He was expelled from the Historical Faculty of Moscow University in 1899 for revolutionary activities and exiled to Nizhnii Novgorod, where he became active as a social agitator and also gained the friendship of Gor'kii.

7. *Zhizn'*, no. 4 (April 1900), 370–71.

8. The fact that these prose poems were published in left-wing journals resulted sometimes in rather incongruous juxtapositions. For example, the prose poem "Krasota" ("Beauty") by Skitalets, a neo-romantic fantasy about the poet's love for a perhaps nonexistent woman, appeared in the Marxist journal *Sovremennyi mir* next to an article entitled "The Theory of Value and Dialectical Materialism: On the 40th Anniversary of *Das Kapital*, 1867–1907." See *Sovremennyi mir*, no. 1 (January 1908), 52–53.

9. Jonathan Monroe, *A Poverty of Objects*, 19.

10. Rolf Hellebust, "Aleksei Gastev and the Metallization of the Revolutionary Body," *Slavic Review* 56, no. 3 (Fall 1997), 505.

11. The only notable exception seems to be the writer S. N. Sergeev-Tsenskii, who retroactively gave to six of his short stories, originally written between 1902 and 1905, the subtitle "Stikhotvoreniia v proze" when they were included in the edition of his collected works in 1955–56 (Moscow: Khudozhestvennaia literatura, 10 vols.). However, none of these stories has the brevity that we associate with the genre of the prose poem. All are at least seven pages long.

12. See on this V. N. Afanas'ev, "I. A. Bunin i russkoe dekadentstvo 90-kh godov," *Russkaia literatura* 11 (1968), vol. 3, 175–81.

13. James B. Woodward, *Ivan Bunin. A Study of His Fiction* (Chapel Hill: The University of North Carolina Press, 1980), 26.

14. Galina Kuznetsova, *Grasskii dnevnik* (Washington D.C.: Victor Kamkin, 1967), 176.

15. "Menia nauchili kratkosti stikhi" ("verses taught me brevity"). "O Chekhove," I. A. Bunin, *Sobranie Sochinenii*, 9 vols. (Moscow: Khudozhestvennaia literatura, 1965–67), 9:172.

16. Maria Langleben, "The Guilty House: A Textlinguistic Approach to the Shortest Prose by I. A. Bunin," *Elementa* 1, no. 3 (1994), 266.

17. *Vozrozhdenie,* April 30, 1931. Quoted in V. P. Prokhodova, "Evoliutsiia zhanra miniatury v proze I. A. Bunina," Ph.D. diss., Moscow State University, 1990, 76.

18. J. K. Huysmans, *Against the Grain* (New York: Dover Publications, 1969), 186.

19. A. I. Kuprin, *Sobranie sochinenii,* 9 vols. (Moscow: Khudozhestvennaia literatura, 1973), 7:474.

20. Bunin, *Sobranie sochinenii,* 5:399.

21. In a later prose miniature, Bunin realized this image literally. "Un petit accident" (1949) describes a driver who has suddenly died at the steering wheel of his car, with his face resembling "a mask." See *Sobranie sochinenii,* 7:343–44.

22. For a more detailed discussion of this text, see Langleben, "The Guilty House," 285–91.

23. In his copy of a review by M. Adrianov (*Novaia Gazeta,* May 1, 1931), Bunin underlined a passage where the reviewer asserts an "amazing similarity" between some of his texts and Turgenev's *Stikhotvoreniia v proze,* and wrote in the margin, "very stupid" (*ochen' glupo*). See Russian State Archive for Literature and Art (RGALI), fond 44, kart. 2, ed. khran. 152, 6. Quoted in Prokhodova, "Evoliutsiia zhanra miniatury v proze I. A. Bunina," Prilozhenie, 8–9. In general, Bunin rejected any comparison of his works with Turgenev's. See on this Iurii Mal'tsev, *Bunin* (Frankfurt am Main: Posev, 1994), 82.

24. Mal'tsev, *Bunin,* 83.

25. Bunin, *Sobranie sochinenii,* 5:147–48.

26. Ibid., 5:456.

27. Ibid., 5:457.

CHAPTER FOUR

1. The only partial exception is Lidiia Zinov'eva-Annibal's cycle of prose miniatures "Teni sna," which was published in the fourth volume of the almanac *Severnye tsvety* in 1905. A description of the contents of the almanac at the beginning of the volume refers to these pieces as "*Stikhotvoreniia v proze.*" However, the actual text is printed as "Teni sna" with no generic subtitle.

2. "Stikhotvoreniia v proze Sharlia Bodlera." *Iziashchnaia literatura: Zhurnal proizvedenii inostrannoi belletristiki,* no. 10 (1884), 141–57. An earlier Russian translation of five prose poems by Baudelaire had appeared already in 1878 in the journal *Zhivopisnoe obozrenie (Art Review).* Perhaps in accordance with the journal's primary function, the editors introduced them as "poems in prose, providing ready-made subjects for paintings, and serving with their style as a link between prose and poetry" (*Zhivopisnoe*

obozrenie, 1878, no. 20, 406). For a general discussion of the early reception of Baudelaire's prose poems in Russia, see Adrian Wanner, *Baudelaire in Russia,* 61–63. Incidentally, the first Anglo-American translation of French prose poems, published by Stuart Merrill in New York in 1890, also appeared under a "painterly" title, *Pastels in Prose.* On this edition, see Murphy, *A Tradition of Subversion,* 15–30.

3. D. S. Merezhkovskii, *Polnoe sobranie sochinenii,* 24 vols. (Moscow: Tip. I. D. Sytina, 1914), 18:218–20.

4. The poem was published in the 1894 collection *Pod severnym nebom (Under Northern Skies).* See K. Bal'mont, *Izbrannoe* (Moscow: Khudozhestvennaia literatura, 1983), 39–42.

5. *Stikhotvoreniia Bodlera* (Moscow: Izdanie Petrovskoi biblioteki, 1894), p. viii.

6. "Proshchal'nyi vzgliad," together with two other prose poems, "Razluka" ("Separation") and "Skazka nochi" ("Fairy Tale of the Night"), first appeared in the newspaper *Russkie vedomosti,* 1894, no. 13. Later, "Razluka" and "Skazka nochi" were included in the first edition of *Pod severnym nebom,* and "Proshchal'nyi vzgliad" reappeared in *V bezbrezhnosti.*

7. "Chaika," without the acompanying prose poem, was republished in *Pod severnym nebom.* As Walter Koschmal has observed, the poem seems inspired by Turgenev's prose poem "Bez gnezda" ("Without a Nest," PSS 10:178). See Koschmal, "Das Prosagedicht," 147. Both texts evoke the flight of a lonely bird over the sea, but with some important differences. Turgenev constructs his prose poem as an allegory that clearly identifies the bird as an emblem of the poet, and provides a clear-cut story line beginning with the bird's search for a safe place to build a nest and ending with its fall into the sea. This allegoric tale of despair turns in Bal'mont's poem into an occasion for aesthetic intoxication. Rhetorical questions about the bird's provenance, destination, and motivation are left unanswered. Instead, Bal'mont evokes metaphorical images of the "north wind's weeping" which fuses with the "sobbing" of the "insane" bird and the poet's own incantatory verbal music.

8. K. Bal'mont, *V bezbrezhnosti* (Moscow: A. A. Levenson, 1895), 59–64.

9. K. Bal'mont, *Pod severnym nebom* (St. Petersburg: Tip. M. Stasiulevicha, 1894), 41–42.

10. "Proshchal'nyi vzgliad," *V bezbrezhnosti,* 59.

11. See "V tsarstve l'dov" (volume "Tishina") in K. D. Bal'mont, *Polnoe sobranie stikhov,* 10 vols. (Moscow: Skorpion, 1908–13), 1:229–32.

12. *Pod severnym nebom,* 79–81. Originally published as part of the triptych "Teni" (see note 7).

13. It is interesting to contrast Bal'mont's approach with Bunin's roughly contemporary sketch "V Al'pakh" ("In the Alps," 1902). After

stressing the inhospitable and threatening character of the Alpine land-scape, Bunin ends with a lyric praise of human brotherhood and spiritual-ity: "We carried into the night and fog the spark of a divine mystery—our thoughts and feelings, our brotherly closeness of man to man and our young friendship, the conscience of which is so delightful in the face of the eter-nal and hostile with which dead nature surrounds us, and which engenders the highest manifestation of the human spirit—poetry!" (Bunin, *Sobranie sochinenii,* 2:440).

14. *V bezbrezhnosti,* 135–37.

15. For a discussion of Bal'mont's reception of Baudelaire, see Wan-ner, *Baudelaire in Russia,* 73–82.

16. *V bezbrezhnosti,* 91.

17. "Cheveux bleus, pavillon de ténèbres tendues, / Vous me rendez l'azur du ciel immense et rond" (Baudelaire, *Oeuvres complètes,* 1:27).

18. A reprint of the seven prose poems excluded from the later edi-tions of *Pod severnym nebom* and *V bezbrezhnosti* can be found in Vladimir Markov, *Kommentar zu den Dichtungen von K. D. Bal'mont, 1890–1909* (Cologne: Böhlau Verlag, 1988), 39, 65–71.

19. As the only partial exception, one could mention Bal'mont's "Malye zerna. Mysli i oshchushcheniia" ("Little Grains. Thoughts and Feel-ings"), published in *Vesy* in 1907, no. 3, 47–56. The style of these min-iatures is quite different from the prose poems of the 1890s, but among the "philosophical" fragments and aphorisms, one also finds a few lyrical pieces.

20. See S. S. Grechishkin and A. V. Lavrov, "Briusov o Turgeneve," in *Turgenev i ego sovremenniki,* ed. M. P. Alekseev (Leningrad: Nauka, 1977), 173.

21. "Miscellanea," XVIII, in V. Ia. Briusov, *Izbrannye sochineniia.* 2 vols. (Moscow: Gos. Izd-vo khudozh. lit-ry, 1955), 2:544. The inclusion of Poe among the authors of successful prose poems is somewhat puzzling. Perhaps Briusov is referring to Mallarmé's French translation of Poe's po-etry, which is written in prose.

22. Barbara Johnson, however, has argued that "Le Thyrse" actually deconstructs the notion of duality in the prose poem by demonstrating its incapacity to serve as a stable model of the relationship between poetry and prose. See *Défigurations du langage poétique,* 62–65.

23. See A. L. Miropol'skii, "Iarko-svetlaia zvezda" ("A Bright-Shining Star"), *Russkie simvolisty,* vyp. 2-i (Moscow: Izd. V. A. Maslova, 1894), 47–48.

24. "Otdalennye dni," in Valerii Briusov, *Neizdannaia proza,* ed. I. M. Briusova (Moscow: Gos. izd-vo khudozh. lit-ry, 1931), 7.

25. See, for example, "Gorod (Putevye nabroski)," Russian State Li-brary, f. 386, kart. 3, ed. khran. 11 (June 21, 1897), a melancholic evocation

of a train ride punctuated with the repeated refrain "Further! I want the new, I search for solitude."

26. One of the leading poets of the French Parnasse, Théodore de Banville, rejected the prose poem with similar arguments in his *Petit traité de poésie française* (1872). See Bernard, *Le poème en prose,* 336.

27. RGALI, f. 6, op. 1, ed. khran. 57.

28. "Stikhotvoreniia v proze," Innokentii Annenskii, *Knigi otrazhenii* (Moscow: Nauka, 1979), 433–37.

29. See A. V. Fedorov, *Innokentii Annenskii: Lichnost' i tvorchestvo* (Leningrad: Khudozhestvennaia literatura, 1984), 82.

30. Annenskii, *Knigi otrazhenii,* 437.

31. Only one of these texts, "Mysli-igly" is dated (March 30, 1906). This is also the only one of Annenskii's prose poems to be published during the poet's lifetime (in the journal *Slovo,* 1906). Annenskii planned to use it as the opening piece of the volume *Kiparisovyi larets* (*The Cypress Chest*). See on this R. D. Timenchik, "O sostave sbornika Innokentiia Annenskogo *Kiparisovyi larets,*" *Voprosy literatury* 8 (1978), 310. Annenskii's four prose poems have been reprinted in Innokentii Annenskii, *Stikhotvoreniia i tragedii* (Leningrad: Sovetskii pisatel', 1990), 213–20.

32. Lidiia Ginzburg, *O lirike* (Moscow: Intrada, 1997), 295–96.

33. "No v samom *Ia* ot glaz *Ne Ia* / Ty nikuda uiti ne mozhezh'." Annenskii, *Stikhotvoreniia,* 205.

34. As Anna Ljunggren shows, Annenskii gives a very similar description of Chekhov's soul in his essay on "Lermontov's Humor." See *At the Crossroads of Russian Modernism: Studies in Innokentij Annenskij's Poetics* (Stockholm: Almqvist & Wiksell International, 1997), 47. The other intertexts that Ljunggren proposes for "Moia dusha" seem less convincing. She mentions Lermontov's "Taman'," because bags are mentioned in this story, and sees a common thread of metempsychosis linking "Moia dusha" with Baudelaire's "La vie antérieure." It seems to me, however, that reincarnation is not the theme of "Moia dusha." Rather, the text presents three different allegories of the poet's soul without implying a chronological sequence.

35. For a discussion of Annenskii's reception of Baudelaire, see Wanner, *Baudelaire in Russia,* 100–12.

36. The quotation is taken from the prose poem "Un roi pleure," which appeared in Paul Fort's journal *Vers et prose* in 1905, vol. 2, 80 (see Ljunggren, *At the Crossroads,* 69).

37. *Mechty i dumy Ivana Konevskogo 1896–1899.* (St. Petersburg: Tip. E. Evdokimov, 1900), 67–76.

38. On Konevskoi's Alpine sketches, see the comments by Zvetelina Staikov in Peter Brang., ed., *Landschaft und Lyrik: Die Schweiz in den Gedichten der Slaven. Eine kommentierte Anthologie* (Basel: Schwabe Verlag, 1998), 424–26.

39. Briusov later remembered that Dobroliubov "was then an extreme 'esthete' and very widely read in the 'new poetry' (French), of which I actually knew only fragments. Mallarmé, Rimbaud, Laforgue, Vielé-Griffin, not to speak of Verlaine and the forerunners of the 'new art,' like Baudelaire, Théophile Gautier and other Parnassians, he knew from cover to cover. He was penetrated with the very *spirit* of Decadence and, so to speak, opened before me that world of ideas, tastes, and judgements which were portrayed by Huysmans in his *A rebours.*" Valerii Briusov, "Avtobiografiia," in *Russkaia literatura XX veka,* quoted in Joan Delaney Grossman, "Aleksandr Dobroliubov: The Making of a Decadent," in Aleksandr Dobroliubov, *Sochineniia* (Berkeley: Berkeley Slavic Specialties, 1981), 11.

40. See "Starukha" ("The Old Woman"), Turgenev, PSS 10:128–29.

41. Dobroliubov, *Sochineniia,* 110.

42. A.M.D., "Obrazy." *Severnye tsvety na 1902 g.* (Moscow: Skorpion, 1902), 84–96. Reprinted in *Sochineniia,* 197–204.

43. Ibid., 200.

44. "Risunki iz sumasshedshego doma." *Severnye tsvety na 1903 g.,* 109–12. Reprinted in *Sochineniia,* 205–8.

45. Aleksandr Dobroliubov, *Iz knigi nevidimoi* (Moscow: Skorpion, 1905. Repr. Berkeley Slavic Specialties, 1983), 202.

46. It is interesting to note that T. S. Eliot rejected the prose poem on similar grounds. "Time has left us many things," he wrote in 1917, "but among those it has taken away we may hope to count *À rebours,* and the *Divagations,* and the writings of miscellaneous prose poets" ("The Borderline of Prose," quoted in Murphy, *A Tradition of Subversion,* 14–15). Margueritte Murphy has speculated whether Eliot's "lack of sustained interest in the prose poem, as well as Ezra Pound's, helped keep the form at the margins of modernist poetry in English." *A Tradition of Subversion,* 60.

47. Andrei Belyi, *Zoloto v lazuri* (Moscow: Skorpion, 1904), 177–96. In contrast to the numbered prose fragments in the notebooks, these texts have been provided with titles. In his selection for publication, Belyi gave preference to pieces with more narrative content, as opposed to purely lyrical mood pieces. For a plot summary, see Ronald E. Peterson, *Andrei Belyi's Short Prose* (Birmingham: Birmingham Slavonic Monographs, 1980), 11–16. Six more fragments from Belyi's notebook have been published by A. V. Lavrov in *Pamiatniki kul'tury: Novye otkrytiia, ezhegodnik 1980* (Leningrad, 1981), 121–25.

48. *Cahiers du monde russe et soviétique* 15 (1974), no. 1, 53–54. Contrary to Belyi's assertion, these texts have not disappeared. They can be consulted in the manuscript division of the Russian State Library, Moscow, f. 25, kart. 1, ed. khran. 1 ("Lyricheskie otryvki v proze"). In addition to the prose pieces, numbered 1–26, the notebook also contains a large number of "lyrical fragments in verse." Although metered and rhymed, they are written as a continuous text without line breaks.

49. A. V. Lavrov, *Andrei Belyi v 1900-e gody: Zhizn' i literaturnaia deiatel'nost'* (Moscow: Novoe Literaturnoe Obozrenie, 1995), 36.

50. *Andrei Belyi's Short Prose,* 16.

51. "Volosatik," *Zoloto v lazuri,* 179. Cf. also titles like "Videnie" (177) or "Son" (195).

52. Fragment No. 14, dated May 1899. Published in *Pamiatniki kul'tury,* 123. In the six pieces slated for publication in *Zoloto v lazuri,* Belyi significantly toned down his use of omission points.

53. Fragment No. 10, dated December 1899 (unpublished).

54. E.g., "Volosatik," or Fragment No. 25 (*Pamiatniki kul'tury,* 124).

55. *Zoloto v lazuri,* 188–90.

56. Ibid., 191–94.

57. Ibid., 184–87.

58. Thirty years later, in his autobiographical letter to Ivanov-Razumnik, Belyi remembered this fragment as one of the texts which could provide a source for merriment.

59. *Andrei Belyi v 1900-e gody,* 40.

60. In his memoirs, Belyi writes that he became captivated by Nietzsche in the fall of 1899, especially by his "amazing musicality" and by his aphoristic style, in which he saw "the limit of symbolization." He continues: "The period from 1899 to 1901 is for me mainly colored by Nietzsche, the reading of his works, the return to him again and again; 'Thus spoke Zarathustra' became my indispensable companion" ("stala moiei nastol'noiu knigoiu"). Andrei Belyi, *Na rubezhe dvukh stoletii* (Moscow: Khudozhestvennaia literatura, 1989), 434–35.

61. Fragments No. 22, dated October 1900, and No. 26, dated December 1900 (unpublished).

62. See "Konets sveta. Son" ("The End of the World: A Dream"), in Turgenev, PSS 10:134–35, and "Son" in *Zoloto v lazuri,* 195–96.

63. Fragment No. 25, dated November 1900. Published in *Pamiatniki kul'tury,* 124–26.

64. *Zoloto v lazuri,* 177–78. In the notebook, this text is entitled "Psalm No. 1" (Fragment No. 24, 1900).

65. As noted earlier, both the thyrsus and the golden cup were used by Baudelaire and Turgenev as metapoetic emblems of the prose poem. See "Le Thyrse" in Baudelaire, *Oeuvres,* 1:335–36, and "Kubok," in Turgenev, PSS 10:178.

66. "Argonavty," *Zoloto v lazuri,* 197–210. For a general discussion of Belyi's "Argonautism," see Alexander Lavrov, "Andrei Bely and the Argonauts' Mythmaking," in Irina Paperno and Joan Delaney Grossman, eds., *Creating Life: The Aesthetic Utopia of Russian Modernism* (Stanford: Stanford University Press, 1994), 83–121. In his unpublished manuscript for a planned collection of poetry entitled "Zovy vremen" ("Calls of times"),

1929–31, Belyi included "Argonavty" in a reworked form as a poem in free verse, together with three other former prose fragments ("Volosatik, "Revun," and "Videnie," which appears under the title "Byl golos"). Belyi added to the latter text a new ending that considerably tempers the optimistic enthusiasm of its dream vision: "Ia—prosypaius': / Noch'!" ("I—wake up: / It is night!"). See John Malmstad, *The Poetry of Andrej Belyj: A Variorum Edition,* Ph.D. diss., Princeton University, 1968, vol. 2, 184–201 and 268–69.

67. Aleksandr Blok, *Sobranie sochinenii,* 8 vols. (Moscow-Leningrad: Gos. izd-vo khudozhestvennoi literatury, 1962), 6:169–73.

68. Ibid., 170.

69. See on this chapter 8.

70. The second volume of the *Grif* almanac (Moscow, 1904) provides a particularly rich source of prose miniatures, with pieces by Aleksei Remizov ("Molitva," 39–40, "Poslednii chas," 41–42, "Ivan-Kupal," 43–46); A. L. Miropol'skii ("Prishlets," 71–73), N. Stal' ("Ia," 86–87); N. Iarkov ("Pustynia," 92–96); Odinokii ("Vozvrashchenie," 102–4); and Nikolai Tabetskii ("Crescendo . . . Fine! [Fantaziia]," 135–38). The third volume (1905) contains an untitled prose fragment by A. Kursinskii (147–48).

71. L. Annibal, "Teni sna," *Severnye tsvety assiriiskie. Al'manakh 4* (Moscow: Skorpion, 1905), 134–46.

72. "Nochnye," *Belye nochi. Peterburgskii al'manakh* (St. Petersburg: Izd. t-va Vol'naia tipografiia, 1907), 166–71. Lundberg (1883–1965), according to his unpublished 1913 autobiography, considered "Nochnye" his best work. See A. V. Chantsev, "Lundberg," in *Russkie pisately 1800–1917. Biografichskii slovar'* (Moscow: Rossiiskaia entsiklopediia, 1994), 3:412–13.

73. Ibid., 170.

74. *Severnye Tsvety. Tretii al'manakh* (Moscow: Skorpion, 1903), 152.

75. See Anna Lisa Crone, *Rozanov and the End of Literature: Polyphony and the Dissolution of Genre in Solitaria and Fallen Leaves* (Würzburg: jal-verlag, 1978). For a discussion of Rozanov as a proto-minimalist, see Rainer Grübel, "Der Text als Embryo. Aus der Vorgeschichte des russischen Minimalismus: Vasilij Rozanovs frühe Prosaminiaturen," in Mirjam Goller and Georg Witte, eds., *Minimalismus: Zwischen Leere und Exzeß* (Vienna: Wiener Slawistischer Almanach, Sonderband 51, 2001), 51–78.

76. *Vesy* 7 (1907), quoted in Roger Keys, *The Reluctant Modernist: Andrei Belyi and the Development of Russian Fiction 1902–1914* (Oxford: Clarendon Press, 1996), 97.

CHAPTER FIVE

1. Fedor Sologub, *Sobranie sochinenii. Vol. 10: Zakliatie sten. Skazochki i stat'i* (St. Petersburg: Sirin, 1913). This volume contains seventy-three "Skazochki" (9–120). Page references to this edition, abbreviated SS,

will be given in parentheses in the text. A first collection of thirty-nine fairy tales was published by Grif in 1904 as *Kniga skazok,* followed by a slim volume of *Politicheskie skazochki* a year later. Five additional stories not contained in *Sobranie sochinenii* appeared in *Politicheskie skazochki* (Moscow: Rodnaia rech', 1916).

2. The most extensive discussion can be found in Stanley J. Rabinowitz, *Sologub's Literary Children: Keys to a Symbolist's Prose* (Columbus: Slavica, 1980), 132–52; and Ulrich Steltner, "Russische Kunstmärchen der Jahrhundertwende: Fedor Sologub," *Jahrbuch der Brüder Grimm-Gesellschaft,* vol. 1 (Kassel, 1991), 161–82.

3. See "Fedor Sologub. Kniga skazok" (*Russkoe bogatstvo,* December 1904), republished in V. G. Korolenko, *O literature* (Moscow: Gos. izd-vo khudozh. lit-ry, 1957), 392–93.

4. *Sologub's Literary Children,* 142.

5. Ibid., 145.

6. "Russische Kunstmärchen," 176.

7. Ulrich Schmid, *Fedor Sologub: Werk und Kontext* (Bern: Peter Lang, 1995), 233.

8. Fedor Sologub, *Stikhotvoreniia* (Leningrad: Sovetskii pisatel', 1979), 248.

9. Baudelaire, *Oeuvres complètes,* 1:306.

10. Ibid., 326 (Baudelaire's italics).

11. *Baudelaire and Le Spleen de Paris,* 61.

12. Yves Vadé, *Le poème en prose et ses territoires* (Paris: Belin, 1996), 191.

13. Rimbaud, *Oeuvres* (Paris: Garnier, 1960), 260.

14. See Barbara Johnson, "La vérité tue: Une lecture de 'Conte'." *Littérature* (October 1973), 68–77.

15. Published in *Novyi zhurnal literatury, iskusstva i nauki,* no. 9 (1905), 289.

16. Sixteen translations appeared in *Strelets,* vols. 1–2 (Petrograd, 1915–16). Eight of these translations, including "Conte," were republished in Artiur Rembo, *Stikhi* (Moscow: Nauka, 1982). The appendix of V. E. Bagno, "Fedor Sologub-perevodchik frantsuzskikh simvolistov," in *Na rubezhe XIX i XX vekov: Iz istorii mezhdunarodnykh sviazei russkoi literatury,* ed. Iu. D. Levin (Leningrad: Nauka, 1991), 129–214, contains an additional twenty-one translations recovered from Sologub's archive (181–92). Thirteen of these texts had previously appeared in "Artiur Rembo-Novonaidennye perevody Fedora Sologuba," *Inostrannaia literatura* 9 (1990), 175–83.

17. See the sixteen texts published in Bagno, "Fedor Sologub-perevodchik frantsuzskikh simvolistov," 192–214. For a discussion of Sologub as a translator of Mallarmé's prose poems, see Roman Dubrovkin, *Stefan Mallarme i Rossiia* (Bern: Peter Lang, 1998), 273–302.

171

18. See O. Uail'd (Oscar Wilde), *Polnoe Sobranie sochinenii.* 4 vols. (St. Petersburg, 1912).

19. Turgenev only made sparing use of folktale elements in his prose poems. "Durak" ("An Idiot," PSS 10:137–38) features the formulaic opening "Zhil-byl na svete durak," and "Vostochnaia legenda" ("An Eastern Legend," PSS 10:138–39), which was written in the same month, has the outward form of an oriental tale. In neither case does Turgenev engage in any subversive narrative experiments.

20. Bagno, "Fedor Sologub–perevodchik frantsuzskikh simvolistov," 138.

21. It seems hard to agree with Rabinowitz, who sees in this story nothing but the depiction of "a trifling phenomenon: a bit of mud on the street, explained in a fresh and delightful manner" (*Sologub's Literary Children,* 146).

22. Daniil Kharms, *Polnoe sobranie sochinenii* (St. Petersburg: Akademicheskii proekt, 1997), 2:159.

23. *Russia's Lost Literature of the Absurd,* ed. George Gibian (Ithaca: Cornell University Press, 1971), 49.

24. "Mukhomor v nachal'nikakh" ("The Mushroom as Chief"), SS 60. "Mukhomor," literally "fly-agaric," can also mean a decrepit, old person. In Sologub's story, this idiomatic meaning of the word is (re-)literalized.

25. "Fedor Sologub," in *A Soviet Heretic: Essays by Yevgeny Zamyatin,* ed. and trans. Mirra Ginsburg (Chicago: University of Chicago Press, 1970), 221.

26. *Narodnye russkie skazki A. N. Afanas'eva.* 3 vols. (Moscow: Gos. izd-vo khudozh. lit-ry, 1957), 3:305.

27. See Afanas'ev no. 531 (3:305) and Sologub, SS 20.

28. Rabinowitz insists on seeing in this story merely a playful, charming prank, written in a style that exudes a "sense of simple innocence, a special kind of poetry which is precisely the author's objective" (*Sologub's Literary Children,* 140). He supports this view by mistranslating the last sentence as "And that's how the misunderstanding ended," thereby endowing the story with a reconciliatory happy ending.

29. "Russische Kunstmärchen," 171, n. 32.

30. *Sologub's Literary Children,* 134.

31. RO IRLI, f. 289, op. 1, n. 539, l. 127. Quoted in Schmid, *Fedor Sologub,* 198.

32. The story was first published in the journal *Zhivoi obraz* in 1898 (see the bibliography in Steltner, 178).

33. See on this Pierre R. Hart, "Functions of the Fairy Tale in Sologub's Prose," in Lauren G. Leighton, ed., *Studies in Honor of Xenia Gasiorowska* (Columbus: Slavica Publishers, 1983), 71–80; Linda Ivanits, "Fairy

Tale Motifs in Sologub's 'Dream on the Rocks'," ibid., 81–87; and Ulrich Schmid, "Märchenmotive," in *Fedor Sologub*, 196–218.

34. *Sologub's Literary Children*, 52.

35. Ibid., 132. The alleged optimism of Sologub's fairy tales has also been questioned by Hart (79) and Ivanits (86).

36. See "Aforizmy" and "Dostoinstvo i mera veshchei" in *Neizdannyi Fedor Sologub* (Moscow: Novoe literaturnoe obozrenie, 1997), 189–206.

37. "Russische Kunstmärchen," 175.

38. See ibid., 168.

39. *Vesy*, no. 11 (1904), republished in Valerii Briusov, *Sredi stikhov, 1894–1924* (Moscow: Sovetskii pisatel', 1990), 125–26.

CHAPTER SIX

1. Natal'ia Kodrianskaia, *Aleksei Remizov* (Paris, 1959), 303.

2. See the two "Sny" in Sologub's *Sobranie Sochinenii*, 10:123–26, mentioned in the previous chapter.

3. Sona Aronian, *The Dream as a Literary Device in the Novels and Short Stories of Aleksej Remizov*. Ph.D. diss., Yale University, 1971, ii.

4. See, in particular, "Pod krov'iu nochi. Sny," *Zolotoe Runo*, no. 5 (1908), 31–37 (25 dreams); "Bedovaia dolia" in *Sochineniia*, vol. 3 (St. Petersburg: Sirin, 1910, repr. Munich: Wilhelm Fink Verlag, 1971), 161–218 (50 dreams); "S ochei na ochi. Sny," in *Podorozhie* (St. Petersburg: Sirin, 1913), 245–54 (7 dreams); "Kuzovok" in *Vesennee porosh'e* (St. Petersburg: Sirin, 1915), 259–313 (33 dreams); and *Martyn Zadeka. Sonnik* (Paris: Opleshnik, 1954). This collection of 100 dreams has been republished in A. M. Remizov, *Izbrannye proizvedeniia* (Moscow: Panorama, 1995), 320–99.

5. *Martyn Zadeka*, 7.

6. According to S. P. Ianovskii's memoirs, Vladislav Khodasevich wrote to Remizov: "From today I forbid you to dream about me!" Quoted in Avril Pyman, "Petersburg Dreams," in Greta N. Slobin, ed., *Aleksej Remizov: Approaches to a Protean Writer* (Columbus: Slavica, 1987), 51.

7. *Martyn Zadeka*, 82. First published in *Podorozhie*, 1913.

8. Sologub's *Mel'kii bes* and Remizov's novel *Prud* (*The Pond*) both appeared in the same journal at the same time (*Voprosy zhizni*, 1905). The success of Sologub's novel completely overshadowed the reception of *Prud*, which caused some resentment on Remizov's part. The two writers did have friendly relations for a while, but cooled toward each other after the death in 1907 of Sologub's sister Ol'ga, who had been a close friend of Remizov and his wife. Another brief rapprochement between Remizov and Sologub occurred after the October Revolution thanks to their common anti-Bolshevik attitude. See on this Alla Gracheva, "K istorii otnoshenii Alekseia

Remizova i Fedora Sologuba (Vvedenie k teme)," http://www.ruthenia.ru:8085/document/397305.html.

9. *Martyn Zadeka,* 93.

10. Ibid., 10.

11. N. V. Reznikova reports that Remizov found Freud "interesting but one-sided." See Pyman, "Petersburg Dreams," 54.

12. Pyman, ibid.

13. *Martyn Zadeka,* 11.

14. Ibid., 13.

15. Ibid., 14.

16. In his diary, Remizov wrote: "Mochul'skii means well, he is cordial and well educated, but his strengths are limited, and what is 'alien' (*ne svoe*) and 'enigmatic' he translates into commonplaces (*obshchepriniatoe*)." Kodrianskaia, *Aleksei Remizov,* 224.

17. *Martyn Zadeka,* 97.

18. Reported by Pyman, "Petersburg Dreams," 52.

19. See "Bedovaia Dolia," 177–78, and *Martyn Zadeka,* 87.

20. The name Vlasov acquired infamous notoriety in the Soviet Union after World War II as the name of the general who led an army of Russian volunteers fighting together with Nazi Germany against Stalin. In Soviet parlance, Vlasov beame the archetypal figure of the traitor (prophetically foreshadowed by Remizov's "treacherous Vlasov"?). Perhaps it was in order to avoid this association that Remizov changed the name to Solonchuk.

21. Strictly speaking, of course, *any* written fixation of a dream is already a secondary revision (the first revision being the recalling of the dream after waking up).

22. See T. V. Tsiv'ian, "O remizovskoi gipnologii i gipnografii," in V. V. Ivanov, V. N. Toporov, and T. V. Tsiv'ian, eds., *Serebrianyi vek v Rossii. Izbrannye stranitsy* (Moscow: Radiks, 1993), 311–12.

23. *Martyn Zadeka,* 15 (emphasis added).

24. Natal'ia Kodrianskaia, *Aleksei Remizov,* 41.

25. *Martyn Zadeka,* 96.

26. The manuscript of Remizov's translation is kept in the Russian State Archive of Literature and Art in Moscow (RGALI, f. 420, op. 1, ed. khran. 42).

27. Horst Lampl, in his article "Innovationsbetrebungen im Gattungssystem der russischen Literatur des frühen 20. Jahrhunderts—am Beispiel A. M. Remizovs," *Wiener Slavistisches Jahrbuch* 24 (1978), classifies several of Remizov's early texts from the collections "Belaia bashnia" and "Posolon'" as prose poems (161), but he considers his dreams as a genre of its own, "the most eccentric and 'avant-garde' of the genres practiced by Remizov" (ibid., 166). Sona Aronian has described Remizov's dream recordings as "prose poems celebrating moments of subconscious experience

as a self-valuable and independent reality," but she did not explore the implications of this generic label. See Sona Aronian, "The Russian View of Remizov," *Russian Literature Triquarterly* 18 (1985), 5.

28. See on this Alex M. Shane, "Rhythm without Rhyme: The Poetry of Aleksej Remizov," in Slobin, *Aleksej Remizov. Approaches to a Protean Writer,* 217–36.

29. See *Chortov log i polunoshchnoe solntse. Rasskazy i poemy* (St. Petersburg: EOS, 1908), 197–246.

30. Aleksei Remizov, *Sochineniia.* 8 vols. (St. Petersburg: Shipovnik, 1910–12), 2:149–202.

31. "Molitva," 39–40; "Poslednii chas," 41–42; "Ivan-Kupal," 43–46.

32. See Miropol'skii's "Iarko-svetlaia zvezda"; Turgenev's "Konets sveta"; and Belyi's "Son" discussed in chapter 4.

33. Greta N. Slobin, *Remizov's Fictions, 1900–1921* (DeKalb: Northern Illinois University Press, 1991), 35.

34. "Konets sveta" ("The End of the World), PSS 10:134–35, and "Vstrecha" ("Encounter"), ibid., 173–74.

35. See "Nasekomoe" ("The Insect"), ibid., 151; "Lazurnoe tsarstvo" ("The Azure Kingdom"), ibid., 152–53; and "Priroda" ("Nature"), ibid., 164–65.

36. See the commentaries in Turgenev, PSS 10:448–49. As has been mentioned earlier, Baudelaire, too, included a category of dreams in his plan for future prose poems, but they remained unrealized. Only one of his prose poems is explicitly narrated as a dream—"Les tentations ou Eros, Plutus et la Gloire" (*Oeuvres complètes,* 1:307–10).

37. See ibid., 455–56. Annenkov criticized Turgenev's inconsistent use of the "dream" heading: "Either everything is a dream, or nothing is a dream in these poems, and there is no reason for conferring to some of them an *excusing* epithet, and not to others." Turgenev seemed to agree with this argument, although he maintained the "son" subtitle in two cases.

38. Aleksei Remizov, *Ogon' veshchei. Sny i predson'e* (Paris: Opleshnik, 1954), 177–78. As we now know, of course, "Starukha" had originally been called a dream. In fact, in the very first draft, the title of this piece was "Son 1-i" ("First Dream"). See Turgenev, PSS 10:479.

39. Turgenev, PSS 10:164–65.

40. Ibid., 128–29.

41. To what extent this story corresponds to an actual dream has to remain an open question. Interestingly enough, Turgenev told it to his German friend Ludwig Pietsch in the summer of 1878 as the alleged report of a recent dream, without mentioning the literary status of the text. Pietsch published his account of the story as "Ein Traum" in *Schlesische Zeitung.* See on this Christa Gasde, "Das Prosagedicht-ein Traum. Zu Turgenevs 'Starucha' und einem Feuilleton von Ludwig Pietsch," in J. Holthusen, ed.,

Beiträge und Skizzen zum Werk Ivan Turgenevs (Munich: Otto Sagner, 1977), 109–34.

42. See "Bab'e leto" ("Indian Summer") in "Bedovaia dolia," 211–12, and its reworked form, "Mat'" ("Mother") in *Martyn Zadeka*, 90.

43. Ibid., 29–30. The rest of the dream recounts how the narrator tries to catch a ride in a cart carrying stones and sand. A mouse-like old woman wants to do the same thing. The cart overturns, the narrator grabs the horse by the tail and gets pulled along the street. He wakes up and finds himself in a Moscow carriage, surrounded by mountains of paper and envelopes. The coachman has fallen asleep and the horse "goes by its own will."

44. Ibid., 94.

45. This becomes evident in Freud's answer to André Breton, who had asked him for a contribution to an anthology of dreams that he was editing. Freud declined, asserting that the manifest dream text in itself had "no interest" for him. Freud's statement in all likelihood would also have reflected his reaction to Remizov's dream project: "A collection of dreams without added associations, without knowledge of the circumstances of dreaming, doesn't mean anything to me, and I can hardly imagine what it could mean to anybody else." See André Breton, ed., *Trajectoire du rêve* (Paris: G.L.M., 1938), 127. The text appears as a facsimile of Freud's handwritten letter at the end of Breton's anthology of dreams. No comment or translation is provided. Readers ignorant of German must have understood it as probably some friendly endorsement of the Viennese master for the project of his French disciple.

46. *Martyn Zadeka*, 7

47. Ibid., 9.

48. Tsiv'ian in fact uses the term *"sdvig"* in referring to Remizov's dreams. See "O remizovskoi gipnologii i gipnografii," 323 and 330.

49. On Guro, see chapter 7. Elena Guro's husband, Mikhail Matiushin, comments in his memoirs on the mutual high esteem Remizov and Guro had for each other's work. See M. Matiushin, "Russkie kubofuturisty," in Elena Guro, *Nebesnye verbliuzhata* (Rostov-na-Donu: Izdatel'stvo Rostovskogo universiteta, 1993), 274.

50. *Apollon*, no. 3 (1909), 23, quoted in Aronian, "The Russian View of Remizov," 5.

51. A. A. Blok, *Sobranie sochinenii*. 8 vols. (Moscow-Leningrad: Khudozhestvennaia literatura, 1962), 5:408. For a discussion of Blok's own use of dreams, see R. D. Timenchik, V. N. Toporov, and T. V. Tsivian, "Sny Bloka i 'Peterburgskii tekst' nachala XX veka," in Z. G. Mints, ed., *Tezisy I vsesoiuznoi (III) konferentsii "Tvorchestvo A. A. Bloka i russkaia kul'tura XX veka"* (Tartu: Tartuskii Gos. universitet, 1975), 129–35.

52. See chapter 7.

53. D. V. Filosofov, *Staroe i novoe* (Moscow: I. D. Sytin, 1912), 22–28.

54. See Andrei Siniavskii, "Literaturnaia maska Alekseia Remizova," in Slobin, *Aleksej Remizov: Approaches to a Protean Writer*, 25–39.

55. Stasiulevich suggested the subtitle "Son" for the politically risky prose poem "Porog" ("The Threshold"), probably because he thought that this would make it easier to pass the text through censorship. As it turned out, Turgenev deemed it unpublishable even in this disguise. This context helps to clarify Annenkov's remark about the subtitle "Son" as an *"excusing epithet."* See Gasde, "Das Prosagedicht-ein Traum," 123.

56. Wim Tigges, *An Anatomy of Literary Nonsense* (Amsterdam: Rodopi, 1988), 47.

57. Ibid., 51, 54–55.

58. *Ogon' veshchei*, 110.

59. See on this Gary Saul Morson, "Gogol's Parables of Explanation: Nonsense and Prosaics," in Susanne Fusso and Pricilla Meyer, eds., *Essays on Gogol: Logos and the Russian Word* (Evanston: Northwestern University Press, 1992), 200–39. Remizov himself briefly commented on "The Nose" as a dream in *Ogon' veshchei*, 73.

60. N. V. Gogol', *Polnoe sobranie sochinenii*. 14 vols. (Moscow: Izd-vo AN SSSR, 1937–52), 10:376–77.

61. In his earliest dream publications in *Zolotoe Runo* (1908), and the collection "Bedovaia dolia" (1910), Remizov added a footnote at the end of the texts, stating that "every dream has the same conclusion: 'And then I woke up'." It is noteworthy that Remizov eliminated this statement in his later dream collections.

62. In her article on surrealism in Russian literature, Liudmila Foster mentions some parallels between the theoretical views of Remizov and the surrealists, in particular with regard to their emphasis on dreams as a valid aspect of reality. However, she claims that Remizov's dreams do not qualify as surrealist literature, because they "clearly delineate the dream as a part of empirical reality." See "K voprosu o siurrealizme v russkoi literature," in *American Contributions to the Seventh International Congress of Slavists*, vol. 2 (The Hague: Mouton, 1973), 218. This seems a somewhat curious argument, since the French surrealists, like Remizov, claimed that their dream-texts were empirical recordings of actual dreams.

63. "Pouchkine: Six rêves," in André Breton, ed., *Trajectoire du rêve*, 33–39.

64. Iurii Annenkov, *Dnevnik moikh vstrech. Tsikl tragedii*. 2 vols. (New York: Inter-Language Literary Associates, 1966), 1:238.

65. In her magisterial investigation of the role of dreams in surrealist literature, Sarane Alexandrian gives the following description of the surrealist understanding of dreams: "For the romantics, a dream is what happens at night during sleep, and during the day in hours of idleness when the

spirit moves about; for the surrealists, it is much more than that, it is a *reality* inherent in the good functioning of the psychic mechanism in any situation of life." *Le surréalisme et le rêve* (Paris: Gallimard, 1974), 9.

66. *Martyn Zadeka*, 98.

67. André Breton, *Manifestoes of Surrealism*, trans. Richard Seaver and Helen R. Lane (Ann Arbor: University of Michigan Press, 1969), 14.

68. Ibid., 26 (emphasis added).

69. D. P. Gallagher mentions the draft of a letter from Remizov to Breton kept in N. V. Reznikova's archive in Paris, in which Remizov "alludes to past conversations with the surrealist leader and expresses a familiarity with surrealist activities." See Daniel Peter Gallagher, *The Surrealist Mode in Twentieth-Century Russian Literature*. Ph.D. diss., University of Kansas, 1975, 30.

70. Kodrianskaia, *Aleksei Remizov*, 41. Perhaps Remizov was simply more honest than the surrealists, whose carefully constructed "automatic writing" gives every appearance of being not all that automatic after all. See on this Herbert S. Gershman, *The Surrealist Revolution in France* (Ann Arbor: University of Michigan Press, 1969), 39.

71. See Alexandrian, *Le surréalisme et le rêve*, 243.

72. Gershman, *The Surrealist Revolution in France*, 38.

73. *Le surréalisme et le rêve*, 151.

74. *La Révolution Surréaliste*, vol. 2 (1924), 27.

75. Ibid., vol. 3 (1925), 2. The killing of a rat also occurs in Remizov's dream "André Gide" (*Martyn Zadeka*, 36–37). The narrator, observing a tête-à-tête between Gide and Verlaine in some kind of crevice, steps into a rathole and frightens the rat. "We have to hack it to pieces!" says Verlaine, and hits the rat with his fist.

76. In his Surrealist Manifesto of 1924, Breton did celebrate childhood as a sort of lost ideal state (40), but he rejected fairy tales, since he believed them to be "tainted by puerility" (15).

77. *Martyn Zadeka*, 98.

78. Ibid., 21.

79. For a discussion of the relationship between nonsense and surrealism, see Tigges, *An Anatomy of Literary Nonsense*, 116–22.

80. Ibid., 117.

81. Breton analyzed two of his own dreams in *Les vases communicants*. 6th ed. (Paris: Gallimard, 1955), 9–83. In this book, Breton tried to reconcile his Freudian understanding of dreams with the tenets of Marxist-Leninist materialism. He went as far as reproaching Freud of being not materialist enough and leaving the door open for idealist explanations. Quoting Lenin, Breton condemned this idealism as a typical product of the "ignorance, the stupidity and absurd savagery of the capitalist contradictions" (25).

82. One wonders, for example, what must have crossed Remizov's mind when he read Pierre de Massot's fawning obituary of Felix Dzherzhinskii in *La Révolution Surréaliste,* which begins with the words: "Alas, on a faraway sky, a star has forever ceased to radiate!" (vol. 8 [1925], 15).

83. *Martyn Zadeka,* 52.

84. Ibid., 61.

85. Aleksei Remizov, *Vzvikhrennaia Rus'* (Moscow: Sovetskaia Rossiia, 1990), 95, 120.

86. See Aleksei Remizov, *Myshkina dudochka* (Paris: Opleshnik, 1953), 93.

87. See Remizov's diary entry of August 31, 1957, in Kodrianskaia, *Aleksei Remizov,* 322. Remizov expresses his frustration over a negative comment about his work that he found in the foreword to one of Prishvin's books, and his (of course hopeless) desire to "respond to Prishvin about this."

88. None of the later surrealist journals contains any dream accounts. See Alexandrian, *Le surréalisme et le rêve,* 260.

CHAPTER SEVEN

1. Baudelaire, *Oeuvres,* 1:275.

2. On the relation between prose poem and painting, see "Poème en prose et description," in Vadé, *Le poème en prose,* 196–202, and "The Descriptive Tendency" in Murphy, *A Tradition of Subversion,* 74–82.

3. "Short Epiphanies," 47.

4. Bernard, *Le poème en prose,* 619.

5. See Vadé, *Le poème en prose,* 198.

6. "Poetry without Verse," in Caws and Riffaterre, eds., *The Prose Poem in France,* 72.

7. "Poshchechina obshchestvennomu vkusu," in *Poeziia russkogo futurizma,* ed. V. N. Sazhin (St. Petersburg: Akademicheskii proekt, 1999), 617.

8. Vladimir Markov, *Russian Futurism: A History* (Berkeley: University of California Press, 1968), 48.

9. Markov mistranslates the title as "The Song of the Peacer" (ibid., 47). Although in modern Russian orthography there is no longer a distinction between "peace" and "world," the prerevolutionary spelling differentiated between миръ (peace) and міръ (world). Khlebnikov uses the latter form.

10. *Poshchechina obshchestvennomu vkusu* (Moscow: Izd. G. L. Kuz'mina, 1912), 53–54.

11. *Collected Works of Velimir Khlebnikov. Vol. 2: Prose, Plays, and Supersagas,* trans. Paul Schmidt, ed. Ronald Vroon (Cambridge, Mass.: Harvard University Press, 1989), 12–13 (the typo "wordrings" has been corrected to read "worldlings").

12. According to Robert McLean's count, 62 of the 307 nouns, verbs, and adjectives in this text are neologisms. The ratio for "Pesn' miriazia" is even higher. See Robert A. McLean, *The Prose of Velimir Xlebnikov*, Ph.D. diss., Princeton University, 1973, 3.

13. See on this A. Uijterlinde, *"Zverinets:* Proza ili poeziia?" in Willem G. Weststeijn, ed., *Velimir Chlebnikov (1885–1922): Myth and Reality* (Amsterdam: Rodopi, 1986), 513–28.

14. See Velimir Khlebnikov, *Neizdannye proizvedeniia,* eds. N. Kharzhiev and T. Grits (Moscow: Khudozhestvennaia literatura, 1940), 279–84.

15. Introduction to *Sobranie proizvedenii Velimira Khlebnikova.* 5 vols. (Leningrad: Izd-vo pisatelei v Leningrade, 1928–33), 1:26.

16. Ibid., 4:36. English translation in Khlebnikov, *Prose, Plays, and Supersagas,* 29.

17. *Neizdannye proizvedeniia,* 296. English translation in *Prose,* 123.

18. Benedikt Livshits, *The One and a Half-Eyed Archer.* Trans. John Bowlt (Newtonville, Mass.: Oriental Research Partners, 1977), 36.

19. Ibid., 54, 41.

20. Benedikt Livshits, *Polutoroglazyi strelets. Stikhotvoreniia, perevody, vospominianiia* (Leningrad: Sovetskii pisatel', 1989), 547.

21. *Gileia* (New York, 1931), quoted in *The One and a Half-Eyed Archer,* 67, n. 30. Alexandra Exter (1884–1949), one of the leading painters of the Russian avant-garde, was known as a "Russian Léger" (see Volkmar Dietsch, "Die Malerei als 'Angelpunkt' in futuristischen Thesen und Texten von Benedikt Livšic," *Festschrift für Wolfgang Gesemann. Band 2: Beiträge zur slawischen Literaturwissenschaft,* ed. Hans-Bernd Harder et al. [Munich: Typoskript-Edition Hieronymus, 1986], 39). It was probably through Exter that Livshits became acquainted with Léger's work. I have been unable to find a painting by Léger with this particular title, however.

22. *The One and a Half-Eyed Archer,* 57.

23. Ibid., 56.

24. Ibid., 51.

25. Ibid., 58.

26. Ibid., 56.

27. *Le poème en prose,* 621.

28. *The One and a Half-Eyed Archer,* 50.

29. See "Die Malerei als 'Angelpunkt'," 40.

30. *Manifesty i programmy russkikh futuristov,* ed. Vladimir Markov (Munich: Wilhelm Fink Verlag, 1967), 139. Dietsch mistranslates "lithoidal" ("stony") as "liquid."

31. *The One and a Half-Eyed Archer,* 51.

32. Ibid., 57.

33. Ibid., 92.

34. Ibid., 58.

35. "Kletka," "Videt'," "Fagot," "Pochemu?" *Poshchechina obshch-estvennomu vkusu*, 81–83. Markov calls these texts the "Russian originals" of the prose poems published in German (*Russian Futurism*, 48). However, as Boris Sokolov has shown, they are in fact a literal translation, almost a calque, of the German text, which differs considerably from the original Russian version. See B. M. Sokolov, "'Kandinskii. Zvuki 1911. Izdanie Sa-lona Izdebskogo.' Istoriia i zamysel neosushchestvlennogo poeticheskogo al'boma," *Literaturnoe obozrenie*, vol. 4, no. 258 (1996), 14–15. For the complete text of *Klänge* in German and English, see Wassily Kandinsky, *Sounds*, trans. Elizabeth R. Napier (New Haven: Yale University Press, 1981). An alternative English translation can be found in Kandinsky, *Complete Writings on Art*, eds. Kenneth Lindsay and Peter Vergo (Boston: G. K. Hall, 1982, repr. New York: Da Capo Press, 1994), 291–339. The Russian version of sixteen pieces, based on Kandinskii's manuscripts kept at the Centre Georges Pompidou in Paris, has been published in D. V. Sarab'ianov and N. B. Avtonomova, *Kandinskii: Put' khudozhnika. Khudozhnik i vremia* (Moscow: Galart, 1994), 164–72.

36. An English translation of this letter can be found in Kandinskii, *Complete Writings on Art*, 347.

37. See the letter to Gabriele Münter of December 9, 1910, quoted in Jelena Hahl-Koch, *Kandinsky* (New York: Rizzoli, 1993), 140.

38. "Kandinskii. Zvuki," 13.

39. See "My Woodcuts," *Complete Writings*, 817.

40. See "Testimonium Paupertatis," "Weiss-Horn," "Immer Zusammen," and "Ergo," published in Wassily Kandinsky, *Concerning the Spiritual in Art* (New York: George Wittenborn, 1947), 84–91 (with English translation). Kandinskii also wrote a few poems in French during this period. See the chapter "Die Pariser Gedichte," in Heribert Brinkmann, *Wassily Kandinsky als Dichter*. Ph.D. diss., University of Cologne, 1980, 408–54.

41. *Concerning the Spiritual in Art*, 40.

42. On the parallels between the Russian symbolists and Kandinskii, see John Bowlt, "Vasilii Kandinsky: The Russian Connection," in John Bowlt and Rose-Carol Washton Long, eds., *The Life of Vasilii Kandinsky in Russian Art. A Study of "On the Spiritual in Art."* (Newtonville, Mass.: Oriental Research Partners, 1980), 1–41, and D. V. Sarab'ianov, "Kandinskii i russkii simvolizm," *Izvestiia Akademii Nauk. Seriia literatury i iazyka*, vol. 53, no. 4 (1994), 16–26.

43. Ibid., 64. Kandinskii's most elaborate attempt at synthetic art is represented by his stage compositions, in particular, *Der gelbe Klang* (*The Yellow Sound*, 1912). For an English translation, see *Complete Writings*, 267–83. Kandinskii's theory and practice of synthesis is discussed in Ulrika-Maria Eller-Rüter, *Kandinsky: Bühnenkomposition and Dichtung als Realisation seines Synthese-Konzepts* (Hildesheim: Georg Olms Verlag, 1990).

44. See the prospect of *Klänge* quoted in Hans Konrad Roethel, *Kandinsky: Das graphische Werk* (Cologne: M. DuMont Schauberg, 1970), 445, and the essay "Mes gravures sur bois," which begins with the words "For many years I have written, from time to time, 'poems in prose' and even some 'poetry'" (*Complete Writings,* 817).

45. See "Kandinskii. Zvuki," 31, 33.

46. Quoted from Sarab'ianov and Avtonomova, *Vasili Kandinskii,* 165–66.

47. For a discussion of Kandinskii's relationship with Remizov, see Peg Weiss, *Kandinsky and Old Russia: The Artist as Ethnographer and Shaman* (New Haven: Yale University Press, 1995), 142–45, with reproductions of Kandinskii's drawings to "Obez'iany" ("Monkeys"), "Tsvetok" ("The Flower"), and "Ved'ma" ("The Witch").

48. *Sounds,* 6. Kandinskii used a very similar image in his essay "Über die Formfrage" ("On the Question of Form") in the *Blaue Reiter* almanac to describe the limits imposed upon an artist's freedom by the spirit of the times: "The little beetle, scurrying in all directions beneath an upturned glass, believes it can see before it unlimited freedom. After a certain distance, however, it comes up against the edge of the glass; it can see beyond it, but it can go no further" (*Complete Writings,* 1: 240).

49. See Patrick McGrady, *An Interpretation of Wassily Kandinsky's* Klänge, Ph.D. diss., State University of New York at Binghamton, 1989, 60–71. An opposite interpretation of the tree is suggested by Claudia Emmert, *Bühnenkompositionen und Gedichte von Wassily Kandinsky im Kontext eschatologischer Lehren seiner Zeit 1896–1914* (Frankfurt am Main: Peter Lang, 1998), 170–71. Emmert sees the tree as part of the problem rather than the solution. As a symbolic reference to original sin, it bars the narrator's way, exuding with its iron leafs and blood-red apples an "oppressing feeling of menace." This seems to me a misreading, which is partially explainable by the fact that Emmert, unlike McGrady, pays no attention to the woodcuts in *Klänge.*

50. See "Kandinskii. Zvuki," 15.

51. Quoted from Sokolov, "Kandinskii. Zvuki," 11.

52. The Lindsay/Vergo translation uses "white crack" (*Complete Writings,* 297). While "crack" is indeed a possible translation of the German "Sprung," it does not work for the Russian "skachok," which can only mean "leap."

53. This explanation seems more meaningful than Sokolov's speculation that Kandinskii used the Russian calque because he did not have access to the original (see "Kandinskii. Zvuki," 9).

54. *Poshchechina obshchstestvennomu vkusu,* 81.

55. Jean Arp, "Kandinsky, le poète," quoted in *Sounds,* 2–3.

56. See, for example, "Blick und Blitz" ("Sight and Lightning"), ibid., 118.

57. See Emmert, *Bühnenkompositionen,* 119.

58. The Russian and German texts both put the opening adjectives in the neutral gender, an aspect that is lost in the English translation. "Sinee" (or in German, "Blaues") thus can mean "something blue," rather than just "blue."

59. *Concerning the Spiritual in Art,* 58, 60.

60. "Yellow has a disturbing influence; it pricks, upsets people, and reveals it true character, which is brash and importunate. The intensification of yellow increases the painful shrillness of its note, like that of a shrill bugle." Ibid., 58.

61. Ibid., 61.

62. *An Interpretation of Wassily Kandinsky's* Klänge, 37.

63. *Bühnenkompositionen,* 119. This interpretation is of course based on the German text and does not work in the same way for the (first) Russian version.

64. *Kandinsky and Old Russia,* 111. Weiss also finds an allusion to shamanist ventriloquism in the text, based on the passage referring to a "humming from every corner." The Russian wording does not seem to support such a reading, however ("ukhnut" means "to cry out" or "to bang"). The German version uses "dröhnen" ("rumble," "roar"), which, although closer in meaning, still is not the same as "humming."

65. The few remarks about cubism in *Über das Geistige in der Kunst* are mostly unkind. Kandinskii accuses the cubists of building their grammar of painting "according to physical laws" as opposed to "the laws of internal necessity, which is of the soul," and berates them for their "concentration on form for its own sake" (*Concerning the Spiritual in Art,* 54, 67).

66. *Sounds,* 122.

67. Ibid., 32.

68. "A blend of black and white produces grey, which . . . is silent and motionless, being composed of two inactive colors, its restfulness having none of the potential activity of green. The immobility of grey is desolate. The darker the gray the more preponderant becomes this feeling of desolation and strangulation." *Concering the Spiritual in Art,* 61.

69. "Two Contextual Approaches," 47 (Beaujour's emphasis).

70. Original-size reproductions of all the *Klänge* woodcuts can be found in Roethel, *Kandinsky: Das graphische Werk.* Smaller reproductions, using only black and white, are also included in Elizabeth Napier's edition of *Sounds* and in *Complete Writings.*

71. Richard Sheppard, "Kandinsky's *Klänge:* An Interpretation," *German Life and Letters,* 33, no. 2 (January 1980), 140.

72. *Kandinsky and Old Russia,* 110.

73. With its close attention to the interaction of image and text in the cycle, McGrady's thesis is more compelling than the three previous disserta-

tions on *Klänge* that were written almost simultaneously in the early 1980s— as it seems, independently of each other: Heribert Brinkmann, *Wassily Kandinsky als Dichter,* Ph.D. diss., University of Cologne, 1980; Juliann Bamberg, *Kandinsky as Poet: The "Klänge,"* Ph.D. diss., Florida State University, 1981; and James Fuhr, *Klänge: The Poems of Wassily Kandinsky,* Ph.D. diss., Indiana University, 1982.

74. "O vystavke," published in *Elena Guro. Selected Writings from the Archives,* eds. Anna Ljunggren and Nina Gourianova (Stockholm: Almqvist & Wiksell International, 1995), 85.

75. Ibid., 109.

76. Ibid., 55. The editors seem to be unaware that "Gavan'" is a translation rather than an original text.

77. See "Stikhotvorenie v proze," ibid., 20.

78. *Russian Futurism,* 21.

79. "O tvorchstve. Vokrug 'Nebesnykh verbliuzhat' (Iz dnevnikov i zapisnykh knizhek," in Elena Guro, *Nebesnye verbliuzhata. Bednyi rytsar'. Stikhi i proza* (Rostov-na-Donu: Izdatel'stvo Rostovskogo universiteta, 1993), 32.

80. Ibid., 118.

81. Elena Guro, *The Little Camels of the Sky,* trans. Kevin O'Brien (Ann Arbor: Ardis, 1983), 53.

82. *Nebesnye verbliuzhata,* 258.

83. Ibid., 121.

84. *The Little Camels of the Sky,* 66.

85. See M. Matiushin, "Russkie kubofuturisty," ibid., 270.

86. See on this Iu. B. Orlitskii, "Malaia forma v sostave prozimetricheskogo tselogo (A. Dobroliubov i E. Guro)," *Studia Slavica Finlandensia* 16, no. 1 (1999), 225–38.

87. See *Elena Guro. Selected Writings from the Archives,* 14.

88. Ibid., 57.

89. *The One and a Half-Eyed Archer,* 124.

90. Elena Guro, *Selected Prose and Poetry.* Eds. Anna Ljunggren and Nils Ake Nilsson (Stockholm: Almqvist & Wiksell International, 1988), 96–97.

91. Ibid., 72.

92. See, for example, Annenskii's "Fortep'iannye sonety" or the poem "Smychok i struny."

93. See chapter 3.

94. *Russian Futurism,* 126.

CHAPTER EIGHT

1. Neil Cornwell, ed., *Daniil Kharms and the Poetics of the Absurd: Essays and Materials* (Houndmills: Macmillan, 1991), 11.

2. Ellen Chances, "Čexov and Xarms: Story/Anti-Story." *Russian Language Journal* 36, nos. 123–24 (1982), 186. Contemporary Kharms scholars such as Jean-Philippe Jaccard or Mikhail Iampol'skii would probably react to such a statement with consternation or scorn. Nevertheless, in juxtaposition to Jaccard's and Iampol'skii's formidable attempts to interpret Kharms' texts as serious philosophy, Chances' genuine bewilderment at the strangeness of Kharms' stories is rather refreshing.

3. Kharms' published diaries and notebooks contain no reference to Chekhov.

4. Daniil Kharms, *Polnoe sobranie sochinenii* (St. Petersburg: "Akademicheskii Proekt," 1997), 2:345.

5. George Gibian, ed. *Russia's Lost Literature of the Absurd: A Literary Discovery. Selected Works of Daniil Kharms and Alexander Vvedensky* (Ithaca: Cornell University Press, 1971), 59.

6. Jean-Philippe Jaccard, *Daniil Harms et la fin de l'avant-garde russe* (Bern: Peter Lang, 1991), 268.

7. Quoting Aristotle and Lacan, Iampol'skii interprets the notion of "encounter" in an even wider existential sense as the fundamental modus of our confrontation with reality. In this sense, the chance encounter typifies the quintessential Kharmsian "sluchai." See Mikhail Iampol'skii, *Bespamiatstvo kak istok (chitaia Kharmsa)* (Moscow: Novoe literaturnoe obozrenie, 1998), 86–88.

8. *Small Worlds,* 16.

9. *Daniil Harms,* 273.

10. Quoted in Cathy Popkin, *The Pragmatics of Insignificance: Chekhov, Zoshchenko, Gogol* (Stanford: Stanford University Press, 1993), 4.

11. Ibid., 213.

12. As an example of a minimal story, Prince offers "John was happy, then he saw Peter, then, as a result, he was unhappy." Rather than a minimal story, Kharms' text would have to be called a "minimal narrative," which Prince defines as the account of a single event ("She opened the door") or a single temporal juncture ("She ate then she slept"). Gerald Prince, *A Dictionary of Narratology* (Lincoln: University of Nebraska Press, 1987), 53.

13. "Dnevnikovye zapisi Daniila Kharmsa." Publ. A. Ustinova i A. Kobrinskogo. *Minuvshee* 11 (1991), 504.

14. Neil Cornwell, "The Rudiments of Daniil Kharms: In Further Pursuit of the Red-Haired Man," *The Modern Language Review* 93, vol. 1 (January 1998), 137.

15. *Polnoe sobranie sochinenii,* 2:42.

16. Graham Roberts has defined metafiction as a key feature of OBERIU poetics. See *The Last Soviet Avant-Garde: OBERIU—Fact, Fiction, Metafiction* (Cambridge: Cambridge University Press, 1997), 171–78.

17. *Polnoe sobranie sochinenii,* 2:71.

18. Ibid., 2:34.

19. On the importance of the number zero for Kharms' poetics and philosophy, see "Le zéro et l'infini" in Jaccard, *Daniil Harms,* 98–102, and "Vokrug nolia" in Iampol'skii, *Bespamiatstvo,* 287–313.

20. See Markov, *Russian Futurism,* 80.

21. Nils Ake Nilsson has argued that these two poems have at least a grammatical meaning. "U-" is a verbal prefix, with the hyphen calling the reader to fill in the missing verb, and "iu" is a morphological marker of the first-person singular, which makes this poem "a programmatic statement of Ego-futurism." See "Vasilisk Gnedov's One-Letter Poems," in *Gorski Vijenats: A Garland of Essays Offered to Professor Elizabeth Mary Hill,* Publications of the Modern Humanities Research Association, 2 (Leeds, 1970), 220–23.

22. Crispin Brooks interprets this poem as an incantation of the "Corn Mother." The allusion to harvest rituals places the death of art into the context of the seasonal fertility cycle. See Brooks, *The Futurism of Vasilisk Gnedov* (Birmingham: The University of Birmingham, 2000), 45–58.

23. In his pamphlet *Futurizm v stikhakh V. Briusova* (Moscow: Tip. Russkogo Tovarishchestva, 1913), Andrei Shemshurin, who liked neither Gnedov nor Briusov, drew a direct connection between Gnedov's minimalist poems and Briusov's monostich (see 20–21).

24. See on this Robert A. Maguire, *Red Virgin Soil: Soviet Literature in the 1920's* (Ithaca: Cornell University Press, 1987), 276–79.

25. In Kharms' poetic works, we do find one-line poems. See on this A. Kobrinskii, *Poetika "OBERIU" v kontekste russkogo literaturnogo avangarda.* 2 vols. (Moscow: Izdanie Moskovskogo Kul'turologicheskogo Litseiia, 1999), 1:19.

26. *Polnoe sobranie sochinenii,* 2:331–32. Another pertinent example of cross-generic labeling are Kharms' two "Symphonies" ("Nachalo ochen' khoroshego letnego dnia. Simfoniia" and "Sinfoniia [sic] No. 2," ibid. 2: 358–59, 159). This generic title clearly alludes to Belyi. As Aleksandr Kobrinskii has shown, there are some direct parallels between "Nachalo" and Belyi's "Second Symphony." See the chapter "Simfonicheskaia forma" in *Poetika "OBERIU,"* 1:33–47.

27. *Bespamiatstvo kak istok,* 348.

28. "Beyond the Turning-Point: An Afterword," *Daniil Kharms and the Poetics of the Absurd,* 258.

29. A. A. Dobrytsin, "'Sonet' v proze: Sluchai Kharmsa," *Philologica,* 1997, vol. 4, no. 8/10, 161–68.

30. See "Daniil Xarms: Poète des années vingt, prosateur des années trente. Les raisons d'un passage," *Revue des études slaves* 67, no. 4 (1995), 653–63.

31. "The Anti-World of Daniil Kharms," in *Daniil Kharms and the Poetics of the Absurd,* 85, 89. Anemone's argument suffers from his reductive

characterization of OBERIU as a "revolutionary and nihilistic attack on the authority of bourgeois traditions in art and politics" (88). This is not to say that there is no connection between the modernist avant-garde and Stalinism, but it lies more in a shared utopian messianism than in anti-bourgeois nihilism. See on this Boris Groys, *The Total Art of Stalinism: Avant-Garde, Aesthetic Dictatorship, and Beyond,* trans. Charles Rougle (Princeton: Princeton University Press, 1992).

32. Baudelaire, *The Parisian Prowler,* trans. Edward K. Kaplan (Athens: University of Georgia Press, 1989), 122.

33. *Polnoe sobranie sochinenii,* 2:337.

34. Ibid., 2:330.

35. Ibid., 2:87.

36. "Khoroshego-po nemnozhku (Podrazhenie 'Stikhotvoreniiam v proze' Turgeneva)." *Strekoza* no. 3 (1883), 3.

37. See on this Kobrinskii, *Poetika "OBERIU,"* 1:13–14.

38. As we know from Kharms' diaries, he held Sologub in high esteem. In a list of poems that he knew by heart, he mentions four pieces by Sologub (see "Dnevnikovye zapisi Daniila Kharmsa," 434). Svetozar Shishman reports that Kharms at one point refused to sit down with Mikhail Zoshchenko at the same table, because the latter had made fun of Sologub in one of his stories (see S. S. Shishman, *Neskol'ko veselykh i grustnykh istorii o Daniile Kharmse i ego druz'iakh* [Leningrad, 1991], 88).

39. *Polnoe sobranie sochinenii,* 2:337–38.

40. Kharms' religious message amounts to a "negative theology" at best. See on this Neil Carrick, *Daniil Kharms: Theologian of the Absurd* (Birmingham: University of Birmingham, 1998).

41. On Sologub's use of the *Anti-Märchen,* see Pierre Hart, "Functions of the Fairy Tale in Sologub's Prose," in Lauren G. Leighton, ed., *Studies in Honor of Xenia Gasiorowska* (Columbus: Slavica, 1983), 71–80.

42. "Daniil Charms' 'Slučai' (Fälle) und die russischen Volksmärchen," *Zeitschrift für Slavische Philologie* 55, vol. 1 (1995/96), 27–52.

43. *Polnoe sobranie sochinenii,* 2:39 and 1:174. Deliberate misspellings play an important role in Kharms' poetics. See on this the chapter "'Bez grammaticheskoi oshibki . . .'? Orfograficheskii 'sdvig' v tekstakh Daniila Kharmsa" in Kobrinkii, *Poetika "OBERIU,"* 1:151–74. Kharms' oeuvre also features a correctly spelled "Skazka," which was published in 1935 in the journal *Chizh.* Although a seemingly "harmless" story for children, "Skazka" contains many of the elements typical for Kharms' "adult" fiction, such as physical violence, senseless repetitions, and self-referentiality.

44. Thomas Grob, *Daniil Charms' unkindliche Kindlichkeit: Ein literarisches Paradigma der Spätavantgarde im Kontext der russischen Moderne* (Bern: Peter Lang, 1994), 90.

45. *Daniil Harms,* 281.

46. See chapter 5.

47. *Polnoe sobranie sochinenii,* 2:60.

48. Sologub, *Sobranie sochinenii,* 10:12.

49. *Polnoe sobranie sochinenii,* 2:346–47.

50. See on this Grob, *Daniil Charms' unkindliche Kindlichkeit,* 271 and 273.

51. "Iz nichego." Remizov, *Martyn Zadeka,* 31.

52. "Pesochnoe sukno," ibid., 68.

53. See "Son" and "Son draznit cheloveka," *Polnoe sobranie sochinenii,* 2:337–38, 349–50. For a list of Kharms' texts concerned with dreams, see ibid., 2:427 and 431.

54. See *Bespamiatstvo kak istok,* 126–28.

55. See A. A. Aleksandrov, "Chudodei," in Daniil Kharms, *Polet v nebesa* (Leningrad: Sovetskii pisatel', 1988), 40–41.

56. Aleksandr Blok, *Sobranie sochinenii,* 6:169–70. On Blok's prose miniatures, see chapter 4.

57. *Russia's Lost Literature of the Absurd,* 60.

58. Their belated publication (only in 1994!) constitutes another parallel between Kandinskii's Russian prose poems and Kharms' mini-stories.

59. See chapter 7.

60. Sokolov, "Kandinskii. Zvuki," 33.

61. Bunin, *Sobranie sochinenii,* 5:449.

62. *Polnoe sobranie sochinenii,* 2:358–59.

63. *Daniil Harms,* 278–79.

64. See Kobrinskii, *Poetika "OBERIU,"* 2:28–36.

65. Stamos Metzidakis, "The Prose Poem's Deconstruction of Literariness," in *Difference Unbound: The Rise of Pluralism in Literature and Criticism* (Amsterdam: Rodopi, 1995), 78.

66. Anna Gerasimova, "OBERIU (Problema smeshnogo)," *Voprosy literatury,* no. 4 (1988), 78. A similar liminal status, but closer to the nonliterary than to the literary pole, characterizes the oeuvre of Vasilii Rozanov (see chapter 4).

67. A related problem consists in the distinction between Kharms' "adult" stories and those written for children. In the latest edition (and most complete to date) of Kharms' work, all texts are printed in chronological order without attention to generic categories. See Daniil Kharms, *Tsirk Shardam,* ed. V. N. Sazhin (St. Petersburg: Kristall, 1999).

68. The complete "Golubaia tetrad'" has been published in *Polnoe sobranie sochinenii,* 2:321–29.

69. Ibid., 2:330.

70. Gibian, 53.

71. By discussing "Golubaia tetrad' No.10" as a minimalist metanarrative, I do not mean to dismiss alternative, complementary readings of

this story, such as a theological interpretation (the red-haired man as the absent God, see Carrick, *Daniil Kharms: Theologian of the Absurd,* 75–78), or a reference to historical reality (the date of composition, 1937, certainly suggests a comment on the Stalinist purges).

72. "Uslovnost'" literally means "convention." The disintegration of the narrative has therefore to be perceived against the backdrop of "convention of representation."

EPILOGUE

1. Quoted in Graham Roberts, *The Last Soviet Avant-Garde,* 175.

2. See ibid., 171–78. On Kharms as a forerunner of postmodernism, see also Grob, *Daniil Charms' unkindliche Kindlichkeit,* 375–98. Grob argues that Kharms' thinking and poetic intention remained within the confines of modernism, but his literary form transcended the modernist tradition in the direction of a new paradigm. To be sure, any discussion that tries to attach either a modernist or postmodernist label to Kharms' writings hinges on the definition that one wishes to give to these notions, and tends therefore to assume a somewhat circular line of argumentation.

3. "O maksimal'no minimal'nom v avangardnoi i postavangardnoi poezii," *Novoe literaturnoe obozrenie* 23 (1997), 290.

4. Ibid., 268.

5. "Lev Rubinshein: Kristall v perenasyshchennom rastvore kul'tury," *Literaturnoe obozrenie* 1.273 (1999), 76.

6. "Vse dal'she i dal'she" ("Onward and onward," 1984), in Lev Rubinshtein, *Reguliarnoe pis'mo* (St. Petersburg: Izd-vo Ivana Limbakha, 1996), 21.

7. Ibid., 10–18.

8. "Kristall v perenasyshchennom rastvore kul'tury," 77.

9. See Gerald Janecek, "Lev Rubinshtein's Early Conceptualism: The Programs of Works," in Marina Balina, Nancy Condee, and Evgeny Dobrenko, eds., *Endquote: Sots-Art Literature and Soviet Grand Style* (Evanston: Northwestern University Press, 2000), 107–22.

10. Published in Lev Rubinshtein, *Domashnee muzitsirovanie* (Moscow: Novoe literaturnoe obozrenie, 2000), 229–64.

11. "Lev Rubinshtein's Early Conceptualism," 115.

12. Stephan Küpper, "Zum Werk Lev Rubinštejns," *Zeitschrift für Slawistik* 40, no. 4 (1995), 446.

13. Lev Rubinshtein, *Reguliarnoe pis'mo,* 6.

14. Ibid., 141–50.

15. See, for example, the series "S chetverga na piatnitsu" ("From Thursday to Friday," 1985), which consists of 41 fragments that all begin with the words "I dreamt that . . ." Published in Rubinshtein, *Domashnee muzitsirovanie,* 70–77.

16. See Aleksandr Solzhenitsyn, *Sobranie sochinenii* (Frankfurt am Main: Posev, 1970), 6:70. For the Russian text of *Krokhotki,* see ibid., 5:221–32.

17. John F. Dunlop, "Solzhenitsyn's Sketches," *Transactions of the Association of Russian-American Scholars in USA,* vol. 6 (1972), 22.

18. "Listvennitsa," "Molniia," and "Kolokol Uglicha," *Novyi mir,* 1997, no. 1, 99–100. "Kolokol'nia," "Starenie," and "Pozor," ibid, no. 3, 70–71. "Likhoe zel'e," "Utro," and "Zavesa," ibid., no. 10, 119–20.

19. Solzhenitsyn's allegoric use of trees is reminiscent of the description of Kondrashev-Ivanov's painting "The Maimed Oak," in *The First Circle* (Evanston: Northwestern University Press, 1997), 251. In isolation from its novelistic context, this ekphrasis could stand alone as another prose miniature.

20. See, for example, Viktor Astaf'ev, *Zatesi* (Moscow: Sovetskii pisatel', 1972), or Vladimir Soloukhin, *Kameshki na ladoni* (Moscow: Sovetskii pisatel', 1977).

21. See "Standart," in Iurii Bondarev, *Mgnoveniia.* 4th ed. (Moscow: Sovremennik, 1987), 28–30.

22. "Iasnaia Poliana," ibid., 446.

23. L. N. Tolstoi, *Polnoe sobranie sochinenii.* 90 vols. (Moscow-Leningrad: Khudozhestvennaia literatura, 1928–58), 30: 94.

24. The connection between Bondarev's *Mgnoveniia* and Turgenev's prose poems has not remained unnoticed. G. B. Kurliandskaia devoted an article to this topic in 1986. Using the customary rhetoric of Soviet criticism, she extolled both Turgenev and Bondarev for their "self-abnegating readiness to serve the cause of progress and the evolution of human thought." See G. B. Kurliandskaia, "'Stikhotvoreniia v proze' Turgeneva i ikh traditsiia v sovetskoi literature ('Mgnoveniia' Iu. Bondareva)," in *I. S. Turgenev: Voprosy mirovozreniia i tvorchestva* (Elista: Kalmytskii gos. universitet, 1986), 134.

25. See Alexander Solzhenitsyn, *Stories and Prose Poems,* trans. Michael Glenny (New York: Farrar, Straus and Giroux, 1971).

26. Western compilers of anthologies have not hesitated to apply the prose poem label both to "certified" *stikhotvoreniia v proze* and to Russian avant-garde texts. Michael Benedikt's collection *The Prose Poem: An International Anthology* (New York: Dell, 1976) contains five of Turgenev's prose poems, Khlebnikov's "Zverinets," ten of Remizov's dreams, fourteen of Kharms' "Sluchai," three of Solzhenitsyn's "Krokhotki," as well as three excerpts from Andrei Voznesensky's "Oza." Stuart Friebert's and David Young's *Models of the Universe: An Anthology of the Prose Poem* (Oberlin: Oberlin College Press, 1995) features three of Turgenev's prose poems in addition to three of Remizov's dreams and three of Kharms' "Sluchai" borrowed from Benedikt's anthology.

Works Cited

Afanas'ev, A. N. *Narodnye russkie skazki A. N. Afanas'eva.* 3 vols. Moscow: Gos. izd-vo khudozhest. lit-ry, 1957.

Afanas'ev, V. N. "I. A. Bunin i russkoe dekadentstvo 90-kh godov." *Russkaia literatura* 11 (1968), vol. 3, 175–81.

Alexandrian, Sarane. *Le surréalisme et le rêve.* Paris: Gallimard, 1974.

Aleksandrov, A. A. "Chudodei." In Daniil Kharms, *Polet v nebesa.* Leningrad: Sovetskii pisatel', 1988, 7–48.

Allen, Elizabeth Cheresh. "Turgenev's Last Will and Testament: Poems in Prose." In *Freedom and Responsibility in Russian Literature. Essays in Honor of Robert Louis Jackson,* eds. Elizabeth Cheresh Allen and Gary Saul Morson. Evanston: Northwestern University Press and The Yale Center for International and Area Studies, 1995, 53–68.

Annenkov, Iurii. *Dnevnik moikh vstrech. Tsikl tragedii.* 2 vols. New York: Inter-Language Literary Associates, 1966.

Annenskii, Innokentii. *Stikhotvoreniia i tragedii.* Leningrad: Sovetskii pisatel', 1990.

———. "Stikhotvoreniia v proze." *Knigi otrazhenii.* Moscow: Nauka, 1979, 433–37.

Anonymous. "Khoroshego-po nemnozhku (Podrazhenie 'Stikhotvoreniiam v proze' Turgeneva)." *Strekoza,* no. 3 (1883), 3.

Aronian, Sona. *The Dream as a Literary Device in the Novels and Short Stories of Aleksej Remizov.* Ph.D. diss., Yale University, 1971.

———. "The Russian View of Remizov." *Russian Literature Triquarterly* 18 (1985), 3–15.

Astaf'ev, Viktor. *Zatesi.* Moscow: Sovetskii pisatel', 1972.

Bagno, V. E. "Fedor Sologub-perevodchik frantsuzskikh simvolistov." In *Na rubezhe XIX i XX vekov: Iz istorii mezhdunarodnykh sviazei russkoi literatury,* ed. Iu. D. Levin. Leningrad: Nauka, 1991, 129–214.

Baker, Kenneth. *Minimalism: Art of Circumstance.* New York: Abbeville Press, 1988.

Bal'mont, Konstantin. *Izbrannoe.* Moscow: Khudozhestvennaia literatura, 1983.

————. "Malye zerna. Mysli i oshchushcheniia." *Vesy* (1907), no. 3, 47–56.

————. *Pod severnym nebom.* St. Petersburg: Tip. M. Stasiulevicha, 1894.

————. *Polnoe sobranie stikhov.* 10 vols. Moscow: Skorpion, 1908–13.

————. *V bezbrezhnosti.* Moscow: A. A. Levenson, 1895.

Bamberg, Juliann. *Kandinsky as Poet: The "Klänge."* Ph.D. diss., Florida State University, 1981.

Battcock, Gregory, ed. *Minimal Art: A Critical Anthology.* New York: Dutton, 1968.

Baudelaire, Charles. *Oeuvres complètes.* 2 vols. Ed. Claude Pichois. Paris: Gallimard, 1975.

————. *Petits poëmes en prose.* Ed. Robert Kopp. Paris: José Corti, 1969.

————. *The Parisian Prowler.* Trans. Edward K. Kaplan. Athens: University of Georgia Press, 1989.

Beaujour, Michel. "Short Epiphanies: Two Contextual Approaches to the French Prose Poem." In *The Prose Poem in France. Theory and Practice,* eds. Mary Ann Caws and Hermine Riffaterre. New York: Columbia University Press, 1983, 39–59.

Beebee, Thomas O. *The Ideology of Genre: A Comparative Study of Generic Instability.* University Park: Penn State University Press, 1994.

Belyi, Andrei. "Liricheskiie otryvki (v proze)." In *Pamiatniki kul'tury: Novye otkrytiia, ezhegodnik 1980,* ed. A. V. Lavrov. Leningrad, 1981, 121–25.

————. *Na rubezhe dvukh stoletii.* Moscow: Khudozhestvennaia literatura, 1989.

————. *Zoloto v lazuri.* Moscow: Skorpion, 1904.

Benedikt, Michael, ed. *The Prose Poem: An International Anthology.* New York: Dell, 1976.

Benjamin, Walter. "The Work of Art in the Age of Mechanical Reproduction." In *Illuminations, Essays and Reflections,* ed. Hannah Arendt, trans. Harry Zohn. New York: Schocken Books, 1968, 217–51.

Bernard, Suzanne. *Le poème en prose de Baudelaire jusqu'à nos jours.* Paris: Nizet, 1959.

Biriukov, Sergei. "O maksimal'no minimal'nom v avangardnoi i postavangardnoi poezii." *Novoe literaturnoe obozrenie* 23 (1997), 290–93.

Blok, Aleksandr. *Sobranie sochinenii.* 8 vols. Moscow-Leningrad: Gos. izd-vo khudozhestvennoi literatury, 1962.

Bogdanovich, Nana. "Pokushaj jedne knizhevne paralele: Pesme u prozi I. Turgeneva i Sh. Bodlera." *Letopis Matice srpske* 375, vol. 6 (June 1955), 562–74.

Bondarev, Iurii. *Mgnoveniia.* 4th ed. Moscow: Sovremennik, 1987.

Bowlt, John. "Vasilii Kandinsky: The Russian Connection." In John Bowlt and Rose-Carol Washton Long, eds, *The Life of Vasilii Kandinsky in*

Russian Art. A Study of "On the Spiritual in Art." Newtonville, Mass.: Oriental Research Partners, 1980, 1–41.

Brang, Peter. *I. S. Turgenev: Sein Leben und sein Werk.* Wiesbaden: Otto Harrassowitz, 1976.

———, ed. *Landschaft und Lyrik: Die Schweiz in den Gedichten der Slaven. Eine kommentierte Anthologie.* Basel: Schwabe Verlag, 1998.

Breton, André. *Les vases communicants.* 6th ed. Paris: Gallimard, 1955.

———. *Manifestoes of Surrealism.* Trans. Richard Seaver and Helen R. Lane. Ann Arbor: University of Michigan Press, 1969.

———, ed. *Trajectoire du rêve.* Paris: G.L.M., 1938.

Brinkmann, Heribert. *Wassily Kandinsky als Dichter.* Ph.D. diss., University of Cologne, 1980.

Briusov, Valerii. *Gorod (Putevye nabroski).* Russian State Library, f. 386, kart. 3, ed. khran. 11.

———. *Izbrannye sochineniia.* 2 vols. Moscow: Gos. Izd-vo khudozh. lit-ry, 1955.

———. *Neizdannaia proza*, ed. I. M. Briusova. Moscow: Gos. izd-vo khudozh. lit-ry, 1931.

———. *Sredi stikhov, 1894–1924.* Moscow: Sovetskii pisatel', 1990, 125–26.

Brooks, Crispin. *The Futurism of Vasilisk Gnedov.* Birmingham: The University of Birmingham, 2000 (Birmingham Slavonic Monographs, No. 31).

Bunin, I. A. *Sobranie Sochinenii.* 9 vols. Moscow: Khudozhestvennaia literatura, 1965–67.

Burliuk, David, Kruchenykh, Aleksei, Maiakovskii, Vladimir, and Khlebnikov, Velimir. "Poshchechina obshchestvennomu vkusu." In *Poeziia russkogo futurizma,* ed. V. N. Sazhin. St. Petersburg: Akademicheskii proekt, 1999.

Burliuk, D., Kruchenykh, A., Maiakovskii, V., and Khlebnikov, V., eds. *Poshchechina obshchestvennomu vkusu.* Moscow: Izd. G. L. Kuz'mina, 1912.

Burton, Richard D. E. *Baudelaire and the Second Republic: Writing and Revolution.* Oxford: Clarendon Press, 1991, 326–28.

Carrick, Neil. *Daniil Kharms: Theologian of the Absurd.* Birmingham: The University of Birmingham, 1998 (Birmingham Slavonic Monographs, No. 28).

Caws, Mary Ann. "Prose Poem." In *The New Princeton Encyclopedia of Poetry and Poetics,* eds. Alex Preminger and T. V. F. Brogan, Princeton: Princeton University Press, 1993, 977–79.

Chances, Ellen. "Čexov and Xarms: Story/Anti-Story." *Russian Language Journal* 36, nos. 123–24 (1982), 181–92.

Chantsev, A. V. "Lundberg." In *Russkie pisateli 1800–1917. Biograficheskii slovar'*. Moscow: Rossiiskaia entsiklopediia, 1994, 3:412–13.

Chernyshevskii, N. G. *Polnoe sobranie sochinenii*. 15 vols. Moscow: Gos. izd-vo khudozh. lit-ry, 1950.

Colpitt, Frances. *Minimal Art: The Critical Perspective*. Ann Arbor: UMI Research Press, 1990.

Cornwell, Neil. "Introduction: Daniil Kharms, Black Miniaturist." In *Daniil Kharms and the Poetics of the Absurd: Essays and Materials*. Houndmills: Macmillan, 1991, 3–21.

———. "The Rudiments of Daniil Kharms: In Further Pursuit of the Red-Haired Man." *The Modern Language Review* 93, vol. 1 (January 1998), 133–45.

Craver, Anne. "Critical Studies of the Prose Poem." *L'esprit créateur* 39, no. 1 (Spring 1999), 84–92.

Crone, Anna Lisa. *Rozanov and the End of Literature: Polyphony and the Dissolution of Genre in* Solitaria *and* Fallen Leaves. Würzburg: jal-verlag, 1978.

Delville, Michel. *The American Prose Poem: Poetic Form and the Boundaries of Genre*. Gainesville: University Press of Florida, 1998.

Dietsch, Volkmar. "Die Malerei als 'Angelpunkt' in futuristischen Thesen und Texten von Benedikt Livšic." *Festschrift für Wolfgang Gesemann. Band 2: Beiträge zur slawischen Literaturwissenschaft,* ed. Hans-Bernd Harder et al. Munich: Typoskript-Edition Hieronymus, 1986, 31–47.

Dobroliubov, Aleksandr. *Iz knigi nevidimoi*. Moscow: Skorpion, 1905; repr. Berkeley Slavic Specialties, 1983.

———. *Sochineniia*. Berkeley: Berkeley Slavic Specialties, 1981.

Dobrytsin, A. A. "'Sonet' v proze: Sluchai Kharmsa." *Philologica* 4 (1997), nos. 8/10, 161–68.

Dubrovkin, Roman. *Stefan Mallarme i Rossiia*. Bern: Peter Lang, 1998.

Dunlop, John F. "Solzhenitsyn's Sketches." *Transactions of the Association of Russian-American Scholars in USA,* vol. 6 (1972), 21–28.

Eikhenbaum, B. M. *L. N. Tolstoi. Semidesiatye gody*. Leningrad: Sovetskii pisatel', 1960.

Eller-Rüter, Ulrika-Maria. *Kandinsky: Bühnenkomposition und Dichtung als Realisation seines Synthese-Konzepts*. Hildesheim: Georg Olms Verlag, 1990.

Emmert, Claudia. *Bühnenkompositionen und Gedichte von Wassily Kandinsky im Kontext eschatologischer Lehren seiner Zeit 1896–1914*. Frankfurt am Main: Peter Lang, 1998.

Eshel'man, Raul'. "'Kakaia, brat, pustota': Minimalizm v sovetskoi novelle." In *Russkaia novella: Problemy teorii i istorii. Sbornik statei*, eds. V. M. Markovich and V. Schmid. St. Petersburg: Izdatel'stvo S.-Peterburgskogo Universiteta, 1993, 249–73.

Evans, Margery A. *Baudelaire and Intertextuality: Poetry at the Cross-roads*. Cambridge–New York: Cambridge University Press, 1993.

Fedorov, A. V. *Innokentii Annenskii: Lichnost' i tvorchestvo*. Leningrad: Khudozhestvennaia literatura, 1984.

Filosofov, D. V. *Staroe i novoe*. Moscow: I. D. Sytin, 1912.

Foster, Liudmila. "K voprosu o siurrealizme v russkoi literature." In *American Contributions to the Seventh International Congress of Slavists,* vol. 2. The Hague: Mouton, 1973, 199–220.

Fowler, Alastair. *Kinds of Literature: An Introduction to the Theory of Genres and Modes*. Cambridge, Mass.: Harvard University Press, 1982.

Friebert, Stuart and Young, David, eds. *Models of the Universe: An Anthology of the Prose Poem*. Oberlin: Oberlin College Press, 1995.

Fuhr, James. *Klänge: The Poems of Wassily Kandinsky*. Ph.D. diss., Indiana University, 1982.

Fülleborn, Ulrich. *Das deutsche Prosagedicht: Zu Theorie und Geschichte einer Gattung*. Munich: Wilhelm Fink Verlag, 1970.

Galand, René. *Baudelaire: poétique et poésie*. Paris: Nizet, 1969.

Gallagher, Daniel Peter. *The Surrealist Mode in Twentieth-Century Russian Literature*. Ph.D. diss., University of Kansas, 1975.

Garshin, V. M. "Stikhotvoreniia v proze" (1875, 1884), in *Sochineniia*. Moscow–Leningrad: GIKhL, 1951, 386–88.

Gasde, Christa. "Das Prosagedicht-ein Traum. Zu Turgenevs 'Starucha' und einem Feuilleton von Ludwig Pietsch." In J. Holthusen, ed., *Beiträge und Skizzen zum Werk Ivan Turgenevs*. Munich: Otto Sagner, 1977, 109–34.

Genette, Gérard. *Palimpsestes*. Paris: Seuil, 1982.

Gerasimova, Anna. "OBERIU (Problema smeshnogo)," *Voprosy literatury*, no. 4 (1988), 48–79.

Gershman, Herbert S. *The Surrealist Revolution in France*. Ann Arbor: University of Michigan Press, 1969.

Gibian, George, ed. *Russia's Lost Literature of the Absurd: A Literary Discovery. Selected Works of Daniil Kharms and Alexander Vvedensky*. Ithaca: Cornell University Press, 1971.

Ginzburg, Lidiia. *O lirike*. Moscow: Intrada, 1997.

Göbler, Frank. "Daniil Charms' 'Slučai' (Fälle) und die russischen Volksmärchen." *Zeitschrift für Slavische Philologie* 55, vol. 1 (1995/96), 27–52.

Gogol', N. V. *Polnoe sobranie sochinenii*. 14 vols. Moscow: Izd-vo AN SSSR, 1937–52.

Goller, Mirjam and Witte, Georg, eds. *Minimalismus: Zwischen Leere und Exzeß*. Vienna: Wiener Slawistischer Almanach, Sonderband 51, 2001.

Gracheva, Alla. "K istorii otnoshenii Alekseia Remizova i Fedora Sologuba (Vvedenie k teme)." http://www.ruthenia.ru:8085/document/397305.html.

Graham, John. *John Graham's 'System and Dialectics of Art,'* ed. Marcia Epstein Allentuck. Baltimore: Johns Hopkins University Press, 1971.

Grechishkin, S. S. and Lavrov, A. V. "Briusov o Turgeneve." In *Turgenev i ego sovremenniki,* ed. M. P. Alekseev. Leningrad: Nauka, 1977, 170–90.

Green, Eleanor. *John Graham, Artist and Avatar.* Washington, D.C.: The Phillips Collection, 1987.

Grob, Thomas. *Daniil Charms' unkindliche Kindlichkeit: Ein literarisches Paradigma der Spätavantgarde im Kontext der russischen Moderne.* Bern: Peter Lang, 1994 (Slavica Helvetica, vol. 45).

Groys, Boris. *The Total Art of Stalinism: Avant-Garde, Aesthetic Dictatorship, and Beyond,* Trans. Charles Rougle. Princeton: Princeton University Press, 1992.

Grossman, Leonid. "Posledniaia poema Turgeneva." *Sobranie sochinenii v piati tomakh.* Moscow: Sovremennye problemy, 1928, 3:75–94.

Grübel, Rainer. "Der Text als Embryo. Aus der Vorgeschichte des russischen Minimalismus: Vasilij Rozanovs frühe Prosaminiaturen." In *Minimalismus: Zwischen Leere und Exzeß*, eds. Mirjam Goller and Georg Witte. Vienna: Wiener Slawistischer Almanach, Sonderband 51, 2001, 51–78.

Grushko, Pavel. "Lev Rubinshtein: Kristall v perenasyshchennom rastvore kul'tury." *Literaturnoe obozrenie* 1.273 (1999), 73–80.

Guro, Elena. *Nebesnye verbliuzhata. Bednyi rytsar'. Stikhi i proza.* Rostovna-Donu: Izdatel'stvo Rostovskogo universiteta, 1993.

———. *Elena Guro. Selected Writings from the Archives*, eds. Anna Ljunggren and Nina Gourianova. Stockholm: Almqvist & Wiksell International, 1995.

———. *Selected Prose and Poetry.* Eds. Anna Ljunggren and Nils Ake Nilsson. Stockholm: Almqvist & Wiksell International, 1988.

———. *The Little Camels of the Sky.* Trans. Kevin O'Brien. Ann Arbor: Ardis, 1983.

Hahl-Koch, Jelena. *Kandinsky.* New York: Rizzoli, 1993.

Hart, Pierre. "Functions of the Fairy Tale in Sologub's Prose." In *Studies in Honor of Xenia Gasiorowska,* ed. Lauren G. Leighton. Columbus: Slavica, 1983, 71–80.

Hellebust, Rolf. "Aleksei Gastev and the Metallization of the Revolutionary Body." *Slavic Review* 56, no. 3 (Fall 1997), 500–18.

Herzinger, Kim. "Introduction: On the New Fiction." *Mississippi Review* 40–41 (1985), 689–98.

Hiddleston, J. A. *Baudelaire and Le Spleen de Paris.* Oxford: Clarendon Press, 1987.

———. "Baudelaire, Manet et 'La Corde'." *Bulletin Baudelairien* 19, vol. 1 (April 1984), 7–11.

Huysmans, J. K. *Against the Grain.* New York: Dover Publications, 1969.

Iampol'skii, Mikhail. *Bespamiatstvo kak istok (chitaia Kharmsa)*. Moscow: Novoe literaturnoe obozrenie, 1998.

Ingold, Felix Philipp, ed. *Geballtes Schweigen: Zeitgenössische russische Einzeiler*. St. Gallen: Erker-Verlag, 1999.

Issova, L. N. *Zhanr stikhotvoreniia v proze v russkoi literature (I. S. Turgenev, V. M. Garshin, V. G. Korolenko, I. A. Bunin). Avtoreferat dissertatsii*. Voronezh, 1969.

———. "Zhanr stikhotvoreniia v proze v tvorchestve V. M. Garshina," *Uchenye zapiski kaliningradskogo universiteta*, vol. 5 (1970), 133–44.

Ivanits, Linda. "Fairy Tale Motifs in Sologub's 'Dream on the Rocks'." In *Studies in Honor of Xenia Gasiorowska*, ed. Lauren G. Leighton. Columbus: Slavica, 1983, 81–87.

Ivanov, V. V., Toporov, V. N., and Tsiv'ian, T. V., eds. *Serebrianyi vek v Rossii. Izbrannye stranitsy*. Moscow: Radiks, 1993, 311–12.

Jaccard, Jean-Philippe. *Daniil Harms et la fin de l'avant-garde russe*. Bern: Peter Lang, 1991 (Slavica Helvetica, vol. 39).

———. "Daniil Xarms: Poète des années vingt, prosateur des années trente. Les raisons d'un passage." *Revue des études slaves* 67, no. 4 (1995), 653–63.

Janecek, Gerald J. "Lev Rubinshtein's Early Conceptualism: The Programs of Works." In Marina Balina, Nancy Condee, and Evgeny Dobrenko, eds., *Endquote: Sots-Art Literature and Soviet Grand Style*. Evanston: Northwestern University Press, 2000, 107–22.

———. "Minimalism in Contemporary Russian Poetry: Vsevolod Nekrasov and Others." *The Slavonic and East European Review* 70, no. 3 (July 1992), 401–19.

Johnson, Barbara. *Défigurations du langage poétique: La Seconde Révolution Baudelairienne*. Paris: Flammarion, 1979.

———. "La vérité tue: Une lecture de 'Conte'." *Littérature* (October 1973), 68–77.

Johnson, Peter. "An Interview with Russell Edson." *The Writer's Chronicle* 31, no. 6 (May/Summer 1999), 30–36.

Kandinsky, Wassily. *Complete Writings on Art*, Eds. Kenneth Lindsay and Peter Vergo. Boston: G. K. Hall, 1982; repr. New York: Da Capo Press, 1994.

———. *Concerning the Spiritual in Art*. New York: George Wittenborn, 1947.

———. *Sounds*. Trans. Elizabeth R. Napier. New Haven: Yale University Press, 1981.

Kaplan, Edward K. *Baudelaire's Prose Poems: the Esthetic, the Ethical and the Religious in the Parisian Prowler*. Athens: The University of Georgia Press, 1990.

Keys, Roger. *The Reluctant Modernist: Andrei Belyi and the Development of Russian Fiction 1902–1914*. Oxford: Clarendon Press, 1996.

Kharms, Daniil. "Dnevnikovye zapisi Daniila Kharmsa." Publ. A. Ustinova i A. Kobrinskogo. *Minuvshee* 11 (1991), 417–583.

———. *Polnoe sobranie sochinenii. Vol. 1: Stikhotvoreniia. Vol. 2: Proza i stsenki. Dramaticheskie proizvedeniia.* St. Petersburg: "Akademicheskii Proekt," 1997.

———. *Tsirk Shardam.* Ed. V. N. Sazhin. St. Petersburg: Kristall, 1999.

Khlebnikov, Velimir. *Collected Works of Velimir Khlebnikov. Vol. 2: Prose, Plays, and Supersagas,* trans. Paul Schmidt, ed. Ronald Vroon. Cambridge, Mass.: Harvard University Press, 1989.

———. *Neizdannye proizvedeniia,* eds. N. Kharzhiev and T. Grits. Moscow: Khudozhestvennaia literatura, 1940.

———. *Sobranie proizvedenii Velimira Khlebnikova.* 5 vols. Leningrad: Izd-vo pisatelei v Leningrade, 1928–33.

Kobrinskii, A. *Poetika "OBERIU" v kontekste russkogo literaturnogo avangarda.* 2 vols. Moscow: Izdanie Moskovskogo Kul'turologicheskogo Litseiia, 1999.

Kodrianskaia, Natal'ia. *Aleksei Remizov.* Paris, 1959.

Konevskoi, Ivan. *Mechty i dumy Ivana Konevskogo 1896–1899.* St. Petersburg: Tip. E. Evdokimov, 1900.

Kornev, A. "Gasnet zaria," *Zhizn',* no. 4 (April 1900), 370–71.

Korolenko, V. G. *O literature.* Moscow: Gos. izd-vo khudozh. lit-ry, 1957.

Koschmal, Walter. "Das Prosagedicht als Gattung des evolutionären Wechsels: Ein Beitrag zur slavischen Komparatistik." In *Russische Literatur an der Wende vom 19. zum 20. Jahrhundert. Oldenburger Symposium,* ed. Rainer Grübel. Amsterdam: Rodopi, 1993, 143–61.

Kovács, Albert. "Zhanr stikhotvoreniia v proze v russkoi literatury kontsa XIX – nachala XX veka." *Romanoslavica* 19 (1979), 263–83.

Kulakov, Vladislav. "Minimalizm: Strategiia i taktika." *Novoe literaturnoe obozrenie* 23 (1997), 258–61.

Kurliandskaia, G. B. "'Stikhotvoreniia v proze' Turgeneva i ikh traditsiia v sovetskoi literature ('Mgnoveniia' Iu. Bondareva)." In *I. S. Turgenev: Voprosy mirovozreniia i tvorchestva.* Elista: Kalmytskii gos. universitet, 1986, 119–36.

Küpper, Stephan. "Zum Werk Lev Rubinštejns." *Zeitschrift für Slawistik* 40, no. 4 (1995), 436–50.

Kuprin, A. I. *Sobranie sochinenii.* 9 vols. Moscow: Khudozhestvennaia literatura, 1973.

Kuznetsova, Galina. *Grasskii dnevnik.* Washington D.C.: Victor Kamkin, 1967.

Lampl, Horst. "Innovationsbetrebungen im Gattungssystem der russischen Literatur des frühen 20. Jahrhunderts—am Beispiel A. M. Remizovs." *Wiener Slavistisches Jahrbuch* 24, 1978.

Langleben, Maria. "The Guilty House: A Textlinguistic Approach to the Shortest Prose by I. A. Bunin." *Elementa* 1, no. 3 (1994), 265–304.

Lavrov, Alexander. "Andrei Bely and the Argonauts' Mythmaking." In Irina Paperno and Joan Delaney Grossman, eds., *Creating Life: The Aesthetic Utopia of Russian Modernism.* Stanford: Stanford University Press, 1994, 83–121.

———. *Andrei Belyi v 1900-e gody: Zhizn' i literaturnaia deiatel'nost'.* Moscow: Novoe Literaturnoe Obozrenie, 1995.

Leiris, Michel. "Le Pays de mes Rêves." In *La Révolution Surréaliste,* vol. 2 (1924), 27–29.

Livshits, Benedikt. *Polutoroglazyi strelets. Stikhotvoreniia, perevody, vospominianiia.* Leningrad: Sovetskii pisatel', 1989.

———. *The One and a Half-Eyed Archer.* Trans. John Bowlt. Newtonville, Mass.: Oriental Research Partners, 1977.

Ljunggren, Anna. *At the Crossroads of Russian Modernism: Studies in Innokentij Annenskij's Poetics.* Stockholm: Almqvist & Wiksell International, 1997.

Lloyd, Rosemary. "Horrifying the Homais: The Challenge of the Prose Poem." *L'esprit créateur* 39, no. 1 (Spring 1999), 37–47.

Lukomnikov, German. "100 tysiach pochemu." *Novoe literaturnoe obozrenie* 23 (1997), 266.

Lundberg, Evgenii. "Nochnye." *Belye nochi. Peterburgskii al'manakh.* St. Petersburg: Izd. t-va Vol'naia tipografiia, 1907, 166–71.

Maclean, Marie. *Narrative as Performance: The Baudelairean Experiment.* London: Routledge, 1988.

Maguire, Robert A. *Red Virgin Soil: Soviet Literature in the 1920's.* Ithaca: Cornell University Press, 1987.

Malmstad, John. *The Poetry of Andrej Belyj: A Variorum Edition.* 2 vols. Ph.D. diss., Princeton University, 1968.

Mal'tsev, Iurii. *Bunin.* Frankfurt am Main: Posev, 1994.

Markov, Vladimir. *Kommentar zu den Dichtungen von K. D. Bal'mont, 1890–1909.* Cologne: Böhlau Verlag, 1988.

Markov, Vladimir, ed. *Manifesty i programmy russkikh futuristov.* Munich: Wilhelm Fink Verlag, 1967.

———. *Russian Futurism: A History.* Berkeley: University of California Press, 1968.

Matiushin, M. "Russkie kubofuturisty." In Elena Guro, *Nebesnye verbliuzhata.* Rostov-na-Donu: Izdatel'stvo Rostovskogo universiteta, 1993, 269–78.

McGrady, Patrick. *An Interpretation of Wassily Kandinsky's* Klänge. Ph.D. diss., State University of New York at Binghamton, 1989.

McLean, Robert A. *The Prose of Velimir Xlebnikov.* Ph.D. diss., Princeton University, 1973.

Merezhkovskii, Dmitrii. *Polnoe sobranie sochinenii.* 24 vols. Moscow: Tip. I. D. Sytina, 1914.

———. "Stikhotvoreniia v proze Sharlia Bodlera." *Iziashchnaia literatura: Zhurnal proizvedenii inostrannoi belletristiki,* no. 10 (1884), 141–57.

Metzidakis, Stamos. "The Prose Poem's Deconstruction of Literariness." In *Difference Unbound: The Rise of Pluralism in Literature and Criticism.* Amsterdam: Rodopi, 1995, 71–95.

Meyer, Holt. "Humilitas, minima modernitas: Für eine historische Pragmatik der 'Untiefen' des Minimalismus (nicht nur) in Rußland (am Beispiel der Karthotek[en] Lev Rubinštejns)." In *Minimalismus: Zwischen Leere und Exzeß,* eds. Mirjam Goller and Georg Witte. Vienna: Wiener Slawistischer Almanach, Sonderband 51, 2001, 447–75.

Milner-Gulland, Robin. "Beyond the Turning-Point: An Afterword." In *Daniil Kharms and the Poetics of the Absurd: Essays and Materials,* ed. Neil Cornwell. Houndmills: Macmillan, 1991, 243–67.

Miropol'skii, A. L. "Iarko-svetlaia zvezda." *Russkie simvolisty,* vyp. 2-i. Moscow: Izd. V. A. Maslova, 1894, 47–48.

Monroe, Jonathan. *A Poverty of Objects: The Prose Poem and the Politics of Genre.* Ithaca: Cornell University Press, 1987.

Monte, Steven. *Invisible Fences: Prose Poetry as a Genre in French and American Literature.* Lincoln: University of Nebraska Press, 2000.

Morson, Gary Saul. "Gogol's Parables of Explanation: Nonsense and Prosaics." In Susanne Fusso and Pricilla Meyer, eds., *Essays on Gogol: Logos and the Russian Word.* Evanston: Northwestern University Press, 1992, 200–39.

———. *The Boundaries of Genre: Dostoevsky's Diary of a Writer and the Traditions of Literary Utopia.* Austin: University of Texas Press, 1981.

Motte, Warren. *Small Worlds: Minimalism in Contemporary French Literature.* Lincoln: University of Nebraska Press, 1999.

Murphy, Margueritte. *A Tradition of Subversion: The Prose Poem in English from Wilde to Ashbery.* Amherst: University of Massachusetts Press, 1992.

Murphy, Steve. "Haunting Memories: Inquest and Exorcism in Baudelaire's 'La Corde'." *Dalhousie French Studies* 30 (1995), 65–91.

Niemojewski, Andrzei. "Eskizy i stikhotvoreniia v proze." *Novoe Slovo* (1897), October, kn. 1 (104–12), kn. 2 (164–70)

———. "Stikhotvoreniia v proze." *Zhizn'* (1899), no. 6, 97–102.

Nies, Fritz. *Poesie in prosaischer Welt: Untersuchungen zum Prosagedicht bei Aloysius Bertrand and Baudelaire.* Heidelberg: Carl Winter, 1964.

Nilsson, Nils Ake. "Vasilisk Gnedov's One-Letter Poems." In *Gorski Vijenats: A Garland of Essays Offered to Professor Elizabeth Mary Hill.* Publications of the Modern Humanities Research Association, 2 (Leeds, 1970), 220–23.

Oehler, Dolf. "Assomons les pauvres! Dialektik der Befreiung bei Baudelaire." *Germanisch-Romanische Monatschrift* 56 (1975), 454–62.

Orlitskii, Iurii. "Malaia forma v sostave prozimetricheskogo tselogo (A. Dobroliubov i E. Guro)." *Studia Slavica Finlandensia* 16, no. 1 (1999), 225–38.

———. "Miniume." *Novoe literaturnoe obozrenie* 23 (1997), 342.

———. "Stikhotvoreniia v proze v tvorchestve V. M. Garshina." In *Vsevolod Garshin on the Eve of the Millennium: An International Symposium in Three Volumes*, eds. Peter Henry et al. Nottingham: Astra Press, 1999, 2:579–80.

Pavlov, Boris. "Turgenevite 'Stikhotvoreniia v proza' i 'Malki Poemi v proza' na Sharl Bodler." *Literaturna Misul* 27, vol. 9 (1983), 25–31.

Perreault, John. "Minimal Abstracts." In *Minimal Art: A Critical Anthology*, ed. Gregory Battcock. New York: Dutton, 1968, 256–62.

Pesterev, V. A. "Zhanr stikhotvoreniia v proze v tvorchestve I. S. Turgeneva i Sh. Bodlera." In *Rol' russkoi klassiki v razvitii i vzaimoobogashchenii literaturnykh zhanrov*. Ordzhonikidze: Severo-Osetinskii gos. universitet im. K. S. Khetagurova, 1986, 119–29.

Peterson, Ronald E. *Andrei Belyi's Short Prose*. Birmingham: The University of Birmingham, 1980 (Birmingham Slavonic Monographs, no. 11).

Polonskii, Ia. P. "Dve fialki." In *Polnoe sobranie stikhotvorenii*. St. Petersburg: A. F. Marks, 1896, 2:125–27.

———. "Stikhotvoreniia v proze." In *Povesti i rasskazy (Pribavlenie k polnomu sobraniu sochinenii)*, ch. 1–2. St. Petersburg: Tip. V. V. Komarova, 1895, 279–80.

Popkin, Cathy. *The Pragmatics of Insignificance: Chekhov, Zoshchenko, Gogol*. Stanford: Stanford University Press, 1993.

Prince, Gerald. *A Dictionary of Narratology*. Lincoln: University of Nebraska Press, 1987.

Prokhodova, V. P. *Evoliutsiia zhanra miniatury v proze I. A. Bunina*. Ph.D. diss., Moscow State University, 1990.

Pyman, Avril. "Petersburg Dreams." In *Aleksej Remizov: Approaches to a Protean Writer*, ed. Greta N. Slobin. Columbus: Slavica, 1987, 51–112.

Rabinowitz, Stanley J. *Sologub's Literary Children: Keys to a Symbolist's Prose*. Columbus: Slavica, 1980.

Rembo [Rimbaud], Artiur. *Stikhi*. Moscow: Nauka, 1982.

Remizov, Aleksei. *Chortov log i polunoshchnoe solntse. Rasskazy i poemy*. St. Petersburg: EOS, 1908.

———. *Izbrannye proizvedeniia*. Moscow: Panorama, 1995.

———. *Martyn Zadeka: Sonnik*. Paris: Opleshnik, 1954.

———. "Molitva," "Poslednii chas," "Ivan-Kupal." *Al'manakh Grif* (vol. 2), Moscow, 1904, 39–46.

———. *Myshkina dudochka*. Paris: Opleshnik, 1953.

———. *Ogon' veshchei. Sny i predson'e*. Paris: Opleshnik, 1954.

———. "Pod krov'iu nochi. Sny." *Zolotoe Runo*, no. 5 (1908), 31–37.

————. *Podorozhie.* St. Petersburg: Sirin, 1913.

————. "Pouchkine: Six rêves." In *Trajectoire du rêve,* ed. André Breton. Paris: G.L.M., 1938, 33–39.

————. *Sochineniia.* 8 vols. St. Petersburg: Shipovnik, 1910–12.

————. *Vesenee porosh'e.* St. Petersburg: Sirin, 1915.

————. *Vzvikhrennaia Rus'.* Moscow: Sovetskaia Rossiia, 1990.

Riffaterre, Michael. "On the Prose Poem's Formal Features." In *The Prose Poem in France: Theory and Practice,* eds. Mary Ann Caws and Hermine Riffaterre. New York: Columbia University Press, 1983, 117–32.

Rimbaud, Arthur. *Oeuvres.* Paris: Garnier, 1960.

Roberts, Graham. *The Last Soviet Avant-Garde: OBERIU—Fact, Fiction, Metafiction.* Cambridge: Cambridge University Press, 1997.

Roethel, Hans Konrad. *Kandinsky: Das graphische Werk.* Cologne: M. Du-Mont Schauberg, 1970.

Rose, Barbara. "A B C Art." In *Minimal Art: A Critical Anthology,* ed. Gregory Battcock. New York: Dutton, 1968, 274–97.

Rozanov, Vasilii. "Mimoletnoe." In *Severnye Tsvety. Tretii al'manakh.* Moscow: Skorpion, 1903, 152.

Rubinshtein, Lev. *Domashnee muzitsirovanie.* Moscow: Novoe literaturnoe obozrenie, 2000.

————. *Reguliarnoe pis'mo.* St. Petersburg: Izd-vo Ivana Limbakha, 1996.

Sarab'ianov, D. V. "Kandinskii i russkii simvolizm." *Izvestiia Akademii Nauk. Seriia literatury i iazyka,* vol. 53, no. 4 (1994), 16–26.

Sarab'ianov, D. V. and Avtonomova, N. B. *Kandinskii: Put' khudozhnika. Khudozhnik i vremia.* Moscow: Galart, 1994.

Schaarschuh, F.-J. "Das Problem der Gattung 'Prosagedicht' in Turgenevs 'Stichotvorenija v proze.'" *Zeitschrift für Slawistik* 10, no. 4 (1965), 500–18.

Schmid, Ulrich. *Fedor Sologub: Werk und Kontext.* Bern: Peter Lang, 1995 (Slavica Helvetica, vol. 49).

Schramm, Caroline. *Minimalismus: Leonid Dobyčins Prosa im Kontext der totalitären Ästhetik.* Frankfurt am Main: Peter Lang, 1999.

Sergeev-Tsenskii, S. N. *Sobranie sochinenii.* 10 vols. Moscow: Khudozh-estvennaia literatura, 1955–56.

Shane, Alex M. "Rhythm without Rhyme: The Poetry of Aleksej Remizov." In *Aleksej Remizov: Approaches to a Protean Writer,* ed. Greta N. Slobin. Columbus: Slavica, 1987, 217–36.

Shatalov, S. E. *"Stikhotvoreniia v proze" I. S. Turgeneva.* Arzamas: Arzamasskii gos. ped. institut, 1961.

Shemshurin, Andrei. *Futurizm v stikhakh V. Briusova.* Moscow: Tip. Russkogo Tovarishchestva, 1913.

Sheppard, Richard. "Kandinsky's *Klänge:* An Interpretation." *German Life and Letters* 33, no. 2 (January 1980), 135–46.

Shishman, S. S. *Neskol'ko veselykh i grustnykh istorii o Daniile Kharmse i ego druz'iakh.* Leningrad, 1991.

Simon, John. "Prose Poem." *Princeton Encyclopedia of Poetry and Poetics.* 2d ed. Eds. Alex Preminger, Frank J. Warnke, and O. B. Hardison. Princeton: Princeton University Press, 1974, 664–66.

———. *The Prose Poem as a Genre in Nineteenth-Century European Literature.* New York: Garland, 1987.

Siniavskii, Andrei. "Literaturnaia maska Alekseia Remizova." In *Aleksej Remizov: Approaches to a Protean Writer,* ed. Greta N. Slobin. Columbus: Slavica, 1987, 25–39.

Skitalets. "Krasota." *Sovremennyi mir,* no. 1 (January 1908), 52–53.

Slobin, Greta N. *Remizov's Fiction, 1900–1921.* DeKalb: Northern Illinois University Press, 1991.

Sokolov, Boris. "'Kandinskii. Zvuki 1911. Izdanie Salona Izdebskogo.' Istoriia i zamysel neosushchestvlennogo poeticheskogo al'boma." *Literaturnoe obozrenie,* vol. 4, no. 258 (1996), 3–41.

Sologub, Fedor. "Aforizmy," "Dostoinstvo i mera veshchei." In *Neizdannyi Fedor Sologub.* Moscow: Novoe literaturnoe obozrenie, 1997, 189–206.

———. "Artiur Rembo-Novonaidennye perevody Fedora Sologuba." *Inostrannaia literatura* 9 (1990), 175–83.

Politicheskie skazochki. Moscow: Rodnaia rech', 1916.

———. *Sobranie sochinenii.* 10 vols. St. Petersburg: Sirin, 1913.

———. *Stikhotvoreniia.* Leningrad: Sovetskii pisatel', 1979.

Soloukhin, Vladimir. *Kameshki na ladoni.* Moscow: Sovetskii pisatel', 1977.

Solzhenitsyn, Aleksandr. "Kolokol'nia," "Starenie," "Pozor." *Novyi mir* 1997, no. 3, 70–71.

———. "Likhoe zel'e," "Utro," "Zavesa." *Novyi mir* 1997, no. 10, 119–20.

———. "Listvennitsa," "Molniia," "Kolokol Uglicha." *Novyi mir* 1997, no. 1, 99–100.

———. *Sobranie sochinenii.* Frankfurt am Main: Posev, 1970.

———. *Stories and Prose Poems,* trans. Michael Glenny. New York: Farrar, Straus and Giroux, 1971.

———. *The First Circle,* trans. Thomas P. Whitney. Evanston: Northwestern University Press, 1997.

Steltner, Ulrich. "Russische Kunstmärchen der Jahrhundertwende: Fedor Sologub." *Jahrbuch der Brüder Grimm-Gesellschaft,* vol. 1 (Kassel, 1991), 161–82.

Stephens, Sonya. *Baudelaire's Prose Poems. The Practice and Politics of Irony.* Oxford: Oxford University Press, 1999.

Terdiman, Richard. *Discourse/Counter-Discourse: The Theory and Practice of Symbolic Resistance in Nineteenth-Century France.* Ithaca: Cornell University Press, 1985.

Tigges, Wim. *An Anatomy of Literary Nonsense.* Amsterdam: Rodopi, 1988.

Timenchik, R. D. "O sostave sbornika Innokentiia Annenskogo *Kiparisovyi larets.*" *Voprosy literatury* 8 (1978), 307–16.

Timenchik, R. D., Toporov V. N., and Tsivian, T. V. "Sny Bloka i 'Peterburgskii tekst' nachala XX veka." In *Tezisy I vsesoiuznoi (III) konferentsii "Tvorchestvo A. A. Bloka i russkaia kul'tura XX veka,"* ed. Z. G. Mints. Tartu: Tartuskii Gos. universitet, 1975, 129–35.

Tsiv'ian, T. V. "O remizovskoi gipnologii i gipnografii." In *Serebrianyi vek v Rossii. Izbrannye stranitsy,* eds. V. V. Ivanov, V. N. Toporov, T. V. Tsiv'ian. Moscow: Radiks, 1993, 299–338.

Todorov, Tzvetan. "Poetry without Verse." In *The Prose Poem in France. Theory and Practice,* eds. Mary Ann Caws and Hermine Riffaterre. New York: Columbia University Press, 1983, 60–78.

Tolstoi, L. N. *Polnoe sobranie sochinenii.* 90 vols. Moscow-Leningrad: Khudozhestvennaia literatura, 1928–58.

Turgenev, Ivan Sergeevich. *"Polnoe sobranie sochinenii i pisem."* 2d ed. *Sochineniia.* 12 vols. Moscow: Nauka, 1978–86.

Uail'd, O. (Oscar Wilde). *Polnoe Sobranie sochinenii.* 4 vols. St. Petersburg, 1912.

Uijterlinde, A. "*Zverinets:* Proza ili poeziia?" In *Velimir Chlebnikov (1885–1922): Myth and Reality,* ed. Willem G. Weststeijn. Amsterdam: Rodopi, 1986, 513–28.

Vadé, Yves. *Le poème en prose et ses territories.* Paris: Belin, 1996.

Wanner, Adrian. "Aleksei Remizov's Dreams: Surrealism *Avant la Lettre*?" *The Russian Review* 58, no. 4 (October 1999), 599–614.

———. *Baudelaire in Russia.* Gainesville: University Press of Florida, 1996.

———. "Cutting Baudelaire's Rope: Ivan Turgenev's Re-Writing of 'La Corde'. *Comparative Literature Studies* 34, no. 1 (1997), 31–40.

———. "From Subversion to Affirmation: The Prose Poem as a Russian Genre." *Slavic Review* 56, no. 3 (Fall 1997), 519–41.

———. "Russian Minimalist Prose: Generic Antecedents to Daniil Kharms' 'Sluchai.'" *Slavic and East European Journal* 45, no. 3 (Fall 2001), 451–72.

Weiss, Peg. *Kandinsky and Old Russia: The Artist as Ethnographer and Shaman.* New Haven: Yale University Press, 1995.

Woodward, James B. *Ivan Bunin. A Study of His Fiction.* Chapel Hill: The University of North Carolina Press, 1980.

Young, David. "Introduction." In *Models of the Universe: An Anthology of the Prose Poem,* eds. Stuart Friebert and David Young. Oberlin: Oberlin College Press, 1995, 17–20.

Zamiatin, Evgenii. "Fedor Sologub." In *A Soviet Heretic: Essays by Yevgeny Zamyatin,* ed. and trans. Mirra Ginsburg. Chicago: University of Chicago Press, 1970, 217–23.

Zhirmunskii, Viktor. "O ritmicheskoi proze." In *Teoriia stikha.* Leningrad: Sovetskii pisatel', 1975, 569–86.

Zinov'eva-Annibal, Lidiia. "Teni sna." *Severnye tsvety assiriiskie. Al'manakh IV.* Moscow: Skorpion, 1905, 134–46.

Zöldhelyi, Zsuzsa D. *Turgenyev prózai költeményei.* Budapest: Tankönyvkiadó, 1991, 341–72.

———. "'Stikhotvoreniia v proze' I. S. Turgeneva: K probleme zhanra." *Russkaia literatura,* vol. 2 (1990), 188–94.

Index

Index

Calf's Head)," 41; "Tuman (Fog)," 38;
"Ubiitsa (The Murderer)," 41; "V
Al'pakh (In the Alps)," 165–66n13
Burliuk, David, 4, 105–6, 110, 115
Burliuk, Nikolai, 106, 110, 114. WORKS:
"Smert' legkomyslennogo molodogo
cheloveka (Death of a Frivolous Young
Man)," 106; "Tishina Ellady (The
Stillness of Hellas)," 106; "Solnechnyi
dom (A Sunny House)," 106
Butor, Michel: *Illustrations,* 104

Cabaret Voltaire (magazine), 120
Cage, John, 6, 146; *4'33",* 132
Carver, Raymond, 3
Censorship, 77, 177n55
Chagall, Marc, 127
Chances, Ellen, 128–29
Chekhov, Anton, 3, 34, 128–29, 131,
167n34; "The Seagull," 64
Chernyshevskii, Nikolai: condemns prose
poem, 15, 16, 36; *Chto delat'? (What Is
to be Done?),* 14
Un chien andalou (film), 102
Children: "literary," 83; stories for, ix, 11
(*see also* Fairy tales)
Collective unconscious, 85
Communism, Soviet, 100, 149. *See also*
Soviet Union
Cornwell, Neil, 11, 128–29, 153–54n4
Cubism, 110–11, 121, 127; literary, 105,
109–14, 126–27, (cubo-futurism) 4, 105,
114, 116, 120, 126; objectives of, 112–13

Dadaism, 102, 116, 120
Dante Alighieri: *Inferno,* 35
Darwinism, social, 26, 42
Death: communication with the dead, 88;
as writer's theme, 51, 57–58, 64, 82, 92,
108, 132, (Bal'mont) 49, 56, (Bunin)
40–42, (Turgenev) 30, 35, 42, 149–50
Decadence: emergence of, in Europe, 45;
influence of, on writing, 36, 38, 58;
necrophilia, 51, 57; in prose poems,
ends, xi; Russian, 67, (in fairy tale) 72;
Russian decadent poets, 38, 45–67,
(difference in) 56; spirit of, 168n39
Delville, Michel, 11
Derrida, Jacques, 147
"Diet Pepsi minimalism," 4
Dietsch, Volkmar, 113

Dobroliubov, Aleksandr, 45, 56–58, 63, 67.
WORKS: *Iz knigi nevidimoi (From the
Invisible Book),* 58, 64, 125; *Natura
Naturans. Natura Naturata,* 56–57, 58,
(musical notations in) 57; "Obrazy
(Images)," 57; "Sketches from a
Madhouse," 57–58
Dobrytsin, Andrei, 133–34
Dobychin, Leonid, 155n5
Dombrovskii, Ivan (John Graham), 4
Dostoevskii, Fyodor, 14, 128; Remizov
comments on the dreams of, 85, 97;
"thrown overboard," 105. WORKS: *Crime
and Punishment,* 87; *Dvoinik (The
Double),* 157n28; "Legend of the Grand
Inquisitor," 35
Dreams, 82, 137, 139, 148; children's,
99–100; "Dream Books," 95; Remizov's,
x, 8, 64, 66, 85–103, 117, 139; as
subgenre of prose poem, 19, 64
Duchamp, Marcel, 5, 15
Dunlop, John, 148
Dzherzhinskii, Felix, 179n82

Edson, Russell, 12
Eikhenbaum, Boris, 34
Eliot, T. S., 168n46
Eluard, Paul, 99, 100–1, 102
Emmert, Claudia, 120, 121, 182n49
England, prose poem studied, 7
Epic of Gilgamesh, 87
Eshel'man, Raul', 155n5
Existentialism, 76, 134
Exter, Alexandra, 110

Fairy tales, 135; anti-fairy tale, 64; and
dreams, 85, 99–100; Sologub's, x, 8, 64,
66, 68–84, 137, 139. *See also Märchen,*
Folklore/folk art, Russian
Fedorov, A. V., 53
Fet, Afanasii, 112
Le Figaro (periodical), 20
Film as minimal art form, 6
Filosofov, D. V., 96
Fin de siècle, 36, 37, 44, 45, 64; European,
49; impressionism, 92, 127; Turgenev
anticipates literature of, 67
Flavin, Dan, 3
Folklore/folk art, Russian, 74, 78–79, 83,
107, 121–23, 127; Göbler's study of, 137;
stylized, 91. *See also* Fairy tales

209

About the Author

Adrian Wanner is a professor of Russian and comparative literature and the head of the Department of Germanic and Slavic Languages and Literatures at Pennsylvania State University.